THE UNCERTAIN MIRROR

© Minister of Supply and Services Canada 1976

Available by mail from

Printing and Publishing
Supply and Services Canada,
Ottawa, Canada K1A 0S9
or through your bookseller

Catalogue No. YC2-282-3-01   Price: Canada: $4.75
                               Other countries: $5.70

Price subject to change without notice

Ottawa 1970

Reprinted 1971
Reprinted 1972
Reprinted 1975
Reprinted 1976

La Cie de l'Éclaireur Ltée
Beauceville, Qué.

Contract No. 08KT. 65826-13253

The Uncertain Mirror

Report of the
Special Senate Committee on Mass Media

Volume I

The Special Senate Committee on Mass Media

The Honourable Keith Davey, *Chairman*
The Honourable L. P. Beaubien, *Deputy Chairman*

The Honourable Romuald Bourque
The Honourable Douglas D. Everett
The Honourable Harry W. Hays, P.C.
The Honourable Mary E. Kinnear
The Honourable J. M. Macdonald
The Honourable Charles R. McElman
The Honourable William J. Petten
The Honourable J. Harper Prowse
The Honourable Josie D. Quart
The Honourable Donald Smith
The Honourable Herbert O. Sparrow
The Honourable Frank C. Welch
The Honourable Paul Yuzyk

Terms of Reference

On Tuesday, March 18, 1969, the Senate of Canada constituted the Special Senate Committee on Mass Media by approving the following resolution:

> That a Special Committee of the Senate be appointed to consider and report upon the ownership and control of the major means of mass public communication in Canada, and in particular, and without restricting the generality of the foregoing, to examine and report upon the extent and nature of their impact and influence on the Canadian public;
>
> That the Committee have power to engage the services of such counsel and technical, clerical and other personnel as may be necessary for the purpose of the inquiry; and
>
> That the Committee have power to send for persons, papers and records, to examine witnesses, to report from time to time and to print such papers and evidence from day to day as may be ordered by the Committee.

The Committee was reconstituted by the Senate during the second and third sessions of the 28th Parliament on October 29, 1969 and October 8, 1970.

Preface

Since I first gave notice of motion in November, 1968, to establish a Special Senate Committee on mass media, the question I have been asked most frequently is what prompted me to propose such a Committee in the first place. I have, of course, had a lifelong interest in the media; and then too, anyone who has been active in public life soon becomes aware of the all-pervasive influence of the mass media. It occurred to me that there had never been a national accounting for the media. Most people agreed that freedom of the press presumes responsibility, but few had really stopped to assess that responsibility. It also occurred to me that Parliament might be the ideal instrument through which the people of Canada could determine whether they have the press they need or simply the press they deserve.

At first we considered a study dealing exclusively with print, but the inter-relation and inter-action between print and the electronic media is so extensive that to be meaningful it was necessary to broaden our study to include all forms of mass media. We have tried, however, to focus on the electronic media as they relate to the whole media spectrum.

Newspaper publishers, in particular, repeatedly told the Committee that they sought no special favours from government. We believe them. Certainly none are required. And yet in the United States, with an equally flourishing press, even while our Committee was meeting, Congress passed a Newspaper Preservation Act which to all intents and purposes legitimizes and extends press concentration. Its easy passage through both Houses of Congress has been popularly attributed, at least in part, to the fact that politicians looking to re-election must depend substantially upon the mass media in the very real world of practical politics.

The Canadian Senate, on the other hand, is structured in a way which allows it to take that detached view which I believe is apparent in this report. None of us doubt that the Senate can be improved. Indeed the press of Canada has been offering us advice in this regard for more than 100 years. We have been grateful for their counsel. But our first concern in approaching this report has not been the welfare of either the press or the Senate, but rather the public interest.

It should be noted for the record that from the moment the Committee was announced until these words were written, we have received the full co-operation of the mass media. Our relationship with the media has been cordial and upon occasion frank and confidential. That confidentiality has been respected.

In all modesty but in simple justice to my colleagues, I must say that it was a hard-working Committee. My gracious deputy chairman, Senator Louis Beaubien; our diligent whip, Senator William Petten; and the other members of our steering committee, Senators Charles McElman, Harry Hays, and John Macdonald, were always available. Every member of the Committee made a useful and effective contribution and I shall always be grateful to each of them: Senators Romuald Bourque, Douglas D. Everett, Mary Kinnear, J. Harper Prowse, Josie Quart, Donald Smith, H. O. Sparrow, Frank C. Welch, and Paul Yuzyk.

Our study began with an intensive research programme under the able direction of Nicola Kendall. Much of this research is appended to this report; that which is not has been made available to the libraries of the University of Western Ontario and Carleton University, which have departments of journalism.

We regret that it was not possible in the time at our disposal to include the situation of the Canadian book-publishing industry in the Committee's study. It deserves attention, because this industry is encountering serious financial difficulties and appears to be coming increasingly under foreign control. We believe it is urgently necessary to consider whether this industry—like banking, uranium, broadcasting, and newspaper and periodical publishing—should not be declared off-limits to foreign takeovers.

Throughout our hearings, which began on December 9, 1969 and concluded on April 24, 1970, we received briefs from some 500 companies, organizations, and individuals. One hundred and twenty-five witnesses appeared personally before our Committee. The value of our hearings was greatly enhanced by the effective performance of our counsel, L. Yves Fortier.

Two staff people deserve special recognition. One of these, Borden Spears, is a newspaperman's newspaperman. As our indefatigable executive consultant, he helped to bridge any credibility gap that may have existed between fifteen Senators and those who collectively comprise the mass media. Marianne Barrie, our administrative director, routinely performed the impossible.

In the deliberative and report-writing phase of our operation we were greatly assisted by Alexander Ross, Gilles Constantineau, and Peter Smith. Our research assistant, Cecile Suchal, was invaluable throughout. We are deeply indebted to the efficiency and devotion of our hard-pressed secretarial staff, Peggy Pownall and Judy Walenstein. It was an effective team, in whose assembly I take great pride. And we owe much to the unfailing assistance of my secretary, Elizabeth Nesbitt, and of Mr. Walter Dean and the staff of the Senate.

The press we need, or the press we deserve? No thoughtful analysis could offer a definitive answer. I present *The Uncertain Mirror*.

December 1970 (KEITH DAVEY), *Chairman*

Table of Contents

	Page
PREFACE	vii
I SPECTRUM	1
II OWNERSHIP	13
1. How Much is Enough?	15
Newspaper Nose-count	19
Group Panorama	22
British Columbia	22
Alberta	23
Saskatchewan	23
Manitoba	23
Ontario	23
Quebec	25
New Brunswick	26
Nova Scotia	26
Prince Edward Island	26
Newfoundland	26
Some Group Profiles	26
The Bassett-Eaton Group	27
Bushnell Communications Limited	27
CHUM Limited	28
The Desmarais-Parisien-Francoeur Group	28
The Dougall Family	28
F. P. Publications Limited	28
The Irving Group	29
Maclean-Hunter Limited	29
The McConnell Family	30
Moffat Broadcasting Limited	31
The Pratte, Baribeau and Lepage Group	31
Radiodiffusion Mutuelle Limitée	31
Rogers Broadcasting Limited	31
Selkirk Holdings Limited	33
The Sifton Group	33
The Southam Group	33
Standard Broadcasting Corporation Limited	35
Télémédia (Québec) Limitée	35
The Thomson Group	35
Toronto Star Limited	37
Western Broadcasting Company Limited	37

	Page
2. Balance Sheet	39
The Message-Bearers	39
Newspaper Costs	40
The Natural Monopoly	42
Newspaper Profits	46
Economics of Broadcasting	56
Broadcasting Profits	60
3. Bucking the Trend	63
Concentration: Pro and Con	63
Press Ownership Review Board	71
For a Volkswagen Press	75
III IMPACT	**81**
1. Change and Response	83
The Constant Bump	83
The Newspapers	85
The Broadcasters	91
2. La Différence	95
Newspapers	96
Periodicals	99
3. Freedom	101
4. Press Council	111
5. Criteria	121
Training for the Job	124
Training on the Job	129
Keeping them on the Job	130
IV MEDIA	**135**
1. Newspapers: The Daily Miracle	137
2. Weeklies: The Community Press	143
3. Periodicals: The Troubled Magazines	153
4. Business Publications: The Invisible Press	169
5. Farm Press: Not for the Family	173
6. Church Press: A Job for Journalists	175
7. Ethnic Press: The Most Mixed Medium	179
8. Student Papers: The Hotbed Press	185
9. Underground Press: Down but not Out	189
10. Broadcasting	193
The Beast of Burden	193
The Public Service	195
The Private Industry	203
Airing the News	210
The Cable Conundrum	213
The Regulator	222
V SUPPORTS	**227**
1. (CP)	229
2. Postal Rates	237
3. Advertising	243
4. Public Relations	249
VI EPILOGUE	**253**
1. And finally	255

I
SPECTRUM

Though it will be apparent to those who read its pages that this is a pre-eminently Canadian document, we make no apology for beginning with a statement by a distinguished American jurist. Justice Hugo Black, in a case involving the right of newspapers to news, wrote that "the widest possible dissemination of information from diverse and antagonistic sources is essential to the welfare of the public ... a free press is a condition of a free society."[1]

This notion is basic to our idea of a free society. The more separate voices we have telling us what's going on, telling us how we're doing, telling us how we *should* be doing, the more effectively we can govern ourselves. In this sense, the mass media are society's suggestion box. The more suggestions there are from below, the better will be the decisions made at the top. This assumption is not limited to parliamentary democracies. The desire to have a voice in ordering the institutions that govern our lives is a universal human constant, from classroom to corporation, from neighbourhood to empire. And in a technological society, the media are one of the chief instruments by which this need is met.

The big trouble with this assumption, the notion that media diversity equals a higher polity, is that it happens to be in flat defiance of economics. More voices may be healthier, but fewer voices are cheaper.

There is an apparently irresistible tendency, which the economists describe as the process of "natural monopoly," for the print and electronic media to merge into larger and larger economic units. The tendency is encouraged by the Canadian tax system, in particular the application of death duties, to the point that the president of Southam Press Ltd. predicted to the Committee: "... it seems apparent that small and medium-sized newspapers will in the long run pass from individual ownership ... all existing

---

[1] *Associated Press v. United States*, 326 U.S. 1, 20 [1944].

independently owned newspapers will come on the market in due course because of the tax implications now facing Canadian business owners."

This tendency could – but not necessarily – have the effect of reducing the number of "diverse and antagonistic sources" from which we derive our view of the public world. It could also – but not necessarily – lead to a situation whereby the news (which we must start thinking of as a public resource, like electricity) is controlled and manipulated by a small group of individuals and corporations whose view of What's Fit to Print may closely coincide with What's Good for General Motors, or What's Good for Business, or What's Good for my Friends Down at The Club. There is some evidence, in fact, which suggests that we are in that boat already.

We have, then, this natural conflict – which isn't terribly unique in any democracy – between what the society needs and what the society can afford. The purpose of this Committee was not to ascertain whether concentration of media ownership is a Good Thing or a Bad Thing. *Of course* it is a bad thing; in a land of bubblegum forests and lollipop trees, every man would have his own newspaper or broadcasting station, devoted exclusively to programming that man's opinions and perceptions.

In the real world, we must try to strike balances. How do you reconcile the media's tendency towards monopoly with society's need for diversity? And if it turns out that there really is no way we can fight this monopolistic trend, is there any way we can still ensure "diverse and antagonistic sources" of information within a diminishing number of media? Which leads us to all kinds of related questions, such as whether we are getting the kind of information service we can afford, or merely the kind we deserve.

These are tricky questions, and the Committee does not presume to have come up with definitive answers for all of them, or even most of them. We would stress, in fact, that this isn't exactly what governments are supposed to be *for*. Further on in this report we suggest some measures which governments could take to encourage the development of a freer, healthier, more vigorous, more Canadian and – yes – a more *diverse* press. But in the same breath, we must recognize that all the medicare legislation in the world, by itself, won't cure a single case of dandruff. To a very limited extent, government can be useful in amending some of the ground-rules under which the mass-media game is played. But it is only the players themselves – the public, the owners of the media, and most crucially of all the journalists – who can improve the quality and relevance of the product.

The extent to which the concentration of media ownership affects this quality is one of the chief concerns of this report. Accordingly, let's state the situation in the baldest possible terms by looking at the 103 Canadian communities where a daily newspaper is published or a primary TV station is located.

Within these 103 communities there are 485 "units of mass communication" – daily newspapers or radio or TV stations – and slightly over half of them are controlled or partially owned by groups. Of Canada's 116 daily newspapers, 77 (or 66.4 per cent) are controlled or partially owned by groups. Of the 97 TV stations (including some relay stations), 47 (or 48.5 per cent) are controlled by groups. Of 272 radio stations, groups control or own a substantial interest in 129 (or 47.4 per cent).

The patterns of concentration take several forms. There are publishing and/or broadcasting chains which control media outlets in several communities. There are local groups which control some or all of the competing media in a given community. There are some groups which fall into both categories – they own newspapers or broadcasting stations in several different places, *and* own print and electronic outlets within a single community. There are also groups – the loose word for them is conglomerates – which have interests in various media outlets that are subordinate to their other investments. With the expansion of cable TV, the growth of suburban weekly newspapers, and the development of new media technologies, these patterns of group ownership could very easily become more intricate and pervasive in the future than they are right now.

But the trend towards fewer and fewer owners of our sources of news and information is already well entrenched. There are only five cities in the country where genuine competition between newspapers exists; and in all five cities, some or all of these competing dailies are owned by chains. Seventy years ago there were thirty-five Canadian communities with two or more daily newspapers; today there are only fifteen – and in five of these cities, the two dailies are published by the same owner.

Of Canada's eleven largest cities, chains enjoy monopolies in seven. The three biggest newspaper chains – Thomson, Southam, and F.P. – today control 44.7 per cent of the circulation of all Canadian daily newspapers; a dozen years ago, the total was only 25 per cent. The conventional wisdom still cherishes the image of the "independent" owner-editor, a tough but kindly old curmudgeon who somehow represented the collective conscience of his community. If this image ever had validity, it hasn't now. Your average daily newspaper editor is the hired branch-manager for a group of shareholders who typically live somewhere else. Fully 77 per cent of the circulation of all Canadian newspapers is now controlled by these chains, a situation which a frontier journalist like Bob Edwards, editor of the *Calgary Eye Opener,* would have found incredible.

In broadcasting, ownership is far more diversified. But the trend towards concentration is present, and it is accelerating. Nearly a dozen TV stations that once enjoyed local control or substantial local participation have come under the control of major broadcasting groups.

But suppose there *are* fewer and fewer owners: is this necessarily a bad thing? There is a lot of evidence to suggest exactly the opposite. Chain ownership has rescued more than one newspaper from extinction. Chain ownership has turned a number of weeklies into dailies. Chain ownership has financially strengthened some newspapers, so they're better able to serve their employees and communities. Chain ownership may in some cases have resulted in a decline in editorial quality; but there are also instances where chain ownership has upgraded it. In other words, there is simply no correlation between chain ownership and editorial performance. There are some great newspapers in Canada and there are a number of distressingly bad ones. But in no case does their quality or lack of it seem to have much to do with where their shareholders live.

In terms of public policy, though, this isn't too relevant. What matters is the fact that control of the media is passing into fewer and fewer hands, and that the experts agree this trend is likely to continue and perhaps accelerate. The logical (but wholly improbable) outcome of this process is that one man or one corporation could own every media outlet in the country except the CBC. The Committee believes that at *some* point before this hypothetical extreme is reached, a line must be drawn. We're not suggesting that the present degree of concentration of media ownership has produced uniformly undesirable effects; indeed, it may be that the country would now have *fewer* "diverse and antagonistic" voices if all these media mergers of the 1950s and 1960s had not occurred. But the prudent state must recognize that at some point, enough becomes enough. If the trend towards ownership concentration is allowed to continue unabated, sooner or later it must reach the point where it collides with the public interest. The Committee believes it to be in the national interest to ensure that that point is not reached.

Would such intervention operate in defiance of economics? The short answer is that it would and it wouldn't. Much of the trend towards media monopoly stems from the stunningly persuasive fact that big newspapers and big broadcasting stations are more profitable than smaller ones. But there are other mergers, lots of them, which appear to confer no benefits of scale. They occur simply because a man gets richer by owning five or ten or fifteen profitable newspapers than he does by owning one.

So there's no reason why a government which acted to stem the tide of media monopoly would find itself, like King Canute, with the waves lapping disobediently at its feet. Anyhow, doesn't the whole Canadian proposition operate in defiance of "economics"? We believe the thing can and should be done, and done quickly. In a later chapter we will suggest how.

But checking the media's monopolistic tendencies is only a small step towards promoting the kind of media the country needs and deserves. Suppose, for instance, that the government decreed tomorrow that control of every newspaper, TV station, and radio station in the country must return to "independent" operators: would it make any difference to the kind of newspapers we read, the kind of programmes we hear and see?

Not likely. No matter who owns the shares, a lousy newspaper is still a lousy newspaper. As Osgoode Hall Law Professor Desmond Morton recently observed: "It doesn't matter whether the North Bay *Nugget* belongs to Roy Thomson, Max Bell, or a local drygoods merchant. They are all, without a single exception, in the same kind of hands. They all belong to the Canadian business community and they all do what that community wants. And if Canadian businessmen assume an automatic, infallible identity between their views and those of every right-thinking Canadian, they are hardly unique among the oligarchs of history."

This gets us closer to the second question into which this Committee was established to enquire. As well as being commissioned to study ownership patterns of the media, we were also asked to consider "their influence and impact on the Canadian public." And this leads us inexorably to a consideration of content – the kind of newspapers we read, the kind of programmes we hear and see. It also leads us into a discussion – and here we tread with extreme diffidence – into the endlessly entertaining subject of What's Wrong With The Press.

Plainly, *something* is wrong. Judgements like this are risky, but it seems to us that there has never been a period in the nation's history when the press has been so distrusted, so disrespected, so disbelieved. "Our profession has moved far from the days of the yellow press and the alcoholic city room," Lee Hills, editor of the Detroit *Free Press*, recently told an audience of American journalists. "And yet, despite this great progress and new knowledge and greater dedication, I believe we are in danger of losing our most important asset: the friendship of our readers." His remarks apply with at least equal force in Canada.

There is something about the media that is turning people off. What is it? It's certainly not "sensationalism," because most newspapers abandoned that shrill technique a generation ago, for the excellent reason that it failed to sell newspapers. It's certainly not "bias." Most consequential news outlets in this country are objective to the point of tedium in their political coverage. And it's certainly not "superficiality," since the news coverage we receive today is more complete, more sophisticated, more exhaustive, than ever before.

No, it's something more basic than the failings which all these archaic weapon-words describe. It's got something to do with society itself, and the way it's changing, and the way people react to it. If the media turn people off, it's because society at large turns them off. If newspapers are losing friends, it's part of the same process by which Parliament is losing friends, and the courts, and the corporations, and the schools, and the churches.

We hesitate to wade too deeply into the swamps of sociology and McLuhanism, but it does seem clear that all the conflict, the hassle, the demonstrations, the social anguish which currently surround us have at least one common characteristic: they're all concerned with people versus institutions. From China's cultural revolution to Czechoslovakia's counterrevolution, from the high-school sit-in to the Red Power movement, this theme is a constant.

The media, precisely because they *are* institutions, are involved in this conflict – and they are involved as participants. One of the truly depressing aspects of our enquiry was the ingenuous view of so many media owners that they are mere spectators. They're *not* spectators. They control the presentation of the news, and therefore have a vast and perhaps disproportionate say in how our society defines itself. It is true, as we were repeatedly reminded by the people who appeared before us, that newspapers can't swing elections any more, that the media's ability to control and manipulate events is vastly overrated. That's like saying an air-traffic controller can't prevent airplanes from landing. Of course he can't; but he can dictate the order in which they land, or send them to another airport. The power of the press, in other words, is the power of selection. Newspapers and broadcasting stations can't dictate how we think and vote on specific issues; but their influence in *selecting* those issues can be enormous. *Of course* the people won't always vote the way the editorial-writers tell them on next week's sewer bylaw; but who decides when they'll start thinking and talking about sewers – or whether they'll worry about pollution at all?

This quaint notion of media-as-spectator appears to be shared by most of the people who control the corporations that control the news. But then, too many publishers and broadcasters seem to harbour a positive affection for the nineteenth century. One eminent publisher, for instance, told us his definition of press freedom included "the right of the public to buy a newspaper each day if they wish, to write letters to the editor, or to start a paper of their own if they don't like it." We are reminded by this of the inalienable right of every Englishman to occupy the royal suite at the Savoy Hotel – *if* he can afford it.

Unfortunately, this flair for sheer, crashing irrelevancy seems to be part of the media's conventional wisdom. Time and again we were presented with similar pious declarations, the sort of thing publishers have been telling service-club luncheons since at least the 1940s. Somehow they always seemed to miss the point.

Item: "Freedom of the press is essential to a healthy democracy." Of course it is; who would disagree? But the question is, is this freedom enhanced or diminished by corporate control of the news?

Item: "We strive to be objective on our news pages, and leave our opinions to the editorial-writers." Great. But what do you mean by "objectivity"? Suppose there's a pulp mill or a nickel refinery dumping millions of gallons of effluent into the nearest river, and the local newspaper says nothing about it unless it's reporting a speech by some local conservationist. Is *that* objectivity? In trying to assess fairness and objectivity, aren't the stories a paper *doesn't* print, the facts it doesn't bother to collect, just as important as the ones it does?

Item: "We're not influenced by advertisers." We believe this. There are very few publishers who will keep a local advertiser's name out of the paper if he's nailed on an impaired-driving charge. But isn't the very *fact* of advertising an influence in itself? Doesn't the very fact that the media live on advertising revenue imply a built-in bias in favour of a consumption-oriented society?

This institutional bias, we suggest, may be one of the chief reasons for the current public disenchantment with the media. But there is an even more compelling reason, and it has to do with the nature of the news itself.

At the annual meeting of a troubled financial corporation in Toronto recently, a woman shareholder stood up and berated the reporters present for printing "all that bad news" about her company. (The bad news consisted of disclosures that the company was earning much less money than previously, that the company's senior executives had borrowed heavily from company-controlled banks, and that the company's founder had got the firm to guarantee loans so he could buy *three* airplanes.)

The applause she received from her fellow-shareholders was literally thunderous. How come? Why this visceral hostility?

Part of it was the well-known tendency of people, when they hear bad news, to blame the messenger. But not all. The sheer prevalence of this shoot-the-messenger syndrome indicates that much of our journalism is failing to prepare its readers for conditions of constant change.

In a static, pre-industrial society, the news must concern itself with isolated events which somehow fracture prevailing patterns: COLUMBUS DISCOVERS AMERICA! The trouble seems to be that today, in a society where hardly anybody will die in the town where he was born, where many of our children's lifetimes will embrace not one but several careers, where exploration into our minds and outward to the stars is a constant process, in a society where *everything* is changing, we're still defining news in the same old pre-columbian way.

If it is to be news, there must be a "story." And if there is to be a "story," there must be conflict, surprise, drama. There must be a "dramatic, disruptive, exceptional event" before traditional journalism can acknowledge that a situation exists. Thus the news consumer finds himself being constantly ambushed by events. Poor people on the march all of a sudden? But nobody told us they were discontented! Demonstrations at the bacteriological warfare research station? But nobody told us such an outfit existed in Canada! People protesting pollution? What pollution? The paper never told us....

We exaggerate, of course. But we think our central point stands up: journalism's definition of what constitutes "news" is still far too narrow. It still concentrates overmuch on the dramatic, exceptional event – the voting, the shooting, the rioting – and not enough on the quiescent but visible situations which could spell trouble later on.

Trouble: that's something else that's wrong with journalism's current definition of the news. There is much more to life than hassle and strife, but the media's entrapment in drama, conflict, and disruption prevents them from reporting it. There are terrible divisions in any technological society, but there are also many places, many ways, in which people are coming together. We should hear more about these scenes than we do.

Part of the trouble is the media's understandable tendency to look for news only in the old, familiar places: city hall, the courts, the police stations, the union halls – places where there's always a man whose institutional credentials ("spokesman," "president," "mayor") allow the news to fit easily into prevailing journalistic pigeonholes. The result often resembles a shadow-play: plastic figures saying plastic things which are transmitted in a plastic way – but we all know that the *real* story, the real news, is happening in some other dimension. It is happening in the streets, in laboratories, within families, beneath the sea, behind the closed doors of foreign boardrooms and, most crucially of all, inside people's heads. But because these exciting developments don't immediately generate "events," they tend to be ignored or – what is worse – distorted by the archaic perceptions of cop-shop journalism.

Let us now, in the words of one authoritative source, make One Thing Perfectly Clear: these are not blanket criticisms. Our best newspapers, our best radio and television reporters, are fully aware of these limitations of the conventional journalism, and have been striving for years to expand its perceptions. In many cases they have succeeded magnificently. In deploring the media's weaknesses, we wish to avoid the old journalistic trap of failing to acknowledge their strengths.

Among these strengths, unfortunately, a penchant for self-criticism is not conspicuous. In the course of our hearings we became astonished that an industry so important, so prosperous, so intelligent as the communications business has developed so little formal machinery for upgrading its personnel and its product.

Apart from the Canadian Managing Editors Conference (an *ad hoc* body which tries to meet once a year) and a couple of excellent local groups, there is no organization worrying about how news is presented and how that presentation can be improved. The American Newspaper Guild worries about salaries. The Canadian Association of Broadcasters, the Canadian Daily Newspaper Publishers Association and its weekly counterpart worry – oh, how they worry! – about revenues.

But nobody seems to worry, outside the office at least, about the quality and relevance of their performance. Nor did anyone from newsrooms or boardrooms appear to be much concerned with the industry's astoundingly offhand approach to recruitment and personnel development. The news business is above all a "people" business. But if IBM had been as unconcerned about the kind of people it attracts and the conditions under which they work, it would still be making adding machines.

This is doubly unfortunate, because government cannot and should not attempt to remedy some of the weaknesses we've been discussing. Only the industry can do that – the people who own the media and the people who work for them. As Victoria *Times* publisher Arthur Irwin told the Committee: "Only journalists can make journalism work."

The job is crucially important, for what is at stake is not only the vigor of our democracy. It also involves the survival of our nationhood. A nation is a collection of people who share common images of themselves. Our love of the land and our instinctive yearning for community implant that image in the first place. But it is the media – together with education and the arts – that can make it grow. Poets and teachers and artists, yes, but journalists too. It is their perceptions which help us to define who and what we are.

We all know the obstacles involved in this task. Geography, language, and perhaps a failure of confidence and imagination have made us into a cultural as well as economic satellite of the United States. And nowhere is this trend more pronounced than in the media. Marquis Childs on the editorial page. Little Orphan Annie back near the classified ads. Nixon and Tiny Tim and Jerry Rubin and Johnny Carson and Lawrence Welk and Timothy Leary on the tube. The Beach Boys and Blind Faith and Simon and Garfunkel on the radio. The latest vc bodycounts courtesy of A.P. and U.P.I. The self-image of an entire generation shaped by Peter Fonda riding a stars-and-stripes motorcycle. Need we continue?

We are not suggesting that these influences are undesirable, nor that they can or should be restricted. The United States happens to be the most important, most *interesting* country on earth. The vigor and diversity of its popular culture – which is close to becoming a world culture – obsesses, alarms, and amuses not just Canadians, but half the people of the world.

What we *are* suggesting is that the Canadian media – especially broadcasting – have an interest in and an obligation to promote our *apartness* from the American reality. For all our similarities, for all our sharing, for all our friendships, we *are* somebody else. Our national purpose, as enunciated in the B.N.A. Act, is "peace, order and good government," a becomingly modest ideal that is beginning to look more and more attractive. *Their* purpose is "the pursuit of happiness," a psychic steeplechase which has been known to lead to insanity.

One of the witnesses who appeared before us, Professor Thomas L. McPhail of Loyola University's Department of Communication Arts, warned that "Canada has one decade remaining in which its members have to make up their minds whether they want to remain a distinct political,cultural and geographical national entity." The C.R.T.C.'s Pierre Juneau, in his testimony, concurred in this assessment. So do we.

The question is, how successful have the media been in helping us to make up our minds? Here again, we must award less than perfect marks. There are too few Canadian stars, although there is plenty of talent. There are too few national news personalities in the manner of Walter Cronkite or Walter Lippmann. There is no *truly* national newspaper, no Canadian newsmagazine, no Canadian hit parade (although Quebec has one), not enough things like the NHL and the CBC that we can all talk about and react to and love and hate and know as our own.

This is hardly the media's fault. In fact, we have cause to be grateful for what the media have already accomplished, against considerable odds, in defining ourselves in non-American terms. But there is vast room for improvement. Later in this report, we will recommend means by which the government and the media can make such improvement possible.

II

OWNERSHIP

1. How Much is Enough?

Communications in Canada is a big business – a billion-dollar business, as a matter of fact, in terms of advertising revenue alone. Does this mean that the news is controlled by Big Business? And if so, how is that affecting the public interest? Finding answers to these questions has been the Committee's main job.

Before we could begin to answer it, though, we had to analyse *to what extent* the media are controlled by various kinds of groups. Strangely enough, no exhaustive comprehensive study of this subject had ever been made in Canada – perhaps because businessmen in the communications field tend to move faster than statisticians.

Accordingly, the Committee commissioned Hopkins, Hedlin Limited, a Toronto-based consultancy firm, to take a long and detailed look at the economics of the communications business in Canada. Their report, which we are publishing as a companion volume to this one, was a massive undertaking. This chapter and the next are a summary of the findings.

We have a few words of caution regarding the data contained in these two chapters: they have nothing to do with people. In the interests of statistical consistency, Hopkins, Hedlin had to make some extremely rigid distinctions between what constitutes a "group" and what constitutes an "independent" owner of a media outlet. But these distinctions bear no direct relation to editorial performance. Some of Canada's best newspapers are owned by groups; some of the worst are owned by independents. The obvious point we're trying to make is this: in the following pages, which analyse the extent of group versus independent ownership, we're not talking about Good Guys and Bad Guys. We're simply describing the ownership situation as it exists, in statistical terms that are wholly consistent but sometimes rather unreal.

To determine the extent of concentration of ownership in the mass media, we limited our study to the 103 Canadian communities where a daily newspaper is published, or where a primary (as opposed to a satellite) TV station is located, or where one of the major groups owns a media outlet. These 103 communities have a total population of about twelve million, but the media involved have a much larger total audience than that. In other words, we're talking here about the most important media outlets in the country, the ones from which the vast majority of the population gets its news, information and entertainment. Weekly newspapers and cable TV ownership aren't included in this chapter, but we'll be dealing with them later on.

On this basis, then, there were a total of 485 units of mass communication in the country in July, 1970. Of this total, 234 are owned by "independents" – that is, by corporations operating in a single community, although they may own more than one media outlet in that community. The rest are owned by "groups" – corporations which own a significant or controlling interest in media outlets in more than one community, or which own media outlets along with other business interests. The short answer to the question, then, is that groups now control 51.8 per cent – more than half – of all the important communications media in the country.

Of the 116 daily newspapers included in the survey, 77 (66.4 per cent) are owned by groups. Of the 97 private TV stations (including satellite stations located in some of the 103 surveyed communities, 47 (48.5 per cent) are group-owned, or groups have a substantial minority interest in them. Among the 272 private radio stations, groups hold controlling or substantial minority interests in 129 (47.4 per cent).

On the basis of this simple nose-count, Quebec's media show the highest degree of concentration of ownership; of 72 media outlets in that province, 47 (65.3 per cent) are group-owned. British Columbia comes next, where 44 (64.7 per cent) of 68 media outlets have group interests. The degree of concentration is least in Nova Scotia, Prince Edward Island, and Manitoba, where the proportion of media outlets in which groups have an interest is below 35 per cent.

Table 1 gives the province-by-province breakdowns.

There's another way of measuring concentration of ownership, and it's probably more meaningful in terms of the way people actually experience the media. That is, *in how many of these 103 communities do the same people own more than one media outlet?* Since so much of our news, information, and entertainment come to us through local outlets, this approach to concentration takes us closer to the realities of the situation. There are probably more potential dangers involved if the same people own all the media outlets in a single community than when a single chain owns several outlets in several towns.

Doing our nose-count on this basis, then, we get a pattern that is hardly reassuring. Of the 103 surveyed communities, there are 61 where groups or independents own two or more of the community's media outlets. There are 34 communities where groups own two or more radio stations, and 26 communities where independents own two or more. There are 31 communities

TABLE 1. GROUP OWNERSHIP BY MEDIA UNITS* IN SELECTED COMMUNITIES

Province	Media Units Total	Media Units Group	Media Units Per Cent	Newspapers Total	Newspapers Group	Newspapers Per Cent	Radio Total	Radio Group	Radio Per Cent	Television Total	Television Group	Television Per Cent
British Columbia	68	44	64.7	18	15	83.3	36	21	58.3	14	8	57.1
Alberta	40	19	47.5	7	6	85.7	23	9	39.1	10	4	40.0
Saskatchewan	28	12	42.9	4	4	100.0	15	5	33.3	9	3	33.3
Manitoba	30	10	33.3	7	2	28.6	16	7	43.8	7	1	14.3
Ontario	183	93	50.8	48	30	62.5	109	50	45.9	26	13	50.0
Quebec	72	47	65.3	14	9	64.3	41	29	70.7	17	11	64.7
New Brunswick	20	11	55.0	6	5	83.3	9	2	22.2	5	4	80.8
Nova Scotia	23	7	30.4	6	2	33.3	13	4	30.8	4	1	25.0
Prince Edward Island	7	2	28.6	3	2	66.7	3	0	0.0	1	0	0.0
Newfoundland	14	6	42.9	3	2	66.7	7	2	28.6	4	2	50.0
CANADA	485	251	51.8	116	77	66.4	272	129	47.4	97	47	48.5

*Total Media Units does not include cable television systems or shortwave radio.

II OWNERSHIP

TABLE 2. MULTIPLE GROUP AND INDEPENDENT INTERESTS BY LISTED COMMUNITIES

Province	Number of Communities	Multiple Interests Total*	Multiple Interests Group	Multiple Interests Independent	Radio Group	Radio Independent	Radio and Television Group	Radio and Television Independent	Mixed Media Group	Mixed Media Independent
British Columbia	15	11	11	4	6	3	7	2	2	0
Alberta	6	5	4	5	1	4	3	3	2	0
Saskatchewan	7	4	2	2	0	0	2	2	1	0
Manitoba	6	3	3	2	3	1	1	2	0	0
Ontario	45	23	20	18	15	16	8	4	2	3
Quebec	12	9	13	0	8	0	8	0	1	0
New Brunswick	3	2	2	0	0	0	1	0	2	0
Nova Scotia	5	3	1	2	1	2	0	1	0	0
Prince Edward Island	2	0	0	0	0	0	0	0	0	0
Newfoundland	2	1	1	0	0	0	1	0	0	0
CANADA	103	61	57	33	34	26	31	14	10	3

*Total number of communities in which multiple interests exist. This may not correspond to the total of multiple group and independent interests because more than one multiple interest may exist in one community.

where groups have common interests in both radio and TV stations, and another 14 communities where "independents" enjoy the same multiple interest.

There are also 11 communities where groups or independents have a common interest in the local newspaper *and* one or more of the broadcasting stations. In eight of these places, the people who own a newspaper also have a financial interest in the TV station. In four of these communities, the newspaper owners have an interest not only in the TV station, but in one or more of the local radio stations as well.

Table 2 gives a province-by-province breakdown of the situation.

NEWSPAPER NOSE-COUNT

When we consider ownership concentration as it applies to daily newspapers, the problem assumes a finer focus. If you accept the notion that "diverse and antagonistic" sources of information promote a healthy democracy, you would have to regard a city with at least two newspapers under separate ownership as being luckier than a city with only one. Well, how many Canadian cities are there where that situation exists? There are ten – or nine if you don't count Vancouver, where the two main dailies are published by a single corporation that is jointly owned by two newspaper groups. You might also discount Moncton and Sherbrooke as competing newspaper towns, since their two dailies are published in different languages. That leaves seven cities; and in most of them, groups control at least one of the competing newspapers.

In fact, there are only *three* Canadian cities – Montreal, Quebec City, and St. John's – where there is major competition involving at least one independent daily. (Toronto and Montreal don't count for the purposes of this study because we're labelling the Montreal *Star*, the Toronto *Star*, and the Toronto *Telegram* as "groups" because of their interests in weekend supplements and suburban weeklies).

On the face of it, this situation represents a significant decline in the number of "diverse and antagonistic" voices available to newspaper readers. According to Professor Wilfred Kesterton, around 1900 there were 66 dailies published in 18 communities with two or more newspapers. By 1958, there were only four communities in this position; between them, they published only 14 dailies. Today there are 23 dailies being published in five cities with two or more newspapers: six in Montreal, six in Vancouver (if you include the four suburban dailies of the Columbian group), four in Toronto (one published in Italian), four in Quebec, and three in Ottawa-Hull.

Putting it another way: just before the First World War, there were 138 daily newspapers in Canada – and there were 138 publishers. In 1953, Canada had the fewest newspapers (89) and the fewest publishers (57) since the first presses rolled out the Halifax *Gazette* in 1752. By 1966 there were 110 newspapers and 63 publishers. Today, 12 publishing groups produce more than two thirds of the country's 116 dailies.

So far in this analysis, we've been counting noses – the number of media outlets controlled by groups and independents. A more meaningful way of looking at the newspaper question, however, is in terms of circulation. Using this approach, we find that the 14 newspaper groups in Canada between them own or hold substantial interests in 77 dailies with a combined circulation of 3,614,354 – about 77 per cent of total Canadian daily circulation.

Newspaper groups control about 95 per cent of the daily circulation in British Columbia and Alberta, 100 per cent in Saskatchewan, 88.3 per cent in Manitoba, 75.9 per cent in Ontario, 92.7 per cent in New Brunswick, 72.6 per cent in Prince Edward Island, 81.1 per cent in Newfoundland, and 97.5 per cent (English) and 50.6 per cent (French) in Quebec, and 9 per cent in Nova Scotia.

The starkest finding, however, is that three of these groups – Southam, Thomson, and F.P. – control about 45 per cent of total Canadian daily newspaper circulation. A dozen years ago, the big three controlled only about 25 per cent.

If you're fond of tables and graphs, Table 3 and Chart 1 summarize the situation.

TABLE 3. PROPORTION OF DAILY NEWSPAPER CIRCULATION

Group	Circulation	Per Cent of Canadian Total
Desmarais-Parisien-Francoeur	319,770	6.8
Thomson	400,615	8.5
Southam	849,364	18.0
F. P.	855,170	18.2
Sifton	115,785	2.5
Toronto *Star*	395,210	8.4
Irving	104,442	2.2
Columbian	26,525	.6
Peladeau	60,045	1.3
Telegram	242,805	5.2
Green	15,142	.3
Montreal *Star*	195,696	4.2
Bowes	12,487	.3
Dingman Estate	21,298	.5
TOTAL GROUP CIRCULATION	3,614,354	77.0
TOTAL CANADIAN CIRCULATION	4,710,865	

On the nose-count basis, once again, the Thomson group, with 30 newspapers, is the largest. But Thomson is a small-town chain, while F.P. and Southam operate mainly in larger cities. The combined circulation of each of these two groups is more than double Thomson's.

Chart 1. CIRCULATION OF DAILY NEWSPAPERS AS A PROPORTION OF POPULATION

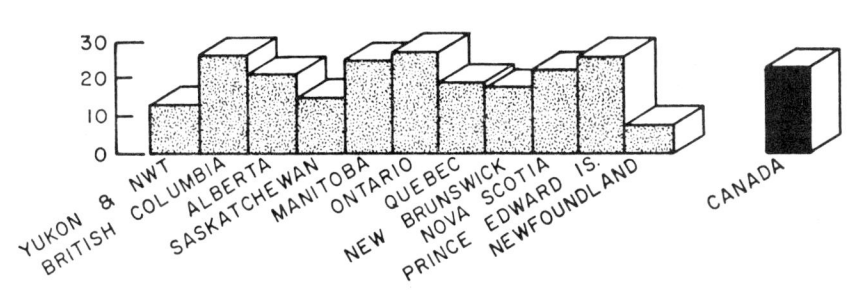

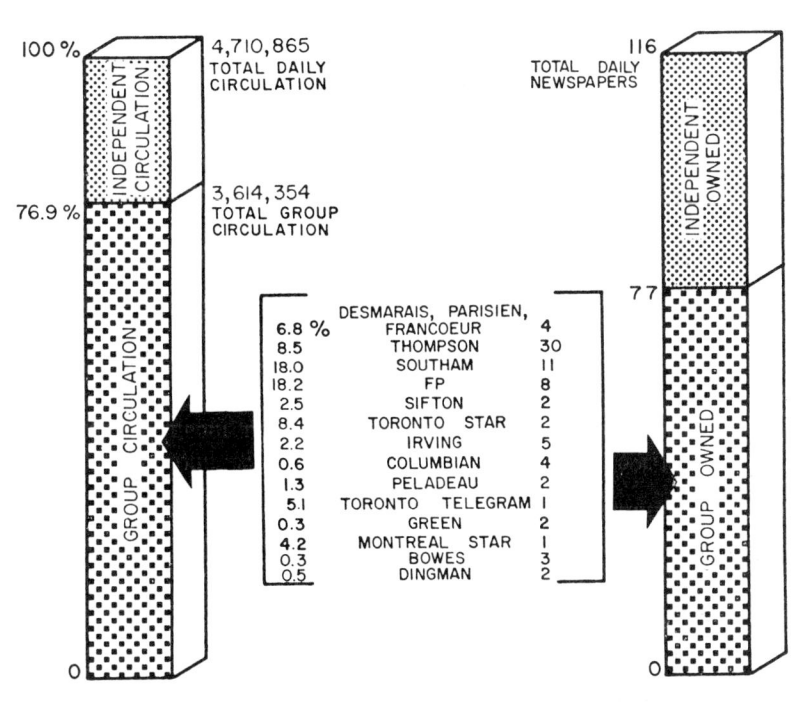

NUMBER OF DAILY NEWSPAPERS DISTRIBUTED FOR EACH 100 OF POPULATION

[Bar chart showing values for: YUKON & NWT, BRITISH COLUMBIA, ALBERTA, SASKATCHEWAN, MANITOBA, ONTARIO, QUEBEC, NEW BRUNSWICK, NOVA SCOTIA, PRINCE EDWARD IS., NEWFOUNDLAND, CANADA]

100% — 4,710,865 TOTAL DAILY CIRCULATION

116 TOTAL DAILY NEWSPAPERS

76.9% — 3,614,354 TOTAL GROUP CIRCULATION

77

%		
6.8 %	DESMARAIS, PARISIEN, FRANCOEUR	4
8.5	THOMPSON	30
18.0	SOUTHAM	11
18.2	FP	8
2.5	SIFTON	2
8.4	TORONTO STAR	2
2.2	IRVING	5
0.6	COLUMBIAN	4
1.3	PELADEAU	2
5.1	TORONTO TELEGRAM	1
0.3	GREEN	2
4.2	MONTREAL STAR	1
0.3	BOWES	3
0.5	DINGMAN	2

PROPORTION OF TOTAL CANADIAN CIRCULATION OF GROUP OWNED NEWSPAPERS

GROUP OWNERSHIP OF NEWSPAPERS IN CANADA

II OWNERSHIP

F.P. publishes the two dailies in Victoria. In Vancouver, F.P. owns the *Sun* and Southam the *Province*; both papers are published by Pacific Press Limited, in which Southam and F.P. share ownership on a 50-50 basis. Edmonton's only daily is owned by Southam, and Calgary's two competing dailies are owned by Southam and F.P. Southam and F.P. also own the two dailies in Winnipeg. In Regina and Saskatoon, the only dailies are owned by the Sifton family. In Ontario, where there are more dailies and their ownership less concentrated, F.P. controls the *Globe and Mail,* Southam owns Hamilton's only daily, and Ottawa's two English-language newspapers are published by Southam and F.P. In Quebec, Southam owns the Montreal *Gazette,* but the most powerful concentration is the one controlled by the Desmarais group which owns *La Presse* in Montreal, three other Quebec dailies, and a number of weeklies. In New Brunswick, K. C. Irving controls all five English-language dailies. In Nova Scotia, where most of the daily circulation is controlled by independents, the only Big Three newspaper is Thomson's New Glasgow *News.* In P.E.I., Thomson owns both Charlottetown dailies. In Newfoundland, two of the province's three dailies are now owned by Thomson.

GROUP PANORAMA

We turn now to broadcasting. Here, the patterns of ownership concentration are much trickier to describe because shared ownership is much more common than in the newspaper business, and because there are a lot more radio and TV stations than there are daily newspapers. Here again, though, the overall pattern seems clear: an accelerating trend towards concentration of ownership. In the past decade alone, nearly a dozen TV stations that started out as "independents" have come under the control of major broadcasting groups. The best way of surveying the situation is briefly to describe which groups own what in each province.

BRITISH COLUMBIA

Probably the province's most important broadcasting group, for the purposes of this survey, is Selkirk Holdings Limited, which controls radio stations in Vancouver, Victoria, and Vernon. Southam Press Limited is Selkirk's biggest (30 per cent) shareholder. Another major group is Western Broadcasting Company Limited, controlled by Frank Griffiths, which owns CKNW, the biggest radio station in the Greater Vancouver area. Western also shares ownership (with Selkirk and Famous Players Canadian Corporation Limited) in British Columbia Television Broadcasting System Limited, which own the private TV stations in Vancouver and Victoria. B.C. Television and Selkirk each hold a one-third interest in Okanagan Valley Television Company Limited, which owns TV stations in Kelowna, Vernon, and Penticton. Another major B.C. group, Skeena Broadcasters Limited, owns a primary TV station in Terrace-Kitimat with relays in Prince Rupert and other smaller communities as well as radio stations in Prince Rupert, Kitimat, and Terrace These groups control seven of B.C.'s 14 TV stations. In November, 1969, according to the Bureau of Broadcast Measurement, the eight group-owned stations accounted for 57.4 per cent of the province's total night-time TV circulation.

ALBERTA

Southam Press Limited which owns daily newspapers in Calgary, Edmonton, and Medicine Hat, also has interests in two radio stations in Edmonton and one in Calgary, either directly or indirectly through its holdings in Selkirk. Selkirk also controls radio stations in Grande Prairie and Lethbridge, and TV stations in Calgary and Lethbridge. The other TV station in each of those cities is controlled by Maclean-Hunter Limited, which also owns a radia station in Calgary. Four of Alberta's ten TV stations, and 40.6 per cent of the province's total TV audience (as measured by B.B.M.) are controlled by these groups.

SASKATCHEWAN

The Sifton family is the province's dominant media owner. Besides controlling both the province's major daily newspapers, they own one of Regina's five radio stations and one of its two TV stations, which has a satellite at Moose Jaw. The other group that counts is the Rawlinson family, which controls radio stations in Regina and Prince Albert, plus Prince Albert's only TV stations. These two families control three of Saskatchewan's nine TV stations, accounting for 30.8 per cent of total daily night-time circulation in the province, according to B.B.M.

MANITOBA

Although there is much independent media ownership, groups are active in Winnipeg, where F.P. owns one daily newspaper and Southam owns the other. Southam also has a 49 per cent interest in the Brandon *Sun*. Western Broadcasting Company Limited controls two Manitoba radio stations, Moffat Broadcasting Limited controls another two plus a TV station and Sifton owns one radio station. The Moffat TV station, one of seven in Manitoba, accounts for 33.9 per cent of total daily night-time circulation.

ONTARIO

Here, ownership patterns are so complex that we'll outline them on a city-by-city basis:

Toronto—Seven of the city's fifteen radio stations are controlled by groups: one by Maclean-Hunter Limited, two by Rogers Broadcasting Limited, two by CHUM Limited, and two by Standard Broadcasting Corporation Limited. Toronto's Italian-language daily newspaper is under independent control, but the three remaining dailies are under group control – the *Globe and Mail* by F.P., the *Star* by the Atkinson-Hindmarsh families, and the *Telegram* by the Bassett-Eaton interests, who also own the city's only private TV station.

Ottawa—*Le Droit,* the city's only French-language daily, is an independent. F.P. owns the Ottawa *Journal*; Southam owns the *Citizen*, as well as a substantial interest in one of the radio stations. The only private TV station is controlled by Bushnell Communications Limited, and broadcasting groups (CHUM, Télémédia Québec, and Raymond Crépault) own another five of the city's eleven radio stations.

Hamilton—Southam owns the only daily newspaper, the *Spectator,* Selkirk – in which Southam is the major shareholder – owns CHCH-TV (founded by Kenneth Soble), the city's only television station. Rogers Broadcasting Limited and Sifton each own Hamilton radio stations, and the Soble estate owns two.

Windsor—The city's only TV station was formerly owned by RKO Distributing Corporation (Canada) Limited which, because of federal restrictions on foreign ownership, was required to divest itself of ownership. The station is now jointly owned by the Bassett-Eaton interests (75 per cent) and the CBC (25 per·cent). Windsor's only daily newspaper is independent, but four of the five radio stations are controlled by groups: two by RKO (which the Bassett-Eaton group have bought subject to C.R.T.C. approval), two by Stirling.

London—The Blackburn family owns the city's only daily newspaper, its only TV station, and two of the four radio stations. Southam, however, holds 25 per cent of the shares of the newspaper – which in turn controls the three stations – plus a further 25 per cent interest in the preferred shares of the broadcasting operation.

Kitchener-Waterloo—Southam has a 48 per cent interest in the area's only daily newspaper, Maclean-Hunter owns two of the radio stations, and Carl Pollock owns the other two, as well as a TV station.

Sudbury—The Sudbury *Star* is controlled by Thomson. Cambrian Broadcasting Limited, owned by the Cooper, Miller and Plaunt families, owns the TV station and two of the four radio stations.

St. Catharines—The *Standard* and two of the four radio stations are controlled by the Burgoyne family.

Oshawa—Thomson owns the newspaper; the two radio stations are independent.

Sault Ste. Marie—Media ownership is mainly independent, although two of the radio stations are controlled by Greco, a small group which also owns radio stations at Blind River and Elliot Lake.

Brantford—The newspaper and two radio stations are independent.

Kingston—The Davies family owns the *Whig-Standard,* and used to have interests in two of the six radio stations and the TV station, but these broadcast holdings were sold to Bushnell Communications Limited in July, 1970.

Niagara Falls—The daily newspaper and the radio station are independently and separately owned.

Sarnia—Thomson owns the newspaper. The two radio stations are separately owned.

Peterborough—Thomson owns the *Examiner.* CHUM and Ralph Snelgrove share control of one radio station. Bushnell controls the other radio station and the TV station.

Guelph—The daily *Mercury* is owned by Thomson, and the one radio station is independently owned.

Oakville—Toronto Star Limited owns the *Daily Journal-Record,* and the radio station is independently owned. Bassett-Eaton interests own the weekly *Oakville Beaver*.

Thunder Bay—Thomson owns the *News-Chronicle* and the *Times-Journal*. The Dougall group owns the city's only TV station and two of its four radio stations.

In the province, groups account for 57.6 per cent of the total TV audience.

QUEBEC

Of Quebec's 14 daily newspapers, nine are group-owned, four by the Desmarais group. Two dailies are published by the Péladeau group. The other group-owned dailies are the Montreal *Star,* the Southam-owned Montreal *Gazette,* and the Thomson-owned Quebec *Chronicle-Telegraph*. Some 29 of the province's 41 radio stations in the surveyed communities are group-owned, including seven by Télémédia (Québec) Limitée, controlled by Philippe de Gaspé Beaubien, five by Crépault, three by a combination of Baribeau-Pratte interests, two each by Standard Broadcasting, Stirling, Tietolman, and Bushnell, one by the Desmarais group, and one by a combination of Baribeau and the Lepage Société. There are only six independent radio stations, the remaining six being owned by the CBC. Eleven of Quebec's 17 TV stations are are controlled by groups, including Télémédia's two stations in Sherbrooke and Rimouski. Desmarais has a minority interest in the

Carleton TV station, as does the Pratte group. Lepage-Baribeau controls the TV station at Jonquière, Famous Players and Baribeau-Pratte control two TV stations in Quebec City, and Bushnell in July, 1970, received C.R.T.C. approval to purchase CFCF-TV in Montreal. Of the province's total TV audience (English and French), 35.3 per cent is controlled by these groups.

NEW BRUNSWICK

K. C. Irving owns all five of the province's English-language dailies, one of Saint John's four radio stations, and its TV station. Since the C.R.T.C. ordered the Moncton TV station to install a satellite station in Saint John, and Irving's station to install a satellite in Moncton, both cities now have alternate TV service. The French-language daily, *L'Évangéline,* is independently owned. Irving reaches 94.9 per cent of New Brunswick's total TV audience.

NOVA SCOTIA

Thomson's New Glasgow *News* and Bowes' Truro *News* are the province's only group-owned newspapers. The Dennis family controls Halifax's two dailies. Of Nova Scotia's 13 radio stations, the Manning family owns two in Truro and one in Amherst, and CHUM owns CJCH radio in Halifax. CTV has a controlling interest in CJCH-TV in Halifax, but Selkirk and Western Broadcasting hold significant minority positions in the same station which, according to the B.B.M. survey cited earlier in this study, accounted for 38.1 per cent of the province's total daily night-time circulation.

PRINCE EDWARD ISLAND

Thomson owns Charlottetown's two dailies. Summerside's only daily is independent, as are two radio stations in the surveyed communities. The CBC owns the only TV station and one radio station.

NEWFOUNDLAND

In 1970, the Herder family sold two of the province's three dailies to the Thomson group. Geoffrey Stirling controls one radio station, and one of the two TV stations in St. John's which accounts for 46.2 per cent of the province's total TV circulation.

SOME GROUP PROFILES

So far in this chapter, we've been attempting to define the extent of concentration of ownership in the media by a statistical analysis of the situation, and by briefly indicating who owns what in each province.

To clarify this latter point, the remainder of this chapter consists of brief profiles of most of Canada's important media ownership groups. These are the corporations whose owners are responsible for most of the nation's daily newspaper circulation, most of its radio and TV distribution. Their influence is considerable, and it appears to be increasing rapidly.

THE BASSETT-EATON GROUP

This group is represented by the Telegram Corporation Limited, the shares of which are held in trust for the three sons of *Telegram* publisher John Bassett and the four sons of John David Eaton, the recently retired head of Canada's biggest retailing chain. One subsidiary, Telegram Publishing Company Limited, publishes the Toronto *Telegram*. Another subsidiary, Inland Publishing Company Limited, owns the following seven suburban Toronto weeklies with a total circulation around 90,000: Bramalea *Guardian*, Burlington *Post,* Mississauga *News,* Newmarket *Era,* Oakville *Beaver,* Stouffville, *Tribune,* Whitby-Ajax *News Advertiser.*

The Telegram Corporation also holds 53.17 per cent interest in Baton Broadcasting Limited (which operates CFTO-TV, the city's only private TV station) and 50.52 per cent of Glen-Warren Productions Limited, a TV production house. Glen-Warren had held 50 per cent of the common shares of Gogers Cable T.V. Limited until ordered by the C.R.T.C. to dispose of this interest. These shares have since been sold to E. S. Rogers. The C.R.T.C. also approved the purchase of CKLW-TV in Windsor, Ontario, by Baton Broadcasting Limited in partnership with the CBC, the latter holding a 25 per cent interest with the option to buy the remaining shares within five years.

BUSHNELL COMMUNICATIONS LIMITED

Bushnell has emerged, fairly suddenly, as one of Canada's major broadcasting groups. Last year the company owned CJOH-TV in Ottawa and CJSS-TV in Cornwall, minority or controlling interests in three cable TV companies, plus several TV production and service firms and a broadcast sales company. This year, as a result of a series of C.R.T.C.-approved acquisitions, Bushnell is in a position to create what amounts to the country's third broadcasting network.

In July, 1970, Bushnell received approval to acquire the Montreal broadcast interests of the Canadian Marconi Company which had been forced to sell because of federal restrictions on foreign ownership. These interests included CFCF-TV, CFCF (Canada's oldest radio station), and CFQR-FM and CFCX (short wave). At the same time, Bushnell acquired all the broadcast interests held separately and jointly by the Davies family of Peterborough and the Thomson group. These include CKWS-AM and FM and CKWS-TV in Kingston, CHEX-AM and FM and CHEX-TV in Peterborough, CKGB-AM and CKGB-FM in Timmins, and CJKL in Kirkland Lake.

The Commission also approved the sale to Bushnell of half the shares of Cablevue (Belleville) Limited which serves Belleville and Trenton, and all the shares of CFCH and CFCH-TV in North Bay. The C.R.T.C. stipulated, however, that Bushnell must resell its interests in Cablevue and in the North Bay stations "as rapidly as possible."

CHUM LIMITED

This is a public company, controlled by Allan Waters, whose main assets are CHUM-AM and FM in Toronto, and a two-thirds interest in Ralph Snelgrove Television Limited, which operates CKVR-TV in Barrie. It also owns CFRA-AM and CFMO-FM in Ottawa, and Waters personally holds a 4.3 per cent interest in CKLC and CKLC-FM in Kingston. CHUM Limited has acquired all the shares of CJCH radio in Halifax and Associated Broadcasting Corp., which operates the Muzak franchise in Ontario and whose ownership was formerly split between Waters and Famous Players Canadian Corporation Limited.

THE DESMARAIS-PARISIEN-FRANCOEUR GROUP

Until recently, Power Corporation of Canada Limited and its Chief Executive Officer Paul Desmarais owned extensive media holdings in Quebec. Last year, apparently in response to public concern (which was reflected in the establishment of a Special Committee on Freedom of the Press by the Quebec Legislature) Power Corporation sold most of its media holdings.

Power Corporation sold 18 newspapers (and one radio station which is associated with the Granby daily) to Les Journaux Trans-Canada Limitée. The latter company's ownership is divided among Desmarais (46.6 per cent), Jacques Francoeur (33.3 per cent), Jean Parisien (15.6 per cent) and Pierre Dansereau (4.45 per cent). Also, Entreprises Gelco Limitée, three-quarters of which is owned by Desmarais (the remaining quarter by Jean Parisien), purchased *La Presse,* Quebec's largest French-language daily (circulation 222,184).

THE DOUGALL FAMILY

This northern Ontario group controls CKPR-TV in Thunder Bay, as well as CKPR-AM and CKPR-FM, plus smaller stations in Dryden, Fort Fances, and Kenora.

F. P. PUBLICATIONS LIMITED

This group is by a slight margin the biggest newspaper chain in the country. It owns or controls eight dailies with a combined circulation of 855,170 and has minority interests in cable TV in Victoria, and in a cable TV company in Calgary that must be sold by C.R.T.C. order. Table 4 lists F.P.'s holdings.

Table 4. MEDIA INTERESTS OF F. P. PUBLICATIONS LIMITED

Newspapers	Circulation	Extent of Interest
		%
Dailies		
Sun (Vancouver, B.C.)	256,806	control
Daily Times (Victoria, B.C.)	31,667	100
Daily Colonist (Victoria, B.C.)	39,158	100
Albertan (Calgary, Alta.)	35,382	100
Herald (Lethbridge, Alta.)	20,844	100
Free Press (Winnipeg, Man.)	134,409	100
Journal (Ottawa, Ont.)	81,171	99.885
Globe and Mail (Toronto, Ont.)	255,733	100
Farm Publication		
Free Press Weekly	550,931	100

Broadcasting	
	%
Cable	
Victoria Cablevision Limited (Victoria, B.C.)	12.5
Community Antenna Television Limited (Calgary, Alta.)	16.7

THE IRVING GROUP

K. C. Irving controls a vast corporate empire in New Brunswick; and almost as an incidental by-product, has achieved the country's highest degree of regional concentration of mass-media ownership. Through the New Brunswick Publishing Company Limited, K. C. Irving owns the *Telegraph-Journal* and the *Evening Times-Globe* in Saint John and the *Times* and the *Transcript* in Moncton. He also controls a majority of the voting shares of University Press of New Brunswick Limited, which publishes the *Daily Gleaner* in Fredericton. The province's only other daily is *L'Evangéline*, a French-language independent. Irving also controls New Brunswick Broadcasting Company Limited, which operates CHSJ and CHSJ-TV in Saint John, with a satellite in Bon Accord, and CHMT-TV, the satellite in Moncton. Of the province's 20 media outlets in the surveyed communities, eight are controlled by K. C. Irving. This is not the place to detail Mr. Irving's extensive non-media interests, which embrace everything from oil to pulp and paper to hardware stores to shipping. But he is by far the most important economic force in the province.

MACLEAN-HUNTER LIMITED

This company is one of the giants of the Canadian communications industry, whose diversified interests in publishing, broadcasting, information services, and industrial and trade shows accounted for net sales in 1969 of more than $58 million. Its publishing interests include three English and two French consumer magazines with a total circulation of 2,262,830; 56 English and

French business periodicals with a total circulation of 516,000; and 21 annuals with an estimated circulation of 289,749. Maclean-Hunter also publishes ten trade periodicals in Britain, five in the U.S., and several in France, Germany and Italy. In the broadcasting field, the company owns CFCN-TV in Calgary and its satellites, including CFCN-TV in Lethbridge. It also owns or controls the following radio stations: CFCN-AM, Calgary; CFCO-AM Chatham; CHYM-AM, Kitchener; CKEY-AM in Toronto; and CFOR-AM in Orillia. Finally, its cable TV holdings include controlling interests in cable operations serving seventeen Ontario communities.

THE McCONNELL FAMILY

The estate of the late J. W. McConnell is locked into a number of trusts that are voted at the direction of his two children, J. G. McConnell and Mrs. P. M. Laing. The estate's corporate cornerstone is Commercial Trust Company Limited, 88 per cent of whose shares are held by Montreal Trust Company as part of a voting trust agreement under which the shares are voted at the direction of Mr. McConnell and Mrs. Laing. Commercial Trust, in turn, holds virtually all the shares in the Montreal Star (1968) Limited and Montreal Standard Publishing Company Limited as a trustee for Starlaw Investments Ltd., the beneficial owner. Starlaw is owned by SLSR Holdings Limited (formerly St. Lawrence Sugar Refineries Limited), and by another corporate entity called The Montreal Star Holdings Limited (formerly The Montreal Star Company). Finally, Commercial Trust, as trustee for Mr. McConnell and Mrs. Laing, owns virtually all the shares of SLSR Holdings Limited and Montreal Star Holdings Limited, the two firms that control Starlaw Investments Limited.

The Montreal Star (1968) Limited publishes the Montreal *Star* (circulation 195,696). The Montreal Standard Publishing Company has a controlling interest in *Weekend Magazine* (and prints it as well) and a 24.7 per cent interest in Perspectives Inc., which publishes *Perspectives* and *Perspectives-Dimanche*. Weekend Magazine is distributed as a supplement in 39 English-language dailies with a total circulation of 1,805,839. *Perspectives* is distributed as a weekly supplement in six Quebec dailies whose total circulation is 828,430. *Perspectives-Dimanche* is distributed as part of *Dimanche-Matin*, a French-language tabloid with a circulation of about 290,000. Weekend's most direct competitor is *Canadian* Magazine, *Canadian Homes* and the *Canadian Star Weekly*. The latter is sold on newsstands, but the *Canadian* and *Canadian Homes* are distributed as supplements in other English-language dailies. All three are owned by Southstar Publishers Limited which is jointly owned by Southam Press Limited and Toronto Star Limited. Despite their editorial rivalry, the competitors co-operate. Montreal Standard prints the Southstar magazines as well as *Weekend* and *Perspectives,* and Southstar and Montreal Standard jointly own a company called Magna Media Limited, which sells advertising for Southstar.

MOFFAT BROADCASTING LIMITED

This is one of the industry's longest-established broadcasting firms, with holdings in five cities in western Canada. Moffat owns 50 per cent (the Misener family owns the other half) of CJAY-TV in Winnipeg, 45 per cent of CHED-AM in Edmonton, and wholly owns the following radio stations: CKLG-AM and CKLG-FM in Vancouver; CKXL-AM in Calgary; CHAB-AM in Moose Jaw; CKY-AM and CKY-FM in Winnipeg. Moffat also holds a 38.75 per cent interest in Metro Videon Limited, which operates a cable TV system serving Winnipeg and Pinawa.

THE PRATTE, BARIBEAU AND LEPAGE GROUP

This group consists of an interlocking assortment of media interests of four groups which are involved in twelve broadcasting outlets in the province of Quebec. They include TV stations in Quebec City, Montreal, Jonquière, and Carleton, and radio stations in Jonquière, Quebec City, Montreal, and Shawinigan. The interlocking nature of the groups' media holdings is illustrated in Chart 2.

RADIODIFFUSION MUTUELLE LIMITÉE—MUTUAL BROADCASTING LIMITED

The holding company for a group of radio stations under the control of Raymond Crépault, consisting of CJMS and CJMS-FM in Montreal, CJRP-AM in Quebec, CJRS-AM in Sherbrooke, CJTR-AM in Trois-Rivières, and CJRC-AM in Ottawa. The group is unique in that it has C.R.T.C. permission to operate as a permanent private radio network.

ROGERS BROADCASTING LIMITED

Rogers is a private company whose shares are controlled by two family trusts. The Rogers group controls CHFI-AM and CHFI-FM in Toronto, CHAM-AM in Hamilton, and CHYR-AM in Leamington, Ontario. Its cable interests include two systems in Toronto, one in Brampton, and one in Leamington.

Prior to September 1970, Rogers Broadcasting Limited held a 13.4 per cent interest in Baton Broadcasting Limited owned by the Bassett-Eaton group (which operates CFTO-TV in Toronto). Through Glen-Warren Productions the Bassett-Eaton group owned 50 per cent of Rogers Cable T.V. Limited. Licences were granted to Rogers' two other cable systems providing that Glen-Warren disposed of its share in the cable company. Hence the two parties sold their interests in each other's operations.

Recently the company's President, E. S. Rogers, applied to the Federal Communications Commission in Washington for a cable licence in Detroit – the first such bid by a Canadian company in the U.S.

Chart 2. MEDIA INTERESTS OF PRATTE, BARIBEAU AND LEPAGE GROUPS

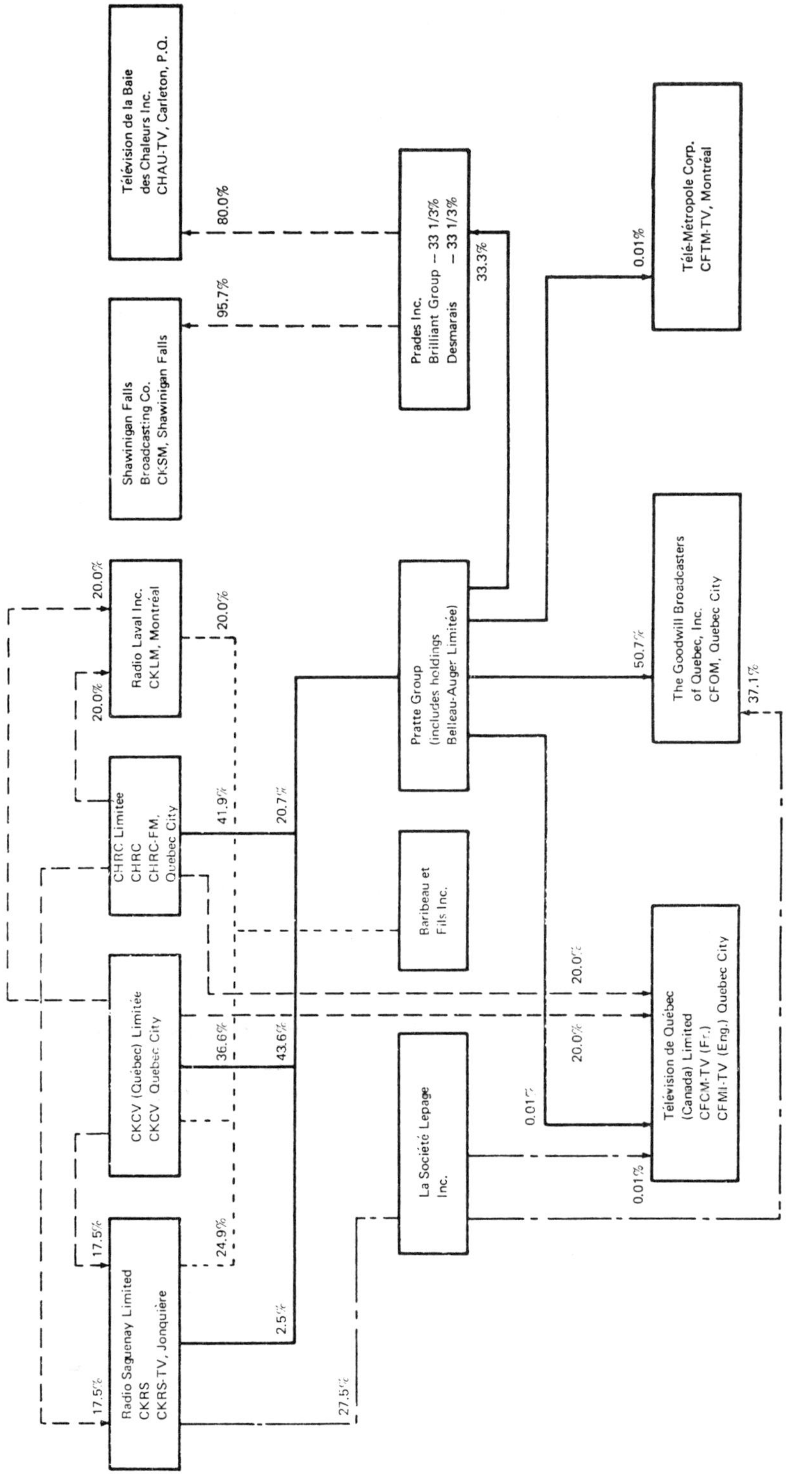

32 THE UNCERTAIN MIRROR

SELKIRK HOLDINGS LIMITED

A public company in which Southam holds a 30 per cent interest. In addition to its joint ownership with Southam of CJCA-AM and CJCA-FM in Edmonton, and CFAC-AM in Calgary, Southam and Selkirk each own 25 per cent of Greater Winnipeg Cablevision Limited. Selkirk wholly owns CHCT-TV in Calgary, with satellites in Drumheller and Banff; CJLH-TV in Lethbridge, which is a partial satellite of the Calgary station, but has relays of its own in Coleman and Burmis, Alberta; CJOC in Lethbridge; CJVI in Victoria; CKWX and CKFX in Vancouver; CJIB in Vernon, CHCH-TV in Hamilton. Selkirk also has a 38 per cent direct interest in CKGP in Grande Prairie, Alberta, and associated interests hold another 36 per cent. Through its minority interests in British Columbia Television Broadcasting Systems Limited, Selkirk has a 36 per cent interest in CHAN-TV in Vancouver, CHEK-TV in Victoria, and CHBC-TV in Kelowna (where its interest through British Columbia Television is supplemented by a direct 33 per cent interest). Selkirk also has substantial minority interests in CJCH-TV in Halifax, Ottawa Cablevision (which wholly owns Pembroke Cablevision) and Cablevision Lethbridge.

THE SIFTON GROUP

This group is controlled by the Clifford Sifton family and operated by Michael Sifton, and functions through Armadale Company Limited which owns all the shares in Armadale Enterprises Limited. Armadale Enterprises in turn owns all the shares in the Regina *Leader-Post* and Armadale Publishers Limited, which publishes the Saskatoon *Star-Phoenix* and *Toronto Life* magazine. Armadale Enterprises also holds 98 per cent of the shares of Armadale Communications Limited, which operates CKCK-AM and CKCK-TV in Regina, CKRC-AM in Winnipeg, and CKJC-AM in Hamilton. Armadale Communications also owns 25 per cent of Eastern Ontario Broadcasting Limited, licensee of CFJR-AM in Brockville. The Sifton group also has 11 per cent of Quality Records Limited, a real estate firm called Jonquil Limited, and a half-interest in Toronto Airways Limited.

THE SOUTHAM GROUP

This is the oldest, largest, and most diversified media group in Canada. It controls eleven daily newspapers with a total circulation of 849,364, and holds substantial minority interests in three other dailies, and owns 50 per cent of Pacific Press Limited, which publishes the Vancouver *Sun* and the Southam-owned Vancouver *Province*. The group also owns half of Southstar Publishers Limited, which publishes the *Canadian* Magazine, *Canadian Homes,* and the *Canadian/Star Weekly*.

Southam also publishes the *Financial Times of Canada,* the weekly *News and Chronicle* in Pointe-Claire, Quebec and, through wholly-owned Southam Business Publications Limited, some 44 trade magazines and 19 annuals. It also owns half of C. O. Nickle Publishing Company, which publishes magazines related to the petroleum industry, and holds a 7.9 per cent interest in *Homemaker's Digest.* The group also operates a large printing operation, owns 11 per cent of Quality Records Limited, and has extensive interests in a wide variety of trade shows. Gross operating revenues in 1969 were $104.7 million, a figure unmatched by any other media company in Canada.

Table 5 lists the publications (apart from the trade magazines) in which Southam exercises a minority or controlling interest.

TABLE 5. PRINT INTERESTS OF SOUTHAM PRESS LIMITED, OTHER THAN TRADE PUBLICATIONS

Newspapers	Circulation	Extent of Interest %
Dailies		
Citizen (Prince George, B.C.)	12,087	100
Province (Vancouver, B.C.)	110,677	Control
Herald (Calgary, Alta.)	100,907	100
Journal (Edmonton, Alta.)	150,130	100
News (Medicine Hat, Alta.)	7,922	100
Tribune (Winnipeg, Man.)	78,024	100
Sun-Times (Owen Sound, Ont.)	14,739	100
Spectator (Hamilton, Ont.)	127,195	100
Nugget (North Bay, Ont.)	17,942	100
Citizen (Ottawa, Ont.)	94,807	100
Gazette (Montreal, P.Q.)	134,934	100
Sun (Brandon, Man.)	14,145	49
Record (Kitchener-Waterloo, Ont.)	52,619	48
Free Press (London, Ont.)	123,488	25
Weeklies		
Financial Times of Canada	46,633	100
News and Chronicle (Pointe Claire, P.Q.)	17,500	100
Weekend Magazines		
The Canadian (weekly)	2,025,664	50
Canadian Homes (monthly)	2,025,664	50
The Canadian/Star Weekly (weekly)	400,000+	50

Southam has a 25 per cent interest in CFPL radio and CFPL-TV in London, Ontario. This interest evolves through its ownership of 25 percent of London Free Press Holdings Limited, which owns virtually all the outstanding shares of CFPL Broadcasting Limited. Southam also owns directly approximately 25 per cent of the preferred shares. Southam has a 38 per cent interest in CKOY in Ottawa, and a 40 per cent interest in CJCA in Edmonton, and CFAC in Calgary. In each case, Selkirk Holdings Limited owns the remainder. Southam also has a 25 per cent interest in Greater Winnipeg Cablevision Limited, in which Selkirk has a similar share.

STANDARD BROADCASTING CORPORATION LIMITED

Controlled by Argus Corporation, one of Canada's leading holding companies. It owns Toronto's largest radio station, CFRB, its FM affiliate CKFM, and CFRX (shortwave) as well as CJAD-AM and CJFM in Montreal. The company also owns Standard Broadcast Sales Inc., a radio sales representative company, Standard Broadcast Productions Limited, which operates Standard Broadcast News, an hourly radio news service for other Canadian stations, and Canadian Talent Library; and Standard Sound Systems Company Limited, which holds the Muzak franchise for Montreal, Quebec, and the Maritimes.

TÉLÉMÉDIA (QUÉBEC) LIMITÉE

In July, 1970, the C.R.T.C. approved the sale of Power Corporation's broadcast holding company, Québec Télémédia Inc., to Philippe de Gaspé Beaubien. The purchase of the new company was financed by a debenture in the amount of $7.25 million in favour of Québec Télémédia Inc. and Trans-Canada Corporation Fund. Since the sale, the new company has purchased CKCH Radio in Hull resulting in holdings which total three TV stations, one a rebroadcasting station in Edmunston, N.B., and nine radio stations in seven Quebec communities.

While Power Corporation has divested itself of the direct ownership of broadcasting interests, it continues to have minority broadcast holding through indirect investments in CHUM Limited, Standard Broadcasting Corporation Limited, and Skyline Cablevision.

THE THOMSON GROUP

Thomson owns thirty daily newspapers in Canada, eleven weeklies, three bi-weeklies, and one triweekly. The family of the late Senator Rupert Davies owns the Kingston *Whig-Standard* and, until recently, shared ownership with Thomson Newspapers Limited in a number of Ontario radio or TV stations. Thomson also owned five radio stations, one TV station and one TV satellite in northern Ontario, but these broadcast assets, together with those in which ownership was shared by the Davies family, have been sold to Bushnell Communications Limited in a deal approved in July 1970 by the C.R.T.C. Table 6 lists the group's current media holdings.

TABLE 6. MEDIA INTERESTS OF THE THOMSON GROUP

Newspapers	Circulation	Extent of Interest
		%
Dailies		
Daily Sentinel (Kamloops)	9,493	100
Daily Courier (Kelowna)	8.115	100
Daily Free Press (Nanaimo)	9,342	100
Herald (Penticton)	6,317	100
Times-Herald (Moose Jaw)	9,318	100
Daily Herald (Prince Albert)	8,189	100
Examiner (Barrie)	10,183	100
Daily Times & Conservator (Brampton)	7,863	100
Daily News (Chatham)	15,129	100
Standard-Freeholder (Cornwall)	14,447	100
Evening Reporter (Galt)	13,824	100
Mercury (Guelph)	17,519	100
Northern Daily News (Kirkland Lake)	6,460	100
Daily Packet and Times (Orillia)	7,953	100
Times (Oshawa)	24,452	100
Observer (Pembroke)	7,861	100
Examiner (Peterborough)	23,026	99
Observer (Sarnia)	18,603	100
Star (Sudbury)	35,362	100
Daily Times-Journal (Thunder Bay)	17,105	100
News-Chronicle (Thunder Bay)	15,766	100
Daily Press (Timmins)	11,779	100
Evening Tribune (Welland)	19,409	100
Daily Sentinel-Review (Woodstock)	10,229	100
Chronicle-Telegraph (Quebec)	4,523	100
Evening News (New Glasgow)	10,055	100
Guardian (Charlottetown)	16,414	100
Evening Patriot (Charlottetown)	4,478	100
Western Star (Corner Brook)	7,884	99.9
Telegram (St. John's)	29,517	99.9
Weeklies		
Enterprise (Yorkton)	7,578	100
Chronicle (Arnprior)	2,828	100
Enterprise-Bulletin (Collingwood)	4,485	100
Chronicle (Dunnville)	3,521	100
Standard (Elliot Lake)	2,500	100
Standard (Espanola)	2,159	100
Herald (Georgetown)	4,589	100
Post (Hanover)	3,271	100
Post and News (Leamington)	5,158	100
Banner (Orangeville)	4,523	100
Northern Light (Bathurst)	5,296	100
Bi-weeklies		
News (Vernon)	6,617	100
Sun (Swift Current)	6,589	100
Free Press Herald (Midland)	5,848	100
Tri-weeklies		
Trentonian (Trenton)	7,313	100

SOURCE: *Canadian Advertising Rates and Data,* December, 1969

TORONTO STAR LIMITED

This is a public company in which the major shareholders are the Atkinson-Hindmarsh families. The company publishes Canada's largest daily (circulation 387,418) and the Oakville *Journal-Record* (7,792), and has interests in eleven Toronto suburban weekly newspapers with a total circulation of 161,810. The company also owns half of Southstar Publishers Limited, which publishes the *Canadian* Magazine, *Canadian Homes,* and the *Canadian/Star Weekly.* Table 7 lists the group's current media holdings.

TABLE 7. MEDIA INTERESTS OF TORONTO STAR LIMITED

Newspapers	Circulation	Extent of Interest %
Dailies		
Daily Journal-Record (Oakville)	7,792	100
Star (Toronto)	387,418	100
Weeklies		
Gazette (Burlington)	9,085	100
Times (Mississauga)	13,202	100
Metropolitan Toronto area:		
Aurora Banner	5,143	100
Richmond Hill Liberal	7,890	100
Willowdale Enterprise	13,472	100
Scarborough Mirror	37,922	50
Don Mills Mirror	53,512	50
The Lakeshore Advertiser	10,000*	75
Weston-York Times	4,149	75
Woodbridge and Vaughan News	3,010	75
The Etobicoke Advertiser-Guardian	19,443	75
Weekend Magazines		
The Canadian (weekly)	2,025,664	50
Canadian Homes (monthly)	2,025,664	50
The Canadian/Star Weekly (weekly)	400,000+	50

*Report by publisher to Committee.

WESTERN BROADCASTING COMPANY LIMITED

Controls CKNW in New Westminster, CNQR in Calgary, CJOB and CJOB-FM in Winnipeg. It owns 44 per cent of British Columbia Television Broadcasting System Limited which operates CHAN-TV in Vancouver and CHEK-TV in Victoria. Part of this is indirect through the company's partnership with Selkirk Holdings Limited in Canastel Broadcasting Corporation Limited, which also owns shares in B.C. Television. B.C. Television also has a one-third interest in Okanagan Valley Television Company Limited which owns CHBC-TV in Kelowna with satellites in Penticton, Vernon, and other communities. Also through Canastel, Western has a 25 per cent interest in CJCH-TV in Halifax. The company also has acquired total ownership of Express Cable Television Limited in North Vancouver.

2. Balance Sheet

THE MESSAGE-BEARERS

The media give us our news, our information, our entertainment, and to some extent our sense of ourselves as a nation. That is their social function, and one of the tasks of this Committee was to enquire how well they are performing it.

To do that, it is first necessary to view the media in the harshest possible light: as economic entities, as capitalist institutions. What, in business terms, are the media *for*? What are they selling? How much does it cost them to produce what they sell? What kind of prices do they get for their product? How much is left over as profit? What do they do with those profits? What happens to costs and profits as the size of the media unit increases? What is the economic advantage of combining several media units under one corporate umbrella?

These are hard-nosed questions, and answering them involves acceptance of one of those little contradictions which make the study of economics such a truly dismal occupation. To view the media in economic terms, we must temporarily suspend our habit of looking at them in human terms. Forget for the moment that the media are purveyors of facts and dreams and sounds and images. Forget the horoscopes, forget Gordon Sinclair's voice, forget the headlines on the front page, forget Bonanza, forget *content* – because, in the strict economic sense, that is not what the media are selling.

What the media *are* selling, in a capitalist society, is an audience, and the means to reach that audience with advertising messages. As Toronto advertising man Jerry Goodis, who appeared before the Committee, put it: "The business side of the mass media is devoted to building and selling the right audience . . . those who buy and, more importantly, those who can choose what they will buy, those whose choice is not dictated by necessity." In this sense, the content – good or bad, timid or courageous, stultifying or brilliant, dull or amusing – is nothing more than the means of attracting the audience. It seems harsh, but it happens to be utterly accurate, that editorial and programming content in the media fulfils precisely the same economic function as the hootchy-kootch girl at a medicine show – she pulls in the rubes so that the pitchman will have somebody to flog his snake-oil to. This notion may collide with the piety with which most media owners view their social responsibilities, but the more you think about the analogy, the apter it seems. Yes, advertisers are concerned with content, but only insofar as it serves to attract an audience. As the Association of Canadian Advertisers delicately expressed it in their brief: "Essentially, the national advertiser views any medium simply as a vehicle for conveying his advertising message... (He is) very definitely interested in the editorial information or program content of any medium, because, of course, the nature of the content determines the particular segment of the public likely to be reached by the medium, or any part of it." In other words, the pitchman would naturally prefer a slender, 17-year-old hootchy-kootch girl to a flabby, 45-year-old hoofer.

Perhaps at this point it would be best to jettison the hootchy-kootch analogy, before she shimmies out of control. Let us do so with the parting observation that, in Canada, she is a very well-paid young lady. The mass media in this country now collect more than a billion dollars a year from advertisers, a total that has more than tripled in the past twenty years. The greatest growth has been in broadcasting, where advertising accounts for 93 per cent of gross revenues in the private sector. But print has also shared in the boom; net advertising revenue for newspapers and periodicals has more than tripled since 1950, and accounts for 65 per cent of the gross income of newspapers and 70 per cent for periodicals. You can see that it is very big business indeed; every time you spend a dollar on consumer goods or services, it means that an advertiser has invested about $2\frac{1}{4}$ cents to persuade you to spend it.

NEWSPAPER COSTS

And so, in strict economic terms, the media exist as message-bearers for people who want to sell us something. The remainder of our economic argument is concerned with what it costs them to deliver that message – in terms of production and content costs – and how much is left over as profit. We'll also see what happens to these factors as the size of the audience increases. To do so, we'll consider print and broadcasting separately.

On the cost side, Table 8 more or less says it all. The D.B.S. statistics we use apply only to publications which both publish and print their own product; thus, they apply most specifically to daily newspapers and, to a lesser extent, to weekly newspapers and magazines. (We should note that while we use D.B.S. aggregates in this discussion, they were supplemented and substantially confirmed by the confidential data supplied to our researchers by representative publishing firms.)

TABLE 8. DISTRIBUTION OF COSTS OF PRODUCTION, PRINTING AND PUBLISHING INDUSTRIES, 1960–1966

Year	Newsprint Paper	Ink	Fuel and Electricity	Other Purchased Material and Supplies	Wages and Salaries	Gross Returns to Capital	Total Revenues
				Dollars			
1960	60,376,000	4,005,000	2,966,000	29,878,000	143,041,000	118,665,000	358,524,000
61	60,002,000	4,180,000	3,071,000	30,129,000	147,855,000	125,052,000	370,327,000
62	60,432,000	4,236,000	3,256,000	31,277,000	157,875,000	128,424,000	385,824,000
63	60,789,000	4,200,000	3,313,000	31,819,000	161,761,000	127,795,000	389,739,000
64	61,156,000	4,387,000	3,428,000	33,862,000	163,639,000	141,447,000	406,716,000
65	65,488,000	4,643,000	3,510,000	36,720,000	179,551,000	156,978,000	446,885,000
66	69,054,000	5,411,000	3,741,000	43,835,000	193,136,000	166,013,000	481,443,000
				Per Cent of Total			
1960	16.84	1.11	.82	8.33	39.89	33.09	100.0
61	16.20	1.12	.82	8.13	39.92	33.76	100.0
62	15.66	1.09	.84	8.10	40.91	33.28	100.0
63	15.59	1.07	.85	8.16	41.50	32.78	100.0
64	15.03	1.07	.84	8.32	40.23	34.77	100.0
65	14.65	1.03	.78	8.21	40.17	35.12	100.0
66	14.34	1.12	.77	9.10	40.11	34.48	100.0
				Index (1960 = 100)			
1960	100.0	100.0	100.0	100.0	100.0	100.0	100.0
61	99.4	104.4	103.5	100.8	103.4	105.4	103.3
62	100.1	105.8	109.8	104.7	110.4	108.2	107.6
63	100.7	104.9	111.7	106.5	113.1	107.7	108.7
64	102.3	109.5	115.6	113.3	114.4	119.2	113.4
65	108.5	115.9	118.3	122.9	125.5	132.3	124.6
66	114.4	135.1	126.1	146.7	135.0	139.9	134.3

SOURCE: Printing, Publishing and Allied Industries, D.B.S., 36–203 (Annual)

The table analyzes the relative economic importance of various cost inputs in the publishing industry from 1960 to 1966. These are the things that publishers must spend money *on,* in order to attract an audience and deliver advertising messages to that audience. An examination of this table provides several useful insights. Among them:

*The publishing industry as a whole (as distinct from the printing industry) spends a much lower proportion of its revenues on outside goods and services than many other manufacturing industries. In general, the industry spends between 25 and 27 per cent of its total revenues on newsprint, ink, fuel, electricity and "etceteras," which include everything from buying paper-clips to chartering helicopters. It is thus correspondingly less dependent than many manufacturing industries on changes in external conditions — like, say, a hike in the price of newsprint. In fact, if the price of *everything* the industry buys from outside were to increase by five per cent, the industry's total costs would increase by only slightly more than one per cent. Again we stress that this observation applies to the industry as a whole, and that there can be glaring individual exceptions. (Some of the biggest newspapers, for instance, must spend more than half their total revenues on newsprint.)

*Wages and salaries constituted the largest proportion of total costs, but this ratio remained fairly constant between 1960 and 1966 when it fluctuated between 39.9 and 41.5 per cent. Capital's share increased slightly over the same period, from about 33.0 per cent in 1960 to 34.5 per cent in 1966. This figure is the gross capital return — which means whatever is left over from revenues after expenses and taxes are met — and this money can be devoted to new capital expenditures, such as printing presses and buildings, or taken as profit. As we shall see later on, profits in fact account for most of the increase. Despite frequent complaints by industry spokesmen about a "cost-price squeeze," the numbers suggest that just the opposite occurred; during the period studied, revenues advanced somewhat faster than costs — not the other way around.

THE NATURAL MONOPOLY

But these internal variables aren't nearly so significant, for the purposes of this study, as what happens to costs as circulation increases. To illustrate, we give you a graph (Chart 3) which plots the cost per column printed and distributed against the circulation of newspapers of various sizes.

That roller-coaster swoop does much to explain the relentless tendency in this or any country towards the one-newspaper town. *The bigger a newspaper's circulation, the lower its per-unit costs.* Average annual cost per 1,000 columns in 1968 for a newspaper with 10,000 circulation was about $1.60. The comparable cost for a newspaper with 250,000 circulation was about 45 cents. The implications are pretty obvious: to produce a product

Chart 3. DAILY NEWSPAPERS, 1968 COST PER 1000 COLUMNS/CIRCULATION

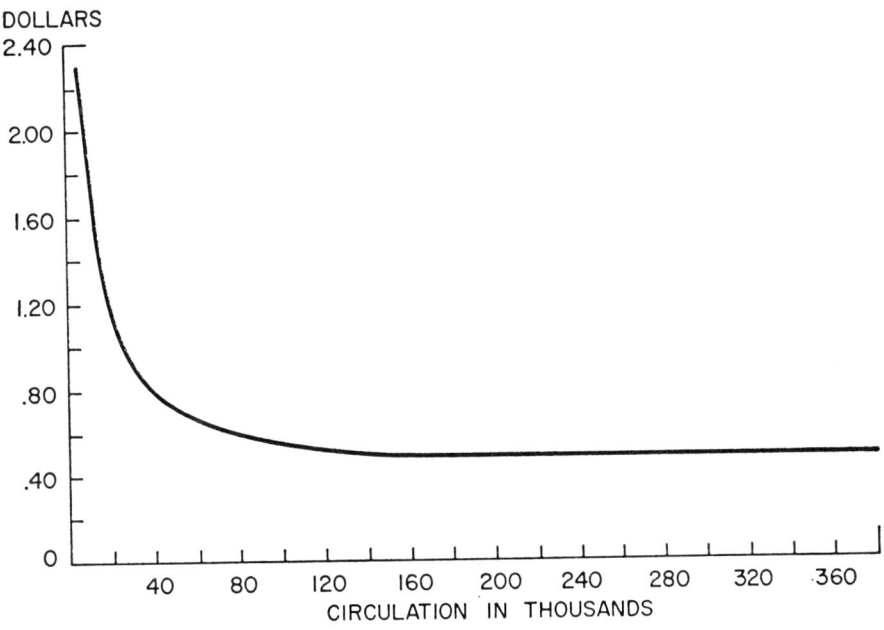

[Chart: X-axis "CIRCULATION IN THOUSANDS" from 0 to 360; Y-axis "DOLLARS" from 0 to 2.40. Curve drops steeply from above 2.40 near zero circulation and flattens near 0.50 for large circulation.]

Source: Special Survey.

of comparable size and quality, the smaller newspaper must raise 3½ times as much revenue per reader as the larger one.[1]

And since our studies show that large newspapers tend to pass on these massive economies of scale to their advertisers, it also means the larger paper's advertising rates will be about 3½ times lower than its smaller competitor's. In classical economics, a curve like that is the certain signature of a natural monopoly.

Classical economics also tells us that, in natural-monopoly industries where two or more firms are competing, their separate shares of the available market are always unstable. They *can't* sit still. If one competing unit is larger than the other, or even if they're of roughly equal size, they battle for supremacy. One firm may cut advertising rates and buy circulation, thus boosting production and lowering its per-unit costs – and in the process forcing the rival's firm's per-unit costs upward.

The larger one newspaper becomes, the easier it becomes to grow larger still. The bigger one newspaper grows, the slimmer are its smaller rival's chances of survival. Its only hope is to cut production costs – which usually means skimping on editorial quality – and to find advertisers willing to pay two or three times more to reach the kind of readers the smaller newspaper attracts.

---

[1] Question: If this is true, how come Canada's smallest dailies are among the most profitable? Answer: Most of these small dailies are the only newspapers in their markets. If they were up against larger rivals, they'd be in trouble. But since they're operating local monopolies, they're in clover.

Naturally, there are several reality-factors which modify the classical perfection of our industry-wide curve. For one thing, because of distribution costs and the local nature of much editorial content, the natural-monopoly rule tends to operate on a local level only. For another, growing newspapers seldom cut advertising rates as low as their reduced per-unit costs would permit; instead, they peg their rates somewhat *above* that level, and invest the difference in improved editorial performance – more pages, more columns, more features, more and sometimes better reporting. The public, as well as the shareholders, thus tend to benefit from profitable newspapers.

Also, it appears that in individual markets, the economies of scale operate even more forcefully than our industry-wide curve would indicate. This is because many newspapers are operating at less than full productive capacity; a circulation increase in such cases can have an especially dramatic effect on per-unit costs. Also, it appears that the larger a paper becomes and the lower its rates, the more advertising it attracts – thus making large newspapers even more profitable than our industry-wide curve might suggest.

The economics of newspapers are a plain expression of the law of the jungle. The name of the game is survival, and the winner is the paper that stays in business. This, in fact, is what has happened in Canada. Apart from cities such as Vancouver where the smaller competitor is kept alive by forcing advertisers to use both newspapers, there are only nine cities with two or more competing newspapers: Calgary, Winnipeg, Ottawa, Toronto, Montreal, Sherbrooke, Quebec City, Moncton, and St. John's.[2]

Competition continues in Sherbrooke and Moncton only because the "rival" papers are published in different languages. Competition continues in Calgary, Winnipeg, and Ottawa because in these cities the rival newspapers are owned by Southam and F.P. – two groups that are so strong, and so evenly matched in terms of capital resources and staying power, that all-out circulation wars are deemed inadvisable.

Of the remaining cities, Toronto and Montreal are the biggest markets in the country, and the scene of the greatest journalistic diversity. Competition continues there because the sheer size of the market allows the smaller papers to generate sufficiently large revenues to remain viable for a long time. The Toronto and Montreal competitors also appear to have achieved separate non-overlapping circulations, so that advertisers continue to patronize several newspapers, even though their rates differ. (If advertisers should decide, though, that one paper largely duplicated the circulation of its larger rival, that smaller paper would be in deep trouble.)

That leaves Quebec City and St. John's. In one case, the smaller French daily, *L'Action,* is subsidized by the Roman Catholic Church. In St. John's, the competition is between the large evening *Telegram* and the smaller *Daily News,* a situation that will not necessarily continue indefinitely.

---

[2] The situation is roughly twice as bad in the United States. With ten times our population, there were only 45 cities in 1968 with two or more competing daily newspapers.

It should be plain from the foregoing that big papers, from a profitability standpoint, are infinitely preferable to little papers in a competitive market. The economies of scale that exist between, say, a paper of 30,000 circulation and a paper of 300,000 circulation are truly dramatic.

But suppose you own *ten* newspapers with 30,000 circulation each: what happens to the economies of scale then? The short answer is, not much. Per-unit costs decline dramatically only when you're producing more and more copies of an identical product. But newspapers in different towns, by their very nature, can't be identical (although some chain owners try hard to make them so.) So how do you explain the existence of newspaper chains? If the economies of scale which apply within a single market *don't* apply over several markets, what's the point of owning lots of newspapers? Wouldn't you make more money by trying to make a single newspaper bigger?

Well, part of the answer is that you can save money by centralizing certain corporate functions. You can save a little money, for instance, by establishing news bureaux that serve all the papers in the chain. But not much – news-gathering costs have already been pooled almost to their economic limits by the existence of the wire services. You can also save some money by centralizing your national advertising sales forces – but again, not much. Most important, a newspaper chain's head office can hire the high-priced managerial talent that few independent newspapers could afford; and since people are by far the most important single asset in the publishing business, this can be a powerful benefit which size confers.

But these advantages are not nearly so significant as the clout which size confers in getting money from other people. Large chains, because they have far more collateral, can borrow more, pay less for it, and refinance more easily, than smaller concerns. It is also easier for them to raise equity capital, by selling shares to the public.

But newspaper groups, like other business enterprises, have a third source of capital: retained earnings, the money they collect as profits but don't pass on to their shareholders as dividends. In terms of explaining the tendency towards ownership concentration, this source of capital is extremely significant.

Under our tax laws, shareholders are taxed only on the earnings they receive as dividends. The remainder, the profits the company keeps in the treasury as retained earnings, aren't taxable until the day they're distributed. The effect is that corporations which keep earning profits build up larger and larger reserves of retained earnings. The shareholders don't mind, because that extra money sitting in the treasury usually means the price of their shares goes up, and the profit they can make by selling them is tax-free. This situation isn't exclusive to the publishing industry, of course. It's a fact of corporate life.

Thus, the typical profitable corporation – and this applies especially to some corporations which publish large newspapers, which are *very* profitable – finds itself with more and more idle money piling up. What to do with it?

Like the Mafia, they're tempted, if not actually forced, to invest it elsewhere. And if you happen to be a newspaper publisher, by far the most plausible place to invest it is in another profitable newspaper.

Where do you find one? You hardly ever start a new newspaper because, as we've seen, that's usually suicidal. The best prospects are family-owned newspapers with aging proprietors. These men, as they approach the Golden Years, are sometimes unable or unwilling to bequeath their property to their heirs. Selling out to a group begins to look attractive – especially if the proprietor is interested in the continuance of his newspaper. A group can afford to pay a good price. More germanely, if the newspaper to be sold is the weaker participant in a competitive situation, chain ownership is much more likely to ensure the paper's survival. Even a small newspaper, if it is owned by a large chain, is unlikely to be the victim of a jugular circulation war. The predator will realize that his victim, now strengthened by the capital resources of its new owner, will be in a much stronger position to fight back. The usual result is a truce, tacit or formal. Both newspapers continue to publish, and to make a profit.

NEWSPAPER PROFITS

The past few pages have been a fairly general discussion of why the newspaper business, in each locality, tends towards a condition of natural monopoly, and how this process works. Its tone has been somewhat theoretical (generalizations usually do sound that way), and the import of it all is somewhat academic – because what we've been describing is a process which has already taken place. We turn now from the theoretical past to the economic present and to that least academic of subjects, profits.

We have already intimated, in earlier sections of this report, that newspaper profits are in general very large. We now propose to document that proposition by presenting what amounts to a huge, collective balance sheet that summarizes the assets, liabilities, revenues, expenses, and earnings of almost every daily newspaper in the country. We compiled this giant balance sheet by asking a representative sample of about half Canada's daily newspapers to provide us with their figures (all of those we asked co-operated splendidly), and by analysing D.B.S. statistics. The result is a composite financial view of the industry; if only one daily were published in Canada, its annual report to shareholders would look something like the data we're about to present.

The first two tables (9 and 10) correspond to the balance sheet that any corporation prepares to describe its financial condition at the moment. (For the non-accountants among us, a brief digression might be helpful to explain how a balance sheet works: it's a two-sided affair, and the sums on each side add up to precisely the same amount. On one side you have "assets" – which includes everything the company owns, and everything owed to it. On the other you have "liabilities," which includes all the money the corporation owes to various lenders, plus the corporation's equity – that is, the money it has received from the people who paid cash into the treasury in return for shares.)

The first table (Table 9) corresponds to the "assets" side of our composite balance sheet. Instead of showing actual amounts, it shows proportionally how various kind of assets are distributed.

You'll notice that, over the period studied, there was a sharp increase in the proportion of assets invested in affiliated companies – from 10.6 per cent in 1958 to 17.8 per cent in 1967. That increase constitutes an accountant's-eye view of where daily newspapers were putting their extra cash. They weren't spending much of it on new buildings and new equipment – that proportion drops slightly over the ten-year period. What they *were* doing was investing it in other companies.

The second table (Table 10) corresponds to the liabilities side of the balance sheet. Again, it's a proportional description.

This table, too, indicates what the daily newspapers have been doing with their extra money. The biggest reduction in the ten-year period is in the "long-term debt" column, which means the dailies were borrowing less and less to finance their long-term growth. So where *did* they get their growth money? By now you should know the answer – from retained earnings, the profits they didn't pass on to their shareholders. Their proportion increased from 37 to 44.4 per cent during the ten-year period.

Now comes the nitty-gritty. The next six tables (11 to 16) document the profitability of daily newspapers in considerable detail. The tables are based on D.B.S. figures which aggregate the financial statements of corporations publishing nearly every daily newspaper in the country. The sixth table (Table 16) provides a comparison between the newspaper business and various other industries.

One of Roy Thomson's most memorable observations was that a television broadcasting permit is "like having a licence to print your own money." These tables demonstrate that ownership of a daily newspaper often amounts to the same thing, except you don't need a licence. There are groups of medium-sized newspapers, the tables show, which in at least one year earned after-tax profits (on equity) of 27.4 per cent! The overall after-tax average, for all newspapers over the ten-year period, as a percentage of total equity, is between 12.3 and 17.5 per cent. In 1965, which was a great year for the industry, after-tax profits of daily newspapers as a percentage of the amount put up by shareholders was 17.5 per cent. The comparable percentage for all manufacturing industries was 10.4 per cent; for retailing industries it was 9.2 per cent. Owning a newspaper, in other words, can be almost twice as profitable as owning a paper-box factory or a department store. The tables follow normal accounting practice by expressing profits in several different ways – (a) as a percentage of total assets, before interest and income taxes are paid; (b) as a percentage of equity, after interest is paid; (c) as a percentage of equity, after interest and income-tax payments; and (d) as a percentage of total revenues, before interest and income tax.

TABLE 9. ASSET DISTRIBUTION AS A PROPORTION OF TOTAL ASSETS: CORPORATIONS PUBLISHING DAILY NEWSPAPERS, 1958–1967

Year	Cash & Securities as a % of Total Assets	Accounts Receivable as a % of Total Assets	Inventories as a % of Total Assets	Current Assets as a % of Total Assets	Land as a % of Total Assets	Net— Buildings and Equipment as a % of Total Assets	Investment in Affiliates as a % of Total Assets	Other Assets as a % of Total Assets (Residuals)
				Per cent				
1958	14.3	11.8	4.5	32.4	6.1	39.8	10.6	11.1
59	13.9	11.8	3.9	31.5	5.7	39.8	12.7	10.3
60	14.6	12.0	3.9	31.6	6.2	40.4	12.2	9.6
61	13.9	11.9	3.7	30.8	6.3	38.2	15.4	9.3
62	14.9	12.0	3.4	31.4	6.5	38.5	14.8	8.8
63	14.9	11.8	3.0	31.2	6.3	39.8	15.1	7.6
64	15.1	11.5	3.9	28.9	6.6	42.1	14.2	8.2
65	12.4	12.2	3.5	29.1	6.0	40.6	17.3	7.0
66	10.9	12.8	3.7	28.6	6.2	40.8	17.1	7.3
67	16.0	12.7	3.1	33.2	5.8	38.0	17.8	5.2

SOURCE: D.B.S.

TABLE 10. LIABILITIES DISTRIBUTION AS A PROPORTION OF TOTAL LIABILITIES AND EQUITY
CORPORATIONS PUBLISHING DAILY NEWSPAPERS, 1958-1967

Year	Bank and Short Term Loans as a % of Total Liabilities and Equity	Accounts Payable as a % of Total Liabilities and Equity	Current Liabilities as a % of Total Liabilities and Equity	Long Term Debt as a % of Total Liabilities and Equity	Total Liabilities as a % of Total Liabilities and Equity	Common Shares as a % of Total Liabilities and Equity	Preferred Shares as a % of Total Liabilities and Equity	Retained Earnings as a % of Total Liabilities and Equity	Equity as a % of Total Liabilities and Equity
					Per Cent				
1958	4.5	7.2	17.8	24.8	46.5	6.7	5.1	37.0	53.4
59	5.1	7.4	19.5	22.5	45.8	6.2	4.7	39.0	54.2
60	2.8	6.5	15.3	25.4	45.8	5.9	4.5	39.4	54.2
61	4.0	6.2	16.3	23.3	44.0	5.7	4.5	41.8	56.0
62	3.9	6.3	16.9	22.6	42.6	5.7	4.3	43.4	57.3
63	4.6	7.2	18.3	21.7	43.4	5.4	3.7	43.8	56.6
64	3.8	8.1	18.4	21.3	45.3	5.3	2.7	43.2	54.7
65	3.7	8.0	17.6	18.3	41.4	8.6	2.0	44.5	58.6
66	3.2	8.3	17.6	17.0	41.2	8.6	1.9	45.1	58.8
67	2.3	7.8	15.9	14.2	37.3	8.8	6.1	44.4	62.7

SOURCE: D.B.S.

TABLE 11. CORPORATIONS PUBLISHING DAILY NEWSPAPERS, 1958–1967

Year	Total Assets Dollars	Equity Dollars	Net Profit A Dollars	Net Profit A / Total Assets Per Cent	Net Profit B Dollars	Net Profit B / Equity Per Cent	Net Profit C Dollars	Net Profit C / Equity Per Cent	Total Revenue Dollars	Net Profit A / Total Revenue Per Cent
1958	183,142,000	97,924,000	26,542,000	14.5	24,083,000	24.6	13,073,000	13.3	224,413,000	11.8
59	199,424,000	108,113,000	34,052,000	17.1	31,067,000	28.7	16,966,000	15.7	250,266,000	13.6
60	208,028,000	112,803,000	31,943,000	15.3	28,546,000	25.3	14,557,000	12.9	259,847,000	12.2
61	218,339,000	122,269,000	32,548,000	14.9	29,965,000	23.7	15,096,000	12.3	263,119,000	12.3
62	222,973,000	127,879,000	35,954,000	16.1	32,345,000	25.3	17,182,000	13.4	272,520,000	13.1
63	233,605,000	132,255,000	34,607,000	14.8	30,945,000	23.4	16,589,000	12.5	278,539,000	12.3
64	240,795,000	131,698,000	39,147,000	16.3	35,484,000	26.9	18,379,000	13.9	288,438,000	13.5
65	273,325,000	160,180,000	52,523,000	19.2	48,816,000	30.5	28,043,000	17.5	335,276,000	15.6
66	292,058,000	171,791,000	50,981,000	17.4	47,293,000	27.5	24,537,000	14.3	348,468,000	14.6
67	307,740,000	192,931,000	53,070,000	17.2	49,435,000	25.6	25,874,000	13.4	383,463,000	13.8

*Net Profit A = Net Profit Before Interest and Income Tax Payments.
Net Profit B = Net Profit Before Income Tax Payments.
Net Profit C = Net Profit After Income Tax Payments.

SOURCE: D.B.S.

TABLE 12. SELECTED CORPORATIONS PUBLISHING DAILY NEWSPAPERS WITH CIRCULATION OVER 100,000, 1958-1967

Year	Total Assets Dollars	Equity Dollars	Net Profit A Dollars	Net Profit A / Total Assets Per Cent	Net Profit B Dollars	Net Profit B / Equity Per Cent	Net Profit C Dollars	Net Profit C / Equity Per Cent	Total Revenue Dollars	Net Profit A / Total Revenue Per Cent
1958	104,863,000	46,986,000	12,259,000	11.7	10,759,000	22.9	5,865,000	12.5	131,537,000	9.3
59	113,756,000	52,132,000	17,438,000	15.3	15,378,000	29.5	8,705,000	16.7	150,468,000	11.6
60	114,139,000	53,073,000	14,544,000	12.7	12,116,000	22.8	6,022,000	11.3	154,190,000	9.4
61	119,319,000	56,398,000	14,780,000	12.4	12,273,000	21.8	6,355,000	11.3	156,500,000	9.4
62	122,096,000	57,953,000	18,033,000	14.8	15,430,000	26.6	8,171,000	14.1	161,833,000	11.1
63	129,847,000	61,218,000	17,234,000	13.3	14,706,000	23.9	7,966,000	13.0	164,320,000	10.5
64	128,020,000	56,624,000	19,683,000	15.4	16,994,000	30.0	8,795,000	15.6	162,220,000	12.1
65	141,353,000	67,176,000	27,512,000	19.5	24,855,000	37.0	14,987,000	22.3	187,243,000	14.7
66	151,634,000	72,965,000	25,401,000	16.8	22,737,000	31.2	11,732,000	16.1	198,538,000	12.8
67	146,518,000	71,066,000	26,244,000	17.9	23,689,000	33.3	11,914,000	16.8	210,187,000	12.5

SOURCE: D.B.S.

TABLE 13. SELECTED CORPORATIONS PUBLISHING DAILY NEWSPAPERS WITH CIRCULATION BETWEEN 50,000 AND 100,000, 1958–1967

Year	Total Assets Dollars	Equity Dollars	Net Profit A Dollars	Net Profit A / Total Assets Per cent	Net Profit B Dollars	Net Profit B / Equity Per cent	Net Profit C Dollars	Net Profit C / Equity Per cent	Total Revenue Dollars	Net Profit A / Total Revenue Per cent
1958	12,471,000	10,606,000	2,628,000	21.1	2,600,000	24.5	1,332,000	12.6	17,945,000	14.6
59	13,355,000	11,348,000	2,732,000	20.5	2,717,000	23.9	1,314,000	11.6	18,562,000	14.7
60	14,384,000	12,457,000	3,115,000	21.6	3,087,000	24.8	1,467,000	11.8	19,476,000	16.0
61	15,662,000	13,605,000	2,847,000	18.2	2,820,000	20.7	1,364,000	10.0	20,239,000	14.1
62	17,021,000	14,211,000	3,037,000	17.8	3,001,000	21.1	1,494,000	10.5	20,787,000	14.6
63	17,246,000	13,244,000	2,664,000	15.4	2,570,000	19.4	1,281,000	9.7	21,382,000	12.5
64	17,377,000	13,302,000	2,888,000	16.6	2,781,000	20.9	1,343,000	10.1	22,725,000	12.8
65	17,788,000	14,167,000	3,546,000	19.9	3,459,000	24.4	1,771,000	12.5	23,945,000	14.8
66	19,414,000	15,637,000	4,349,000	22.4	4,285,000	27.4	2,134,000	13.6	26,509,000	16.4
67	20,627,000	16,957,000	4,615,000	22.4	4,564,000	26.9	2,262,000	13.3	28,490,000	16.2

SOURCE: D.B.S.

TABLE 14. SELECTED CORPORATIONS PUBLISHING DAILY NEWSPAPERS WITH CIRCULATION BETWEEN 10,000 AND 50,000, 1958–1967

Year	Total Assets Dollars	Equity Dollars	Net Profit before Int. and Inc. Tax Dollars	Net Profit A / Total Assets Per cent	Net Profit after Int. Dollars	Net Profit B / Equity Per cent	Net Profit after Int. and Inc. Tax Dollars	Net Profit after Int. and Inc. Tax / Equity Per cent	Total Revenue Dollars	Net Profit A / Total Revenue Per cent
1958	35,311,000	23,256,000	4,464,000	12.6	3,980,000	17.1	2,056,000	8.8	30,548,000	14.6
59	38,990,000	24,670,000	5,113,000	13.1	4,623,000	18.7	2,353,000	9.5	32,528,000	15.7
60	46,207,000	26,653,000	5,350,000	11.6	4,795,000	18.0	2,398,000	9.0	35,098,000	15.2
61	48,410,000	28,743,000	5,507,000	11.7	4,801,000	16.7	2,465,000	8.6	34,447,000	16.0
62	47,824,000	30,731,000	5,180,000	10.8	4,512,000	14.7	2,295,000	7.5	35,448,000	14.6
63	49,415,000	32,147,000	5,353,000	10.8	4,676,000	14.5	2,318,000	7.2	36,800,000	15.0
64	55,461,000	36,091,000	6,484,000	11.7	5,853,000	16.2	2,964,000	8.2	41,307,000	15.7
65	68,736,000	50,551,000	7,461,000	10.9	6,802,000	13.5	3,458,000	6.8	44,763,000	16.7
66	71,692,000	52,338,000	8,316,000	11.6	7,721,000	14.8	3,814,000	7.3	48,408,000	17.2
67	87,728,000	69,136,000	8,695,000	9.9	8,117,000	11.7	4,059,000	5.9	51,449,000	16.9

SOURCE: D.B.S.

Table 15. SELECTED CORPORATIONS PUBLISHING DAILY NEWSPAPERS WITH CIRCULATION UNDER 10,000, 1958–1967

Year	Total Assets Dollars	Equity Dollars	Net Profit before Int. and Inc. Tax Dollars	Net Profit A / Total Assets Per cent	Net Profit after Int. Dollars	Net Profit B / Equity Per cent	Net Profit after Int. and Inc. Tax Dollars	Net Profit after Int. and Inc. Tax / Equity Per cent	Total Revenue Dollars	Net Profit before Int. and Inc. Tax / Total Revenue Per cent
1958	6,008,000	3,429,000	473,000	7.9	433,000	12.6	360,000	10.5	8,652,000	5.5
59	6,441,000	3,884,000	766,000	11.9	721,000	18.6	557,000	14.3	9,957,000	7.7
60	6,464,000	4,358,000	776,000	12.0	725,000	16.6	582,000	13.4	10,531,000	7.4
61	7,114,000	5,071,000	791,000	11.1	744,000	14.7	401,000	7.9	9,961,000	7.9
62	7,204,000	5,100,000	851,000	11.8	807,000	15.8	449,000	8.8	11,102,000	7.7
63	7,917,000	5,550,000	883,000	11.1	833,000	15.0	476,000	8.6	11,486,000	7.3
64	7,795,000	5,313,000	1,084,000	13.9	1,025,000	19.3	554,000	10.4	12,203,000	8.9
65	9,258,000	5,121,000	1,811,000	19.6	1,728,000	33.7	981,000	19.2	13,935,000	13.0
66	9,950,000	6,082,000	2,068,000	20.8	1,963,000	32.3	1,088,000	17.9	16,010,000	12.9
67	10,442,000	6,319,000	2,268,000	21.7	2,164,000	34.2	1,183,000	18.7	17,154,000	13.2

Source: D.B.S.

TABLE 16. INTER-INDUSTRY COMPARISONS OF CAPITAL STRUCTURE AND PROFIT RATES, 1965 AND 1966

	Manufacturing Industries		Retail Trade Industries		Service Industries		Public Utilities		Daily Newspaper Industry	
	1965	1966	1965	1966	1965	1966	1965	1966	1965	1966
	Per Cent		Per Cent		Per Cent		Per Cent		Per Cent	
Current Assets Total Assets	46.5	46.0	62.4	63.2	26.6	27.8	7.9	7.3	29.1	28.5
Net Buildings and Equipment Total Assets	33.9	34.5	17.5	18.5	46.6	46.3	75.1	75.2	40.7	40.8
Retained Earnings Share Capital	32.6	32.1	29.7	29.6	16.5	18.7	13.9	16.2	44.6	45.1
Total Liabilities and Equity	18.7	17.2	13.4	12.7	16.4	15.5	23.5	23.3	10.7	10.5
Long Term Debt Total Liabilities and Equity	11.3	11.3	8.5	9.1	23.5	23.4	43.1	40.9	18.3	17.0
Profit (Before Tax) Total Assets	10.9	10.0	8.3	8.0	7.2	8.5	8.3	8.2	19.2	17.4
Profit (Before Tax) Equity Capital	18.0	16.9	15.3	15.9	14.5	17.5	13.8	13.4	30.5	27.5
Profit (After Tax) Equity Capital	10.4	10.0	9.2	9.8	9.4	11.7	8.6	8.3	17.5	14.3
Profit (Before Tax) Total Revenue	9.3	8.7	3.3	3.1	7.7	8.5	26.4	24.8	15.6	14.8

SOURCE: Corporation Financial Statistics, D.B.S. 61–207 (Annual)
D.B.S. Special Aggregation of Income Tax Returns

A few other observations on the profitability of daily newspapers, as set forth in the profitability tables:

*If you want to own a newspaper, it's better to own a small one or a large one than a medium-sized one. Companies publishing newspapers with circulation below 10,000 or above 100,000 consistently earned after-tax profits of more than 16 per cent from 1965 onward. Newspapers with circulations between 10,000 and 50,000 were less than half as profitable as the industry as a whole.

*During the period studied, labour costs increased about as much as did total revenues – 71.5 per cent. Gross returns to capital, however, increased by 95.2 per cent over the same period. (It is one of our regrets, incidentally, that the Committee could not make a detailed study, without unduly prolonging its existence and delaying this report, of the effect of labour costs on the ability of the media to survive and serve their audience. It has been suggested that rising labour costs are killing off newspapers, particularly in the United States. But on the evidence available to us, it would appear that while publishing and broadcasting are subject to the same inflationary pressures as everyone else, on an industry-wide basis both productivity and returns to capital are increasing faster than labour costs.)

*Retained earnings – the profits which a corporation holds back and usually invests in expansion or in other corporations – are much higher in the daily newspaper business than in other manufacturing industries. This indicates that the industry has been highly profitable in the past, and that its members are probably hungry to acquire other newspapers.

*Share capital and long-term debt make up smaller proportions of total liabilities and equity for daily newspapers than they do for corporations in other industries. This underlines what we know already: that newspapers are less likely than other corporations to borrow or to issue new shares when they need extra money; usually, they can finance expansion and acquisitions from their profits.

ECONOMICS OF BROADCASTING

We turn now to the economics of broadcasting, where many of the same considerations apply. We're going to argue that broadcasting, like newspaper publishing, is another industry where large economies of scale can be achieved as circulation increases. We think the data indicate that if broadcasting existed in a regulatory vacuum, individual stations would behave as newspapers do – the big ones would swallow the little ones. The main reason this hasn't happened is that broadcasting is subject to stringent federal regulation, and that the existence of a public broadcasting network drastically alters the rules of the media monopoly game.

There are 395 AM and FM radio stations in Canada, 45 of them owned by the CBC and 119 others affiliated with the CBC. There are 77 primary TV stations in Canada. Four are independent, 18 are owned by the CBC and 43 affiliated with the CBC, and 12 are affiliated with the CTV network. In 1968, Canada's TV and radio stations attracted a total of $210 million in advertising revenue.

These revenues have increased enormously in the past decade or so. Net advertising revenues in the TV industry have grown from $8.6 million in 1954 to about $118 million in 1968 – an increase of 1,272 per cent! Radio revenues almost tripled between 1954 and 1968.

The major reason for this spectacular growth, of course, is the fact that TV started from scratch. The other reason is that the *supply* of broadcasting time is limited by federal regulation, and by the nature of the medium, while the *demand* has been constantly increasing. (A newspaper will print as many ads as it can sell; but broadcasting stations are limited by the fact that there are only so many minutes in the day, and most of them have to be devoted to programming.) With more and more dollars chasing a fairly fixed amount of available advertising slots, the inevitable has occurred: TV stations and networks have substantially increased their rates in recent years.

An examination of these rates reveals that, in general, broadcasting works the way publishing does: the bigger your audience, the lower your unit cost of reaching that audience. As in publishing, substantial economies of scale exist. Table 17 indicates how great those economies can be. By dividing the amount of money the station charges for a minute of advertising by the average number of viewers who tune in during night-time hours (6 p.m. to 1 a.m.), you get a figure that corresponds to the advertiser's cost-per-viewer. As the table shows, this cost declines sharply as the audience size increases.

TABLE 17. AVERAGE TELEVISION ADVERTISING RATES-PER-THOUSAND BY STATION SIZE

Size Category (Number of viewers)	Average Size of Stations	Number of Stations in Sample	Rate-Per-Thousand ¢
Under 75,000	55,140	10	89.8
100,000–200,000	135,820	10	76.8
300,000–500,000	383,790	10	62.4
Over 500,000	1,017,000	7	43.7

The reason is pretty obvious. It costs a certain amount of money to put a programme on the air, and to attract viewers. But it costs you very little extra if your audience is twice as large. As we have seen in our study of newspapers, this declining unit-cost curve is characteristic of natural monopolies. In the newspaper business, the natural tendency is for larger units to drive the smaller ones out of business. This is much less true in broadcasting, though, for several reasons. For one thing, the C.R.T.C. won't grant licences unless it feels the station has a good chance of survival. For another, the cost structure of the industry is such – especially in radio – that a number of competing stations can survive by appealing to different segments of the total available audience.

Now let's look briefly at this cost structure, and see what happens to costs as the station's circulation increases. Table 18 shows what TV stations of various sizes spend their money on. The figures are expressed as a proportion of total costs. We're assuming here that the larger a station's revenues, the larger its audience, although there are probably exceptions to this rule. The figures are taken from D.B.S., which lumps the stations into revenue categories that are rather broader than we wish they were. The figures, then, should be regarded as educated estimates, rather than hard fact.

TABLE 18. PRIVATE TELEVISION: DISTRIBUTION OF PRODUCTION COSTS PER VIEWER* CIRCULATION BY REVENUE GROUPS

Revenue Group	$1,500,000 +	$1,000,000–1,499,999	$500,000–999,999	$250,000–499,999
Number of Stations	16	9	13	15
Total Circulation	8,106,600	1,551,800	1,558,400	1,119,900
Representative Commission	$0.355	$0.207	$0.248	$0.119
Rent, Repairs, etc.	0.421	0.413	0.362	0.421
Fuel, Electricity	0.059	0.083	0.084	0.109
Salaries, Wages	2.203	2.091	1.976	1.994
Staff Benefits	0.128	0.095	0.089	0.087
Performing Rights	0.168	0.117	0.095	0.099
Telephone, Telegraph	0.067	0.061	0.071	0.082
Micro-Wave, Wire Line	0.067	0.021	0.014	0.067
Films, Tapes	1.667	0.675	0.618	0.454
Advertising Promotions	0.292	0.199	0.167	0.157
Office Supplies, Other Expenses	0.054	0.050	0.043	0.061
Artist and Other Talent Fees	0.421	0.064	0.067	0.042
Total Production Costs	5.902	4.076	3.834	3.692
Total Operating Expenses	7.241	5.332	4.841	4.968
Total Operating Revenue	9.101	5.804	5.806	5.156
Net Operating Revenue	1.860	0.472	0.966	0.188

*Average night-time circulation, 6 p.m. to 1 a.m.
SOURCE: D.B.S. 56-204.

Chart 4 is drawn from Table 18, and it reveals an interesting phenomenon. Programming costs – including salaries, films, tape, talent fees, and performing rights, climb slowly or not at all as the size of the audience increases – *until* you get to the largest revenue category. Then they climb steeply. The biggest TV stations, in other words, spend far more on "quality" than the smaller ones do. This may be associated with the fact that many of the smaller TV stations are the only ones in their market. The stations with the largest revenues are operating in metropolitan markets, where competition exists and where quality programming becomes a competitive factor.

The "quality curve" does *not* mean, though, that small stations are more profitable than large ones. Although large TV stations spend relatively more on "quality," this factor is more than offset by various economies of scale. Productivity per employee is much higher for stations in the biggest revenue category than for smaller TV stations, for instance.

Chart 4. AVERAGE COSTS PER VIEWER FOR SELECTED COMPONENTS BY REVENUE GROUP

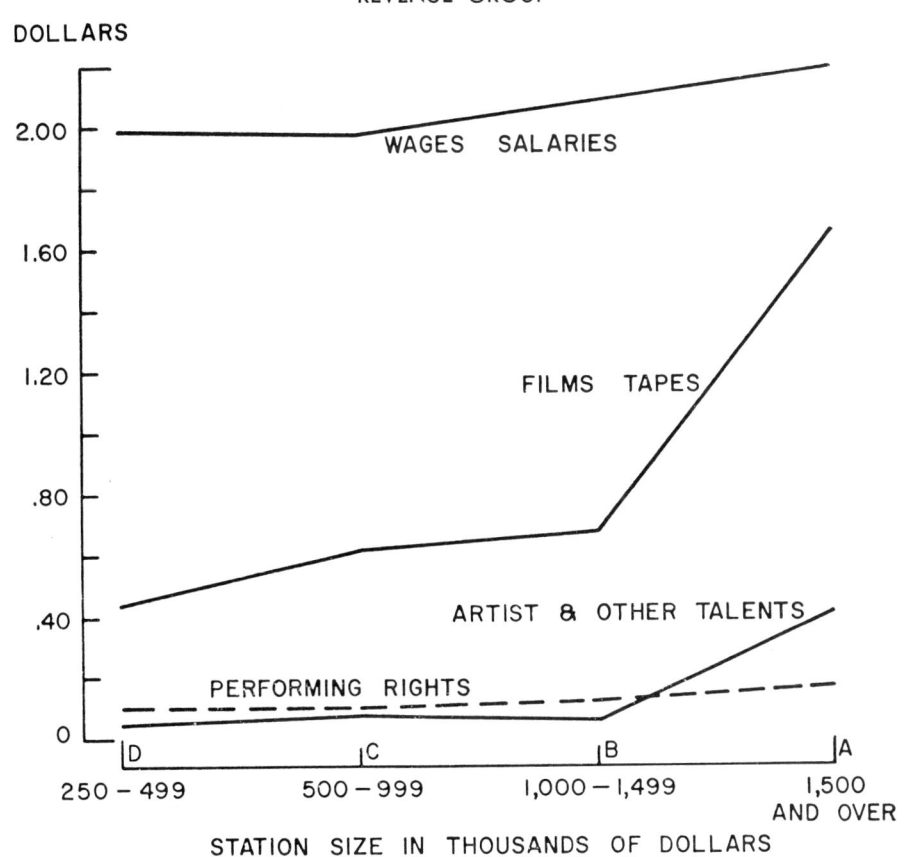

Source: D.B.S., 56-204.

BROADCASTING PROFITS

But the most significant benefits of bigness can be seen in the profitability figures. Table 19 tells the story. As with newspapers, we've expressed profits in various ways: as a percentage of equity, before taxes; as a percentage of assets before taxes; and as a percentage of sales before taxes. The figures were compiled for the Committee by D.B.S. and the C.R.T.C. from the balance sheets of individual private stations. The figures for "radio" refer to companies which operate radio stations but do not also own TV stations. The TV figures are for companies which do not also own radio stations. The combined figures are for those companies owning both radio and TV stations.

TABLE 19. RATES OF PROFITS IN PRIVATE BROADCASTING, CANADA 1964–1968

Type of Broadcaster by Revenue Group	1964	1965	1966	1967	1968
			BEFORE TAX RETURN ON EQUITY		
*Radio**					
Less than $100,000	−11.0	− 9.2	−17.3	− 8.0	−32.3
$100,000 to 249,999	10.3	12.4	15.6	8.3	6.9
$250,000 to 499,999	13.8	28.0	11.8	11.8	12.8
$500,000 to 999,999	60.5	22.6	27.8	31.5	28.4
$1,000,000 and over	33.2	37.0	37.9	39.6	43.1
All Stations	22.1	21.1	22.8	23.9	25.8
Television†					
Less than $250,000	−27.3	−31.2	− 0.9	+ 7.0	− 5.8
$250,000 to 499,999	3.4	22.3	9.4	8.3	11.7
$500,000 to 999,999	32.7	16.7	3.3	19.9	27.5
$1,000,000 to 1,499,999	31.4	42.0	9.5	35.4	23.3
$1,500,000 and over	98.5	91.0	56.3	40.1	60.8
All Stations	56.0	64.4	42.3	36.3	50.7
Combined Radio and Television‡	29.9	50.2		56.8	29.6
All Stations	42.1	48.1	49.1	47.4	21.1
			BEFORE TAX RETURN ON ASSETS		
*Radio**					
Less than $100,000	− 0.7	− 1.5	− 2.7	− 1.2	− 7.0
$100,000 to 249,999	8.2	7.7	9.9	6.1	5.4
$250,000 to 499,999	7.9	4.6	6.8	6.9	8.1
$500,000 to 999,999	14.9	9.3	10.5	18.5	14.3
$1,000,000 and over	21.8	27.5	26.0	25.0	25.6
All Stations	12.0	11.6	12.6	14.2	14.3
Television†					
Less than $250,000	− 5.9	− 8.4	− 0.6	+ 6.5	− 1.6
$250,000 to 499,999	4.6	11.2	5.6	4.8	6.5
$500,000 to 999,999	25.3	10.0	2.0	13.2	18.3
$1,000,000 to 1,499,999	16.7	39.9	5.7	30.7	21.4
$1,500,000 and over	22.6	31.2	26.0	21.1	31.9
All Stations	18.5	25.5	19.4	19.6	27.9

THE UNCERTAIN MIRROR

TABLE 19. RATES OF PROFITS IN PRIVATE BROADCASTING,
CANADA 1964-1968—Concluded

Type of Broadcaster by Revenue Group	1964	1965	1966	1967	1968
Combined Radio and Television‡	16.3	22.5		24.6	16.8
All Stations	22.1	27.1	26.0	20.4	12.4

BEFORE TAX
RETURN ON TOTAL OPERATING REVENUE

	1964	1965	1966	1967	1968
Radio*					
Less than $100,000	− 4.5	− 4.1	− 6.3	− 4.3	−12.3
$100,000 to 249,999	6.2	7.6	10.2	4.7	3.4
$250,000 to 499,999	5.5	3.5	5.9	6.4	6.8
$500,000 to 999,999	11.0	6.2	8.9	12.5	12.7
$1,000,000 and over	16.0	19.8	21.3	23.9	24.1
All Stations	9.5	9.9	11.7	12.8	13.2
Television†					
Less than $250,000	−12.9	−15.3	− 0.6	+ 3.2	− 4.7
$250,000 to 499,999	1.9	11.1	5.1	5.9	5.7
$500,000 to 999,999	19.4	8.1	2.1	12.8	15.5
$1,000,000 to 1,499,999	8.4	17.5	10.6	17.3	13.3
$1,500,000 and over	16.9	22.4	22.7	19.5	23.8
All Stations	14.1	19.1	19.5	18.3	21.4
Combined Radio and Television‡	13.4	17.0		14.4	11.2
All Stations	18.9	20.4	16.1	12.0	8.1

*Privately owned radio stations operated by companies which do not operate television stations.
†Privately owned television stations operated by companies which do not operate radio stations.
‡Privately owned radio and television stations which are operated jointly by the same company (and which therefore have consolidated balance sheets for the radio and television operations).
SOURCE: Calculated from accompanying tables.

There are several points to note concerning these figures:

*The smallest stations – radio stations with revenues of less than $100,000 and TV stations with less than $250,000 annually – were consistent money-losers. The rate of loss was greater for the small TV stations than for the small radio stations.

*Profitability, no matter how you measure it, tends to vary widely from year to year. Among companies operating only radio stations, however, the losses of some appear to be offset by the profits of others, so that the profitability of this group as a whole maintained a fairly steady upward trend between 1964 and 1968.

*The tables show a striking correlation between size and profitability. In 1968, for instance, only 22 of the country's 221 private radio stations without TV connections had revenues of $1 million or more. Yet these stations – 8.4 per cent of the total – accounted for slightly more than 68 per cent of the total net operating revenue of all such stations. Similarly, only eight of 29 TV stations without radio affiliates had revenues of $1.5 million or more. But these eight large stations accounted for 92 per cent of the total net operating revenue for all such stations!

*The other thing to note is how wondrously profitable some broadcasting operations can be. The largest revenue-group of TV stations, for instance, earned a before-tax profit (on equity) of 98.5 per cent in 1964. At that rate, even after taxes, shareholders would recover their entire investment in two years! The big TV stations' worst year was 1967, when pre-tax profits declined to 40 per cent; in most other industries, that kind of margin would be considered fabulous.

3. Bucking the Trend

CONCENTRATION: PRO AND CON

We think the figures set forth in the previous chapter are astonishing. There are a number of individual newspapers and broadcasting stations that are having trouble meeting their payrolls. But *on the average,* media corporations are onto a very good thing indeed. If the brewing industry made profits half this large, and the people knew it, we suspect there would be sit-ins in the beer stores. Most media corporations, fortunately for them, don't have to disclose these earnings. Because their very large profits allow them to pay for expansion and acquisitions out of retained earnings, most continue as private companies. And so we are confronted with a delicious irony: an industry that is supposed to abhor secrets is sitting on one of the best-kept, least-discussed secrets, one of the hottest *scoops,* in the entire field of Canadian business – their own balance sheets!

The daily-newspaper and broadcasting industries make profits that are, on the average, *very* generous. In most cases, these large profits are made possible by conditions of natural monopoly. In the case of broadcasting, federal licensing policy protects broadcasters against excessive, uneconomic competition. In the case of newspapers, the circulation wars of yester-year have created monopoly or near-monopoly situations which now confer large benefits on the survivors.

In a few cases, the corporations concerned are making genuine efforts to deliver quality editorial content and quality programming in return for their privileged economic position. But the general pattern, we regret to say, is of newspapers and broadcasting stations that are pulling the maximum out of their communities, and giving back the minimum in return. This is what, in contemporary parlance, is called a rip-off.

In traditional usage, you have a monopoly rip-off when the corporations concerned use their privileged position to charge their customers more than the traffic would otherwise bear. In the case of the media, we think, the problem is reversed: it's not that the companies are charging too much – but that they're spending too little. The profit margins in broadcasting, for instance, indicate that the industry as a whole can readily afford to supply its audience with the Canadian content that the country has long needed, and which the C.R.T.C. is now demanding. The industry hasn't supplied it voluntarily, for the excellent reason that it can make more money by relying on canned American re-runs. In the same way, many Canadian daily newspapers could readily afford to develop their own editorial-page columnists, their own cartoonists, their own commentators. But it's cheaper, far cheaper, to buy syndicated American columnists and reprint other papers' cartoons, and to skimp on staff news coverage in the hope that one of the wire services will do the same job almost as well.

Too many newspapers and broadcasting stations, in other words, are delivering a product that is not as good as they could afford to make it. They don't try hard enough to improve their product because there is no economic incentive to do so – quite the reverse, in fact. That paragon of candour, Lord Thomson, expressed the matter rather well in an encounter with Douglas Fisher, a syndicated political columnist for the Toronto *Telegram*. Mr. Fisher referred to this revealing exchange in his brief to the Committee:

> I remember asking Lord Thomson several years ago when I was the M.P. for Port Arthur two questions: was the *News-Chronicle* a good money-maker? Would he consider having my column bought or that of George Bain or Peter Newman bought for the *News-Chronicle,* my point being that I thought the interpretation of Ottawa politics was covered rather slightly considering the high political interest in the area? The answers were: "Port Arthur is a dandy, one of the best profit-makers in our Canadian operations, and I got a great deal on the building from the federal government." The second answer went: "Frankly, what would be the point of it? It wouldn't sell one more paper in the market area."

Precisely. The paper is earning a pile already; why reduce profits by putting out a better product? The examples of such a cheese-paring approach to journalism could be multiplied endlessly. When the Prime Minister made his fence-mending tour of the prairie provinces in 1969, no one from the Ottawa bureau of F. P. Publications went with him, because the chain's head office in Winnipeg decided the tour could be covered more cheaply by having Winnipeg *Free Press* staffers accompany the Manitoba portion of the tour, and letting CP cover the rest.

There are hardly any Canadian newspapers that *cover* travel news the way they cover sports, say, or politics. Instead, they run their travel pages as adjuncts of their advertising departments. The editorial content consists either of verbatim handouts from tourist bureaux, or of staff-written stories by writers whose travel expenses have been paid by hotels or airlines. Once again, the industry's profit margins suggest that there are many newspapers that could afford to pay these costs themselves. Most don't. As a result, everything in your average travel section reads like a press release, and the newspaper's audience is denied any objective, unvarnished, trustworthy assessment of what these exotic destinations are really like.

There's no point in spinning this out further. Any reporter, any broadcast newsman, could supply additional examples of robustly profitable media corporations skimping on their news product. A cursory reading of almost any Canadian newspaper, or two hours spent with a radio or TV set, serves to confirm this.

This give-'em-as-little-as-possible syndrome is reflected in the industry's approach to personnel. Outside those communities where genuine journalistic competition exists, the hiring criterion is frequently not how good a man (or woman) is at the job, but how low a salary they're willing to accept. In another section of this report we document how, in both print and broadcast media, increases in productivity have consistently outrun increases in wages and salaries — and that, as a result, capital's share of available revenues is increasing faster than labour's. Once again, we see the same situation: many newspapers and broadcasting stations operating under monopolistic conditions could afford to pay better salaries to attract better people. But they don't.

As a result, newsrooms are chronically understaffed, the turnover in personnel is scandalous, and the best people, unless they have a penchant for personal philanthropy, frequently move on to some other industry, such as advertising or public relations, where talent is recognized and rewarded.

This isn't just a matter between owners and employees. The public is affected very directly, because staff shortages and salary-scrimping mean they're not getting the kind of information service that the industry's profit margins entitle them to expect. The best in-depth stories are often the costliest to get, in terms of both time and money. We quote Thomas Melville, editor-in-chief of the Regina *Leader-Post*, who in his testimony before the Committee pointed out that he would like to give "more of our reporters more time for more detail." And he continued: "We do have some who would like to work on a story for six weeks, but their time is limited."

It's not merely the time involved; it's also the gamble. Many promising leads take days or even weeks of checking, and then simply don't pan out. Every editor knows this, and wishes he had more financial latitude to gamble on the long shots. But in monopoly situations, journalistic enterprise is seldom encouraged. The shareholders are the gainers as a result. The public are the losers.

The most insidious effect of journalistic monopolies, however, is the atmosphere they breed. Every reporter soon learns that there are only a few newspapers where excellence is encouraged. If they are lucky or clever or restless, they will gravitate to those newspapers. If not, they will stay where they are, growing cynical about their work, learning to live with a kind of sour professional despair. Often you can see it in their faces. Most Canadian city-rooms are boneyards of broken dreams.

We think it is interesting that Jerry Rubin, the American Yippie, was radicalized by this very spectacle. Speaking of his days as a bright young reporter in Cincinnati, he told an interviewer:

> On the paper, I came on really full of fire, excitement, really loved reporting, etc. Everybody was really bored at the paper—at 4:30 everybody left to go home, no matter what they were doing, they went right to the elevator. People just sat around doing nothing—and they weren't hippies, either. Here were these guys, 40, 50 years old and their lives were just *wasted*.
>
> So at the age of 17 I came into contact with the whole community of people with wasted lives. They weren't happy with what they were doing, they had nothing to look forward to except maybe a three-week vacation once a year or maybe retiring. They knew they weren't going to rise in the newspaper hierarchy—there was nowhere to go. They were all very cynical, and they said to me, "Why do you want to be a reporter?" And of course they were all right in their own terms . . .
>
> What I discovered at the paper was that the people were great, each individual was fantastic, you know, go out to lunch with the reporters—I loved them all as individuals. It was like a dream in their stomachs that had been destroyed and I got a tremendous sympathy for them and began to hate the editor and the whole thing. I think I got to be an instinctive Communist.

We wish we could report that most Canadian newspapers are exciting places to work, that they're charged with the kind of tension and creative joy you'd find in a well-run university classroom. When that atmosphere is present, you can *feel* it in the city-room, you can see it in the product. It is no accident that many Canadian newspapers look and read as though they were produced by people who are profoundly bored. Too many of them *are* bored. The economics of the industry, and the placing of profits ahead of product, have made them so. That is the tragedy of practising journalism in a commercial culture: unless you are very strong or very lucky or very good, it will murder your dreams.

The sort of conditions we've been describing are a frequent consequence of monopoly situations. Without the spur of competition, it is easy for a news organization to lapse into mediocrity. Similarly, in cities where competition is vigorous, such as Toronto and Montreal, the odds are strong that editorial excellence will be sought after and rewarded.

But not always. The existence of two or more competing newspapers is not an automatic guarantee of improved performance, although it certainly widens the odds. And there is no law that says a monopoly outlet *has* to be mediocre, although there is ample economic incentive for it to become so. The forces of economics are influential, but the intentions of people can be even more decisive.

London, Ontario, for instance, is a classic monopoly situation. The Blackburn family owns the London *Free Press,* CFPL radio, and CFPL-TV. On the face of it, this would constitute one of the tightest information monopolies in the country. And yet the *Free Press* is a very good community newspaper; and CFPL and CFPL-TV are among the best local programmers in the country. It is significant that in five cities near London – Sarnia, Chatham, St. Thomas, Woodstock, and Stratford – the *Free Press* has achieved an average combined circulation that totals 41 per cent of the circulation of the local dailies. This is a tribute to the editorial performance of the *Free Press* – and, we suspect, a commentary on the performance of the five local daily newspapers, three of which are owned by Thomson. Both the radio and TV outlets are *serious* about local news and entertainment programming – to the point where local programmes frequently draw larger audiences than do the CBC network offerings.

In his appearance before the Committee, Walter Blackburn forcefully argued that his properties do *not* enjoy an information monopoly. In the seven-county area served by the *Free Press,* CFPL and CFPL-TV, his presentation outlined that there are forty-two newspapers (including six dailies), thirteen radio stations, two TV stations and fourteen cable-TV systems. But very few, if any, of these outlets provide the kind of direct, forceful journalistic competition that leads to better newspapers and better programming. The Blackburn media are providing good service to their community, we suggest, because their owner *wants* them to provide good service, and is willing to spend to get it.

Montreal provides another exception to the apparent rule that monopoly promotes mediocrity, competition promotes quality. Editorial competition among French-language dailies in Montreal has been vigorous. But while the two competing English-language dailies, the *Star* and the *Gazette,* compete keenly for advertising revenues, their editorial performances over the past twenty years or so have been less than distinguished. Both newspapers have improved in recent years – the *Star* dramatically so – and this appears to be due, not to altered competitive conditions, but to a new-found determination by owners and management to improve their product.

We cite these exceptions because we think they are important in any consideration of how to safeguard the public interest against the increasing concentration of media ownership. <u>Media monopolies seem to operate against the public interest only when the owner allows it to happen. But if the owner has a genuine commitment to public service</u>, if he places his readers' interests ahead of his own dividends, <u>he can readily offset what the Committee has come to regard as the intrinsic dangers of ownership concentration. The public interest can be served or ignored</u>, in other words, <u>according to the personal preoccupations of the people who own the media.</u>

And this leads us to what may be the Committee's most fundamental conclusion: that this country should no longer tolerate a situation where the public interest in so vital a field as information is dependent on the greed or goodwill of an extremely privileged group of businessmen.

We are not suggesting that the state should reward or punish individual newspapers on the basis of some "official" assessment of their editorial performance. The moment any government decides it is better qualified than a publisher or editor to decide what to print, we are in serious trouble. The freedom to publish is crucial to all our freedoms. Government's role is to protect this right, not infringe on it. This is so basic to our notions of freedom that it should hardly require elaboration.

But the power to merge, the power to expand, the power to form large concentrations of media holdings, is another matter. We think the findings of this Committee demonstrate that concentration of ownership has proceeded to the point where some form of intervention by the state is desirable and necessary. There are some media acquisitions which appear to have served the public interest. There are others which we think have led to its abuse. The principle is now well established that the state has a right to safeguard the public's right to information by approving, disapproving, or disallowing various property transactions within the broadcasting industry. The Committee believes it is time for this principle to be extended to include the print media.

There are several different forms of ownership concentration: (a) newspaper chains, (b) mixed-media holdings operating within a single market or in different markets, and (c) media holdings by companies whose main business interests are other than publishing or broadcasting. We are satisfied that there is no sweeping regulatory principle that is applicable to all of them.

The advantages and disadvantages of newspaper groups or chains, from the public-interest point of view, are especially finely balanced. Although chain ownership can lead to the sort of numbing journalistic conformity that characterizes the Thomson newspapers, it can also confer benefits that are unquestionably in the public interest. <u>The most compelling benefit</u>, of course, <u>is that group ownership tends to prevent more newspapers from dying</u>. When two group-owned dailies are competing in the same town, the result is usually a "truce" instead of a winner-take-all struggle for circulation. In Vancouver, it is probable that the smaller of the city's two dailies, the *Province,* would have folded years ago if it weren't for the fact that two large groups jointly own the company that publishes both papers. The same can be said of a number of cities with more than one daily, including Winnipeg and Ottawa: <u>the existence of newspaper chains is actually contributing to diversity by maintaining two newspapers when</u>, by the inexorable logic of economics, <u>there eventually would be only one</u>. Indeed, our best hope for *more* daily newspapers seems to lie with chains; only corporations with access to large amounts of capital can be expected to sustain the high risks, and the long initial period of non-profitability.

In the thoughtful brief submitted by F. P. Publications Limited, R. S. Malone observed that a city the size of Edmonton – which is now a one-newspaper town – should have a second editorial voice; both F.P. and the

Thomson group have investigated the possibility of starting a second newspaper there, he said, but so far neither group has been willing to accept the financial risks involved. Mr. Malone continued:

> While our combines branch here in Ottawa might take a rather jaundiced view of any attempt of, say, the Southams and ourselves cooperating to publish joint morning and evening papers in Edmonton, you might ask yourselves—might this not be a benefit to the city of Edmonton—having two separate editorial voices, with competing news staffs, foreign services, columnists and leader writers, commenting with conflicting views?

If you're serious about the advantages of media diversity, you have to concede that, yes, it would be better for Edmonton.

Group ownership can confer other benefits which, though they may be less tangible than the preservation of an existing newspaper, are nevertheless real. They can afford high-priced managerial talent in the head office, an asset from which all members of the chain can benefit. Chains can also offer greater opportunity and mobility to their staffs than could a separate newspaper; in the editorial context, this can contribute to a better overall understanding of the country among writers and readers. (Southam, for instance, feels that its acquisition of the Montreal *Gazette* will add depth to the whole group's understanding of French Canada.)

The most pervasive benefit of group ownership, however, is that groups tend to be profitable. This in itself is no guarantee of excellence; but it obviously increases the chances of achieving it. Profitable media outlets are less susceptible to pressures from advertisers and special-interest groups, and better able to accept the risks – such as lawsuits – which sometimes accompany the practise of gutsy journalism.

The moral seems to be that there is no moral. There is no such thing as a "good" chain or a "bad" chain – only good and bad owners. Even then, the situation can be pretty ambiguous.

We believe the evidence is overwhelming, for instance, that the Thomson chain is doing an inadequate job for its readers in terms of the profits it earns. But having said that, we must now quote from an informal brief from G. J. Rowland, publisher of the Penticton *Herald:*

> For many years I was the sole owner and publisher of the Penticton *Herald.* Since 1956, when I sold to the Thomson organization, I have remained as publisher. I have thus been able to study both phases of ownership.
>
> For the first seven years of the new ownership there where no profits whatever. Losses in some years were formidable. From 1964 onward modest net profits were accumulated. But not until this year (1969) could it be said that the total net gain in operating statements offset accumulated losses, to say nothing of acquisition cost and capital outlay.
>
> Meanwhile the community has had a regular annual infusion of much larger wage payments to a much larger staff—the basic cause of the drought in profit which I doubt would be contemplated by any other type of investor in this-sized community.

> In knowledge of this background, you may perhaps appreciate my recoil from the superficial type of criticism that the Thomson organization—which has dealt so much with this size of market—is cheap and repressive with regard to expense. I was the one who, as publisher, made more profit in my last year of publication as an owner than the Thomson interests have made in over-all net in the past dozen years. And why? Basically because I had to overwork the smaller staff I underpaid. I cannot focus the whole matter more sharply than by confessing that.

The case for (or against) newspaper chains is finely balanced. As for the two other forms of ownership concentration – mixed-media holdings and conglomerate holdings – the cost-benefit equation is less ambiguous. In general, we feel, these forms of media ownership are a Bad Thing, unless individual circumstances indicate otherwise.

New Brunswick, of course, is the outstanding example of conglomerate ownership. K. C. Irving, who owns almost everything else in the province, owns five of the six dailies, and TV and radio stations in Saint John. We discuss the journalistic implications of this situation in another chapter; but for now, we'll simply quote approvingly from the brief of Beland Honderich, publisher of the Toronto *Star*. "Mr. Irving," he wrote, "has in effect created a private empire of New Brunswick, complete with its official press – print and electronic."

But even in this case, which is about as flagrant an example of abusing the public interest as you're likely to find in Canada, there is something to be said for it. Dalton Camp, of all people, said it to the Committee. After astounding us by speaking warmly of the Irving newspapers – feeding the hand that bites him, you might say – Mr. Camp continued:

> The presence of a newspaper monopoly in New Brunswick, at least in the English-language market, is held by some to be sinister. I suspect the concern is excessive. It is remarkable to find, anywhere on this continent, much less in New Brunswick, a population of 620,000 people serviced by six newspapers. New Brunswick may have more daily newspapers, per capita, than any state or province on the continent, other than an obvious exception, Prince Edward Island. The economics apparently allow for it, and perhaps it is only the monopoly which perpetuates it.

The man is dead right. New Brunswick *does* have more newspapers per capita than anyplace else in Canada, except Prince Edward Island. We don't think they quite qualify as "diverse and antagonistic voices." But it is at least arguable that the province is better off with a home-owned media monopoly than with one controlled from Toronto or Winnipeg.

Even in the case of mixed-media ownership, it is easy to find extenuating circumstances. We have already described how, in London, Ontario, good management and responsible ownership have avoided the abuses that could result from what we persist in regarding as a monopoly situation.

But there are even more persuasive grounds for arguing that <u>mixed-media ownership can</u>, in some instances, <u>contribute to media diversity instead of lessening it</u>. Putting it simply, the argument goes that the day may come when a newspaper's participation in the electronic media may spell the difference between survival and collapse. Mr. Honderich told us he felt that the rival Toronto *Telegram's* interest in CFTO-TV could place his newspaper at a competitive disadvantage: "A newspaper publisher who is in the fortunate position of having such a lucrative licence may, if he chooses, use his TV profits to subsidize his newspaper in order to gain the upper hand over a competitor."

Similarly, it was argued, a newspaper's involvement in cable TV could be regarded in the long term as survival insurance. Once again, Mr. Honderich: "It is technically possible to transmit a newspaper physically into homes via cable. Although this is not yet commercially practical, it may become so. And if that happens, a newspaper without access to cable will be finished."

Again, the moral is that there is no moral. There are not, nor can there be, any sweeping criteria that will determine now and for all time which ownership-concentration situations militate against the public interest, and which ones are operating in its favor. In every case the arguments for and against are quite finely balanced. Each case much be judged in the light of individual circumstances.

PRESS OWNERSHIP REVIEW BOARD

And that brings us to one of our major recommendations: *we urge the government to establish a Press Ownership Review Board with powers to approve or disapprove mergers between, or acquisitions of, newspapers and periodicals*. The Board should have one basic guideline, spelled out in its enabling legislation: *all* transactions that increase concentration of ownership in the mass media are undesirable and contrary to the public interest – unless shown to be otherwise.

The Board's authority should be restricted to transactions involving print media only. The Canadian Radio-Television Commission now has authority over broadcasting mergers, and has exercised this power in a series of licensing decisions which add up to an evolving policy on ownership concentration. The intent of this series of decisions, as we define it, is that the C.R.T.C. is already following the same broad guideline that we propose for the Press Ownership Review Board: concentration is bad – unless proved otherwise.

We would like to see this principle enunciated in an amendment to the Broadcasting Act. This guideline, together with the proposed Ownership Board's terms of reference, would constitute a two-part legislative framework that would help to protect the public against some of the undesirable effects of media ownership concentration.

The Ownership Board would examine any future newspaper or periodical takeovers that are proposed, to determine whether or not they are in the public interest. The Board should function as the C.R.T.C. does – as a tribunal empowered to issue binding decisions, not merely recommendations to cabinet – but should of course be subject to the provisions of the Federal Court Act, which provides for appeals to the courts against the rulings of such tribunals.

We believe it is important that the Board's powers be carefully circumscribed by its enabling legislation. It should *not* be empowered, for instance, to rule on changes in newspaper ownership arising from gifts and bequests. There are still a large number of family-owned newspapers in the country; transfer of these assets from one generation to the next should not be among the Board's concerns.

Similarly, the Board should not be given authority to intervene retroactively. There are a number of areas, the Committee believes, where existing newspaper or cross-media ownership patterns have operated to the detriment of the public interest. But it should be beyond the Board's powers to intervene in such situations – *unless* the chain or group involved should seek to expand through the acquisition of another newspaper or periodical. In other words, the Board would not have authority to order a publisher to divest himself of assets acquired before the coming into force of the new enactment recommended by this report.

Legislation similar to what we propose has been in force in Britain since August 5, 1965. The legislation, Subsection 1 of Section 8 of the Monopolies and Mergers Act, declares that the transfer of a newspaper to another newspaper proprietor, in any case where this would bring the total circulation of his papers to 500,000 or more a day, is unlawful unless he has the written consent of the Board of Trade, after the Board has received a report on the matter from the Monopolies Commission. The Committee's research showed that the British Monopolies Commission, in its five years of operation, has not so far withheld its approval of any proposed merger. But the very existence of the legislation, we were told, has had a deterrent effect; newspaper mergers that are plainly against the public interest don't need to be disallowed – because they don't get proposed.

The Committee feels the circulation restriction in the British legislation is inapplicable to Canadian conditions. There should be no limit, on the basis of circulation, on the Board's powers to rule on proposed mergers or takeovers. (Although we would expect that the Board, as a matter of policy, would automatically approve mini-mergers between, say, two small weeklies.)

In deciding whether or not a proposed merger is in the public interest, the Board would have to use criteria of a fairly subjective nature. In Britain, the criteria used by the Monopolies Commission are quite broad. Under section 8(3) of the Monopolies and Mergers Act, 1965:

> The Commission shall report whether or not the transfer may be expected to operate against the public interest, taking into account all matters which appear in the particular circumstances to be relevant and having regard (amongst other things) to the need for accurate presentation of news and free expression of opinion.

Individual judgements made by the British Commission have revealed other criteria. In ruling on the proposed merger between the London *Times* and the *Sunday Times*, for instance, the Commission posed three questions: (a) whether the merger would cause an excessive concentration of newspaper power; (b) whether the merger would be a threat to the survival of other newspapers; and (c) whether "changes in the nature of the *Times* are likely to result which would rob it of qualities which make its preservation a matter of public interest."

Regarding another proposed merger, the Commission asked: (a) whether there can be any serious danger of a change in policy on editorial freedom; (b) whether the grouping of a number of local newspapers under Thomson control is liable to lead to some loss of contact by editors and their staffs with the local community to the detriment of the service provided; and (c) what effect an attitude on the part of the proprietor of neutrality in editorial matters, subject only to commercial success, is likely to have upon the character of the newspaper concerned.

Beyond the broad guidelines we propose, it would be up to the Board to define its own criteria of the public interest. But we recommend that any such definitions should include consideration of (a) whether the proposed merger would lengthen the odds on survival of a newspaper that might otherwise die; and (b) what would be likely to happen to the editorial character of the newspaper to be purchased, in view of the purchaser's past performance on the newspapers he already owns, *in relation to the profits they generate*. The onus should be on the purchaser, in other words, to demonstrate that he is in as good or a better position to serve the public interest than is the present owner.

One immediate objection arises to this proposal: the "stable-door" argument that, since 77 of Canada's 116 daily newspapers are already owned by chains or groups, there would be little for the proposed Board to do. We can't buy this argument; the stable door is still wide open. Many more newspaper mergers are still possible, and it is possible to imagine many combinations that would have serious effects on the public's access to diverse and antagonistic sources of information. Suppose K. C. Irving wished to buy the last remaining independent newspaper in New Brunswick. Suppose Southam and Thomson deemed it expedient to join forces. Suppose F. P. Publications Limited wanted to buy the *Columbian*. Would such transactions be in the public interest? It seems almost unarguable that the state should be empowered to watch over the public interest if any such transactions were proposed. So there would be plenty of work for a Press Ownership Review Board.

Since the Committee was established, there has been considerable merger activity in newspapers and periodicals. The three Newfoundland dailies changed hands, the Thomson group buying the Corner Brook *Western Star* and St. John's *Telegram;* Southam Press Limited bought the Prince George *Citizen*, the Owen Sound *Sun-Times*, and the Montreal *Gazette;* Southam

Business Publications Limited purchased National Business Publications Limited, acquiring ten business periodicals and four annuals. In Ontario, Toronto Star Limited purchased the 50 per cent Thomson interest in the Oakville Daily *Journal-Record* and became the sole owner. In Nova Scotia, the Truro *News* was sold to an Ontario publishing firm which also owns the daily in Grande Prairie, Alberta. This may seem like an exceptionally busy period, but in fact it was fairly typical. There has been no period in the past five years when the Board wouldn't have had several merger proposals before it.

In considering establishment of such a Board, the government would have to weigh the matter in relation to any proposed changes in existing anti-combines legislation. The Consumer and Corporate Affairs Department has already proposed new anti-combines legislation that would establish a Competitive Practices Tribunal. This change would enable some restrictive practices to be controlled by the Tribunal, instead of through the Criminal Code, and would permit regulation of service industries to an extent not now possible. We feel strongly that the Press Ownership Review Board we propose should be included in the context of a broadened system of anti-combines legislation, but that the Board should be established as a separate entity. Failing that, and assuming the Board's functions were incorporated as part of a broadened anti-combines authority, we urge that the guidelines we propose be spelled out in legislation that would be binding on the general authority.

The Committee is aware that the establishment of such a Board, since it would involve the application of federal power in a specialized area of anti-combines activity, is a problem fraught with constitutional pitfalls. Indeed, it is the existence of these earlier uncertainties – which are now being reconsidered under new light – that has postponed reform of existing anti-combines legislation, which almost everyone agrees is long overdue. But this shouldn't be taken as a justification for doing nothing. Rather, we feel that the urgent need for regulation of ownership concentration in the printed media provides an additional reason for resolving the constitutional problems involved. Our advice on the matter indicates that the federal government has sufficient constitutional justification for legislating in this particular area; the Consumer and Corporate Affairs Department's contemplated legislation indicates that it feels equally confident with regard to the subject as a whole.

The tribunal we propose could not operate within the constitutional framework on which existing anti-combines legislation is based. *That* legislation derives its authority from the federal government's competence in the field of criminal law. The Press Ownership Review Board couldn't operate under the same authority. By definition, its job would be to approve or disapprove of acts not yet committed, and for this it would have to draw its powers from sources beyond criminal law. Its role, therefore, would be regulatory, not punitive.

This is not to be construed as a suggestion that the Board should have powers to make regulations concerning the content or conduct of individual publications. Its sole concern – and the source of its constitutional authority – would be <u>the investigation and regulation of ownership concentration in the printed media,</u> an area that at present appears to be outside the competence of existing anti-combines laws, and which cannot be effectively regulated by purely provincial enactments.

We say this because we think the problem of ownership concentration in the printed media is especially acute, and because newspapers, emphatically, are not just another business. What happens to the catsup or roofing-tile or widget industry affects us *as consumers;* what happens to the publishing business affects us *as citizens.* Because of this, we can't regard the operations of newspapers and periodicals as purely local pursuits, of concern only in the areas served by these publications. Their impact, their effect on the national consciousness, their ability to influence public opinion on national issues, make publishing a matter of national concern. As businesses, their concerns may be local; but as institutions they are of national importance.

FOR A VOLKSWAGEN PRESS

The Press Ownership Review Board, if it operated under the guidelines we've suggested, would be limited in its effects. It could be useful in preventing or deterring undesirable newspaper mergers, thus preventing a bad situation from becoming worse. But it would have no retroactive powers, and so could do nothing to encourage more independent ownership of newspapers and periodicals than already exists.

But even if the Board were able to achieve a reduction in chain ownership and a corresponding increase in independent ownership, we doubt that this would have much effect on the kind of journalism the public receives. As we've already indicated, neither type of ownership is in itself a guarantee of editorial excellence. If anything, the evidence suggests that this is rather more likely to occur under chain ownership than otherwise.

So it seems futile to yearn for a return to the journalistic status quo of fifty years ago, when most cities of any size were served by several competing dailies. The economics and technology of publishing simply won't allow it any more. This is regrettable but unavoidable. We also mourn the demise of the Marmon, the Pierce-Arrow, the Duesenberg, the Packard, and the Stutz Bearcat – *especially* the Stutz Bearcat – but the relentless economics of mass production seem to dictate that three large automobile companies are about all this continent can afford.

The analogy is a very serviceable one. Detroit has "rationalized" its production to the point where its customers have less choice than they used to have. So have newspaper publishers. Detroit products manage to satisfy most of the people most of the time. So do our newspapers. Detroit cars are sometimes fat, clumsy, poorly made, and loaded with useless options. Must we pursue the analogy any further?

We will, to this extent: what this country now needs, to achieve the sort of editorial competition that is our best guarantee of a good society, is a journalistic equivalent of the Volkswagen.

The Volkswagen[3] challenged all the assumptions that Detroit used to make about its customers. The Volkswagen offered basic transportation, stripped of all considerations of status. The Volkswagen appealed to people who disliked waste and who believed in the importance of real alternatives. And the Volkswagen stole a substantial portion of the available market, forcing Detroit to produce the kind of cars that a lot of people – by their votes in the marketplace – had said they wanted. If it hadn't been for Volkswagen, there would be no Maverick. If it hadn't been for the MG, there probably would be no Mustang. Real competition produced more choices for more people.

The Committee believes a "Volkswagen press" is just beginning to emerge in this country, and that it is the most hopeful development in print journalism for many years. The Volkswagen press usually appears weekly or monthly, not daily. The Volkswagen press has no room for such journalistic tailfins as lavish colour, comic strips, boiler-plated travel sections, and other assembly-line features that are convenient for advertisers but frequently useless to readers. The Volkswagen press can be produced relatively cheaply – usually on offset presses – and it does not aim at the total market. It concentrates on basics; telling what's going on in a personal and opinionated manner. The Volkswagen press is primarily designed for readers, not for advertisers. We believe there is a large minority of the Canadian public that will buy that kind of product.

We wish we could point to a single example of a financially successful Volkswagen newspaper or magazine. There are none yet, but a few promising attempts are being made. Among them:

Last Post: Produced by an editorial co-operative in Montreal, *Last Post* specializes in radical investigative journalism, done up slickly in the manner of *Ramparts* or *Scanlon's* Magazine. *Last Post* tackles subjects that are important, and usually handles them with flair, wit, and professionalism. Almost a monthly, in that it appears as often as the co-operative's members, and the readers who support it through donations and subscriptions, can afford to produce an issue.

The Mysterious East: Edited for love by a group of academics from the University of New Brunswick whose lack of journalistic experience has not prevented them from producing a lively, provocative magazine. Editor Donald Cameron says his magazine wouldn't be needed if the province's Irving-owned dailies were as alert as newspapers are supposed to be.

---

[3] Lest the Committee be accused of showing an unseemly commercial preference, we stress that our remarks apply equally to Austin, Morris, Peugeot, Datsun, Toyota, and many others.

The 4th Estate: Is doing for Nova Scotia what *The Mysterious East* is doing for New Brunswick: providing the kind of journalism that the province's monopoly newspapers fail to deliver. Probably closer to financial viability than most Volkswagen periodicals, since *The 4th Estate* has managed to attract some advertising. (Although its editor complains that its no-holds-barred editorial posture has scared off some large advertisers.)

Canadian Dimension: Edited by C. W. Gonick, Manitoba MLA and economics professor, *Dimension* is left-of-Waffle nationalist, but serves up more ideology than information. Probably the most authoritative and thoughtful of the Volkswagen periodicals, but sadly deficient in a sense of humour.

This is a partial list, and we offer it more to define the *genre* than to enumerate its occupants. The fact that the three periodicals we mentioned are primarily concerned with left-of-centre politics doesn't mean we think that's the only kind of Volkswagen periodicals there could be. There are a number of others in print now, and there could and should be more. *Take One,* a lively film bi-monthly published in Montreal, certainly qualifies. So does *Canada Month,* a financially troubled conservative monthly. So does Vancouver's *Georgia Straight,* which is more concerned with lifestyles than with politics *per se.* So does *The Atlantic Reporter,* a beautifully designed general-interest weekly newspaper which, at this writing, was struggling to get off the ground. So do a lot of other promising newspapers and magazines that either never got off the ground, or perished after a few issues: Peter Desbarat's *Parallel;* Peter Gzowski's *This City;* Peter Lebensold's *Five Cent Review;* Donald Cromie's *Vancouver Life;* and quite a few others.

These periodicals were diverse in their format, their frequency, their editorial approach, their ideology, their competence. Some sought advertising, some attempted to survive on circulation revenue alone. Some may have been aimed at too narrow an audience ever to achieve financial stability. Some, on the basis of their editorial performance, probably deserved to die. Others deserved to survive, and to prosper. But all these Volkswagen publications, living, dying, stillborn, and dead, have at least one thing in common: *they never received a fair trial.*

There are no instant hits in the publishing business. It takes *time* for readers to grow accustomed to the new offering, time to persuade advertisers that a new medium is worth supporting. Usually it seems to take about twice as long as the promoters pessimistically expect, and sometimes longer. *Sports Illustrated* lost money for almost a decade before readers' and advertisers' acceptance moved it into the black. *Toronto Calendar* published more than fifteen money-losing issues before it began attracting substantial advertising (and imitators).

A lack of time – which is another way of saying a lack of money – is (apart from subsidized foreign competition) probably the chief cause of stillbirths in the Canadian publishing business. At least a few of the Volkswagen periodicals that have been launched in this country in the past decade might be alive and prospering today *if* – and this is a big *if* – they'd been able to find the capital that would recognize their potential before the public did. The observations of publisher Peter Lebensold on the demise of *The Five Cent Review* are quoted in the Toronto *Star* (November 1, 1969) this way:

> Unfortunately the economics of magazine publishing are such that no matter how successful a new publication may be, its publishers must be prepared to wait two or three years before advertisers – and especially advertising agencies – come to accept it as a valid advertising medium. It's almost impossible to begin a new magazine unless the publisher is independently wealthy or has secured long-term financing. And the most likely investors in a magazine are people who are already in the publishing industry, which is one reason why so much control over the mass media is more and more concentrated in the hands of a powerful few.

The traditional sources of capital – private "angels," the banks, the stock market – are obviously inadequate to provide this kind of high-risk financing. Existing government agencies, such as the Industrial Development Bank, are precluded by their terms of reference from providing loan or equity capital to publishing ventures. And yet additional capital sources – along with the elimination of subsidized foreign competition – are what the Volkswagen press needs most, if it is to develop into a viable and socially important industry.

The Committee therefore recommends the establishment by the government of a Publications Development Loan Fund, with an available annual "draw" of not less than $2 million, that would assist Canadian publishing ventures in achieving economic viability. Among the Fund's guiding principles:

1. It would *not* be in business to underwrite the establishment of new publications *ab initio*. That would be to invite a flood of petitions from publications which, however potentially "deserving," could never hope to achieve economic viability. Rather, the Fund would receive applications only from publications which have got themselves started and have demonstrated their seriousness by producing a minimum number of issues (say six issues in the case of a monthly).

2. The Fund would consider assistance to publications only if they have attracted sufficient readership to indicate that a readers' need exists and is being adequately served.

3. The applicant publication would be required to have secured a substantial portion of the new financing it requires from private sources; the Fund would not supply it all from the public purse.

4. The applicant would be required to have developed a feasible, acceptable plan for allocating the additional funds to future development.

5. As a condition of loan, the Fund would nominate one independent director to serve on the board of the applicant company as a watchdog for the public interest, such director to serve until the loan is discharged. (This

condition should be gratefully accepted by the borrowers; one reason for the failure of many young publications is that while they may have brilliant editorial direction, they lack a business balance wheel.)

We think the Fund could be organized with a very small staff. It should operate with the widest possible mandate: to allocate its funds in whatever manner will best encourage the development and financial viability of diverse and antagonistic media voices in Canada. Naturally, this guideline implies an obligation to avoid loans to publications, however worthy, that appear unlikely to be able to repay them.

In making this recommendation, the Committee is aware of the policies, and apparent success, of the Canadian Film Development Corporation, and we suggest that the Fund be set up as a corporation on similar lines. The C.F.D.C., set up to administer a $10 million revolving loan fund, has had a major impact on the recent growth of the Canadian feature-film industry. It too operates on the "matching" funds principle; as a matter of policy, the C.F.D.C. demands that an applicant producer have secured a distribution contract involving a financial commitment of at least half the film's projected budget. We note that the C.F.D.C. is also empowered by its enabling legislation to make grants to film-makers "to assist them in improving their craft." Although the Loan Fund we envision would not be in business to give handouts to "worthy" publications, we don't think it should be precluded from making small-scale development grants in cases where this seems advisable.

The Committee is hopeful that implementation of this recommendation, together with the other measures we are proposing, would have an encouraging effect on the Canadian periodical industry. Government investment in this direction appears to us to be the most hopeful form of encouraging a diversity of voices in an industry that is tending increasingly towards monopoly.

III

IMPACT

1. Change and Response

THE CONSTANT BUMP

Soap companies commission attitude surveys to find out what the public thinks about soap. Car manufacturers commission motivational surveys to find out which kinds of sexual fantasy can most successfully be translated into automobile design. But to our knowledge, no one in Canada has ever commissioned a public-opinion survey to find out what people think about the media as a whole – their roles, their effectiveness, their weaknesses.

We did. Martin Goldfarb Consultants, a Toronto-based opinion-polling firm, conducted in-depth interviews on this subject with 2,254 Canadians from all provinces. The sample was scientifically selected to represent a cross-section of the population, and the interviews lasted from two to six hours each. The interviewers talked to teenagers, farmers, housewives, university professors, junior executives, carpenters, factory workers, teachers, retired people – all sorts of Canadians representing various ages, incomes, education levels, and geographic regions. We are satisfied that the sample was more than adequate, that the structuring of the questionnaires was free of built-in bias, and that results are novel and important.

Perhaps the most striking thing about the results is the discovery that what people think about the media, and what media managers *think* people think about the media, are two very different things. What publisher could have imagined, for instance, that close to half his audience suspects that "criminal elements" influence the news? And how many owners of TV stations could have suspected what the survey indicates – that roughly four out of ten Canadians actually *talk out loud* to their radio or TV sets? Or that three out of ten Canadians feel the media are not sufficiently critical of government? Or that about half feel that newspapers and radio should be censored?

There are areas, however, where the perceptions of media producers and media consumers appear to coincide. Most Canadians think news coverage has generally improved in the past five years, and most are generally satisfied with the *amount* (as distinguished from quality) of news they receive. Newspapers are regarded by most Canadians as the best medium for detailed information. Television is regarded as the most exciting and influential medium, but newspapers remain the least dispensable over the long term. Radio is regarded as the most important medium in case of public emergency; at other times, most seem to regard radio mainly as a source of background noise demanding little attention. Magazines are regarded as the least essential of the mass media.

Some of the public's fears and reservations concerning the media are shared by media people themselves. Some obviously aren't. About half the people fear that newspapers might invade their privacy; their fear of radio and TV isn't as great in this respect. Most feel there is too much sex and violence on TV, and too many programs about drugs. A large majority felt they were getting biased information about politicians (but also felt that in general the media do a good job in reporting politics.) About two thirds of the sample felt that "big business" was to blame for press bias, and four out of ten felt that newspapers serve the interests of advertisers or the government, rather than the public at large.

The results of the Goldfarb survey are published separately, so we won't deal with it in greater detail here. What they seem to indicate is that Canadians, by and large, despite a number of reservations, are satisfied with the job their media are doing for them. The existence of this attitude has also been claimed by a number of broadcasters and publishers, who cite audience and circulation figures as evidence of public acceptance of their product.

We believe this to be true in many parts of the country. There is no question that many newspapers and a number of TV and radio stations have made strenuous efforts in the past few years to upgrade the quality and relevance of their editorial product. The Goldfarb study indicates that these efforts have not been in vain; nearly nine out of ten Canadians feel they are better informed today than they were five years ago.

But in too many cases, public acceptance of the media may be said to exist only in the sense that the public "accepted" large Detroit automobiles before Volkswagens became available. "Acceptance" exists only because no better alternative is available. This is true even in Nova Scotia and New Brunswick, two provinces that the Committee has come to regard as journalistic disaster areas; Nova Scotians feel better informed than Ontarians do, and New Brunswickers feel better informed than do British Columbians.

We are treading in a highly subjective area here. Perhaps it would be best, before we continue, to define what we mean by "good" and "bad" media. There can be endless disagreement in such an area, because the criteria can vary so widely. The standard we choose to employ is pretty straightforward: *how successful is that newspaper, or broadcasting station, in preparing its audience for social change?*

This involves no partisan judgements. Change is *the* constant of our times, and the media, by definition, must deal with change – not only through reporting the isolated, dramatic event, but by probing the hidden shifts in attitudes and institutions by which most change is accomplished. To insist that this is the media's main job is not to suggest any built-in bias for or against the notion of "progress." A new pulp mill on the edge of town may or may not be "progress"; but it is definitely change. The media's job is to bring forward as many facts, as many informed judgements on that change as possible. As Frank Walker, editor-in-chief of the Montreal *Star,* put it:

> We try as a conscious editorial policy to take the surprise out of living. ... the shock value out of things that happen ... .we discuss a trend or predict an event or a change in attitude and by putting that into the paper early enough, stop this constant bump you get by being surprised almost every day.

THE NEWSPAPERS

Some newspapers dig. Some newspapers are a constant embarrassment to the powerful. Some manage to be entertaining, provocative, and fair at the same time. There are a few such newspapers in Canada. The Vancouver *Sun*. The three Toronto dailies. *Le Devoir*. The Montreal *Star*. The Windsor *Star*. *La Presse*. The Edmonton *Journal*. A handful of others. There should be more.

There are also newspapers which, despite occasional lapses into excellence, manage to achieve a consistent level of mediocrity. The Montreal *Gazette,* and the dailies in Ottawa, Winnipeg, and Calgary fit into this category.

There is a third kind of newspaper in Canada – the kind that prints news releases intact, that seldom extends its journalistic enterprise beyond coverage of the local trout festival, that hasn't annoyed anyone important in years. Their city rooms are refuges for the frustrated and disillusioned, and their editorial pages are a daily testimony to the notion that Chamber-of-Commerce boosterism is an adequate substitute for community service. It is our sad impression that a great many, if not most Canadian newspapers fall into this classification. Interestingly enough, among them are some of the most profitable newspapers in the country. A number of these newspapers are owned by K. C. Irving. A much larger number are owned by Roy Thomson. And some of them, unhappily, are owned by respected residents of the communities they profess to serve.

In general, you can say that the best of them are published in big cities, the worst in small ones. But there are plenty of exceptions. Halifax, Canada's twelfth-largest city, is served by daily newspapers which are either mediocre or dreadful, depending on the rigor of your standards. The Peterborough *Examiner,* until Thomson acquired it, had one of the most urbane editorial pages in the country. And, as we've noted several times already, there is no easy one-to-one correspondence between mediocrity and group ownership. The dailies published in Canada by the Thomson chain are almost uniformly disappointing. The dailies published by F.P. range from competent to excellent. The only reliable rule appears to be that good newspapers usually happen when (a) the operation is financially secure and (b) people who care more about journalism than about balance-sheets control the editorial product.

In such salubrious circumstances, you tend to get situations like this:

*In Vancouver, the c.p.r. wanted to build a shopping centre on some land it owned in Kerrisdale. Many residents thought it would destroy the neighbourhood's character. They met, they organized, they fought the proposal — and were supported every step of the way by the f.p.-owned Vancouver *Sun,* whose special articles, columnists, and news stories reported the issue critically but fairly. In so doing, they helped mobilize public opinion against the project, which was eventually dropped. It was a textbook demonstration of the proposition that people who own a newspaper don't *have* to treat its news columns as their personal property; one of the c.p.r.'s major shareholders is Max Bell, who is also one of the major shareholders in F.P. Publications Limited.

*The editors of the Toronto *Star,* concerned that opinionated comment was becoming too much the preserve of professional journalists, opened their Page Seven to — of all people — the people. They devoted an unprecedentedly large amount of space to letters-to-the-editor. They sponsored public forums on various public issues, and reported the meetings in great detail. Instead of buying syndicated U.S. columnists on the cheap (as too many Canadian editorial pages do) they spent money to fill their columns with articles by people who don't normally write for newspapers. It was an attempt to give a voice to the voiceless, and it was a success. The volume of mail doubled, and the New York *Times* is now imitating the *Star's* approach.

*Some of the most eloquent put-downs that came to the Committee's attention were directed at the Fredericton *Gleaner,* formerly owned by Brigadier Michael Wardell, now controlled by K. C. Irving. We think much of it was justified. But we should point out that the *Gleaner* carried the second-highest proportion (after *La Presse*) of staff-written material in the thirty dailies whose contents were tabulated by the Committee's researchers. We should also quote from Dalton Camp's presentation:

> The daily newspapers of New Brunswick have improved more in the past ten years than the press from any other comparable region. The *Daily Gleaner,* prior to its purchase by Brigadier Wardell, was an outrage to journalism. It was probably the only newspaper in Canada in which the disinterest of the publisher was fully matched by the boredom of its readers.
>
> After Mr. Wardell assumed responsibility for the *Gleaner,* it began to acquire a resemblance to a daily newspaper. It manifested a lively interest in the community, embarked on a number of editorial crusades reflecting the special interests of the province and the Atlantic area and, if its opinions were often stringent, at least they were opinions and, as such, invoked community interest, involvement, discussion and debate. Fredericton had never known a newspaper like it or, more properly, Fredericton had never known what a newspaper was like. The *Gleaner* became a reasonable facsimile.

It would be easy to devote several chapters to similar examples, for there are a lot of newsmen who are dedicated, in the most highly professional way, to this ideal of documenting change – even if some of their bosses aren't. Several million Canadians – but not, we fear, the majority – are served by newspapers that have earned the wary respect of local Establishments. That is as it should be.

Regrettably, we could devote an entire book to examples of how newspapers are failing to do their job. The Committee was made aware, formally and informally, of dozens of cases of "news suppression" – instances where editors or publishers were said to have trimmed, killed, slanted, or displayed a reporter's story in such a way as to support an "official" version. Most such cases are practically impossible to document. Human error, honest disagreement over modes of presentation, fear of libel laws and so on could be cited to explain most of them. But we are satisfied – as are most reporters – that a "party line" does in fact exist in many newsrooms. But like pressure from advertisers, it operates subtly and capriciously when it operates at all.

Frankly, we don't view *deliberate* suppression of the news by owner-publishers as much of a problem. It happens, but seldom blatantly. More often, it is the result of a certain atmosphere – an atmosphere in which boat-rocking is definitely not encouraged – and of news editors trying to read the boss's mind. This leads to journalistic sins (of omission, mostly) that result from lassitude, sloppiness, smugness, and too chummy a relationship with the local power structure. One-newspaper towns are the most frequent victims. For example:

**The Mysterious East,* a young muckraking monthly published in Fredericton, printed a truly astonishing scoop last July: that the chairman of the New Brunswick Water Authority, the body charged with, among other things, enforcing anti-pollution laws against pulp mills, was also for a time secretary-treasurer and general manager of the New Brunswick Forest Products Association – a lobbying organization for the pulp and paper industry! There are newspapers in this country which would have joyously trumpeted a fact like that, and probably forced the official's resignation from one body or the other. No daily newspaper in New Brunswick did, however. The uncharitable might be led to suspect that this lack of journalistic enterprise was connected to the fact that K. C. Irving, owner of one of the province's largest pulp mills, also owns all five New Brunswick English-language dailies.

*One of *The Mysterious East's* contributing editors, Dr. Donald Cameron, supplied another example. When Laurier LaPierre, in October, 1969, addressed a student gathering outside Moncton, he devoted nearly all his speech to the shortcomings of capitalism, the press, and K. C. Irving, and to a plea for "decentralized socialism" as a solution to the problems of the Maritimes. *En passant,* Dr. LaPierre also mentioned that he was against Maritime union, since he favoured less, not more, centralization. According to Dr. Cameron, the New Brunswick dailies covered the story this way:

> On Monday, October 27, the Moncton *Times* headlined its front-page story MARITIME UNION "WASTE OF TIME AND RESOURCES."

It devoted twenty column-inches to LaPierre's speech in a story labelled "Staff Special." Of those twenty inches, one and a quarter was devoted to the attack on Irving. Two inches covered the comments on the press. The rest of the article was devoted to Maritime union and economic development, but the economic development was made to appear as simply a variant of the existing economic system, and the word "socialism" did not appear anywhere in the article.

The Saint-John *Telegraph-Journal* clipped the inessential last paragraph from the story, and instead of calling LaPierre simply "the head" of McGill's French-Canadian Studies programme it called him "the articulate head." Otherwise the *Telegraph-Journal* story was, word for word, identical with the Moncton *Times* story. Naturally the Moncton evening paper, the *Transcript,* followed its morning sister. So did the *Evening Times-Globe* in Saint John. And the Fredericton *Wiener* picked up the *Telegraph-Journal* story complete. So far as any New Brunswick reader could tell, LaPierre simply came down from Montreal to tell us what to do about Maritime union. Oh, these cheeky bastards from central Canada!

What is even more puzzling, however, is the fact that the story printed by the Irving press contains a good deal that is not in the transcript. Why? Very simply, because the reporter who wrote the *Times* story did not hear Mr. LaPierre. Instead he relied on some mimeographed notes which Mr. LaPierre passed out in advance. When he actually spoke, Mr. LaPierre threw away the notes and delivered a rousing committed speech. But the reporters had taken the handout and left – with one exception. The one exception, the one New Brunswick daily to report the story reasonably accurately, the one daily to mention socialism, to quote the vigorous criticism of the Irving empire, was the one daily in the province *not* owned by Mr. Irving: I mean, of course, *L'Evangéline,* the Moncton French-language daily.

*The news columns of the Peterborough *Examiner,* in December, 1968, virtually ignored one of the year's biggest local stories – the strike at the *Examiner* by members of the American Newspaper Guild. The *Examiner's* publisher and general manager, William J. Garner, when questioned on this point by the Committee, explained: "If we gave day-to-day coverage of the strike, of our side of it, it could be termed biased." This is perhaps understandable but is it good enough? "Objectivity" is one of the shibboleths of the Thomson chain; deliberately playing down strike news seems to reflect, at the very least, a lack of confidence in the *Examiner's* ability to achieve this ideal.

*As a final entry in this random and admittedly incomplete assortment of journalistic cop-outs, we must refer at some length to the situation in Halifax. The city's two dailies, the *Chronicle-Herald* and the *Mail-Star,* are both owned by the Dennis family; according to the publisher, they are essentially morning and evening editions of the same newspaper. They enjoy a virtual monopoly on print communication in Halifax, and there is probably no large Canadian city that is so badly served by its newspapers. The *Mail-Star* prints a ringing (and rhyming)[1] declaration of editorial

---
[1] "For the cause that lacks assistance,
gainst the wrong that needs resistance,
For the future in the distance,
and the good that we can do."

prowess on its masthead. But there is probably no news organization in the country that has managed to achieve such an intimate and uncritical relationship with the local power-structure, or has grown so indifferent to the needs of its readers.

The Dennis newspapers, which are highly profitable, have for years been guilty of uncaring, lazy journalism. This is not merely our opinion. It appears to be shared by a substantial minority of the reading public in Nova Scotia. How else do you explain the remarkable growth of *The 4th Estate,* a boat-rocking bi-weekly (now a weekly) that has achieved a circulation of 8,000 in less than a year, and a readership estimated at several times that number? Or that this Committee received more letters from unhappy newspaper readers in Halifax than from any other area in the country?

Nick Fillmore, *The 4th Estate's* managing editor, provided the Committee with a list of news stories that broke in his newspaper:

> August 14, 1969 – A report that a study to determine the feasibility of harnessing the Bay of Fundy tides showed that the project was technically feasible but financially impractical. (A major story on the same subject, carried by the *Chronicle-Herald* several weeks later. It was also picked up by the Canadian Press.)
>
> Nov. 20, 1969 – A report of irregularities in the handling of liquor seized by a Police Committee Chairman in the town of Liverpool, N.S. (Attorney General's Department later invited the town's former police chief to present facts about the administration of justice in the town.)
>
> Dec. 3, 1969 – Report that the first international fisheries agreement was being made to limit the catch of species of fish off the east coast of Canada. (Item reported in early February in the daily press.)
>
> Dec. 25, 1969 – Report that the U.S. Defence Department withdrew a signed $3.5-million contract from Fairey Canada Ltd. of Dartmouth, N.S. for defence equipment because of pressure after Canada announced cuts in its NATO forces. (Item unreported so far as I know.)

These are important regional stories. It seems odd that a two-man operation like *The 4th Estate* could scoop an organization with the resources of the *Chronicle-Herald* and the *Mail-Star* on all four of them. It seems even stranger that the Dennis newspapers, once scooped, didn't follow up these stories immediately – either to enlarge on them or to knock them down.

This may be because the Dennis newspapers appear reluctant to publish anything that might embarrass the government. At the hearings, L. F. Daley, vice-president of the Halifax Herald Limited which publishes the *Chronicle-Herald,* was questioned about the charge – contained in the December 20, 1969 issue of the *Globe Magazine* – that "in the twelve years in which Robert Stanfield was Premier there wasn't one word of criticism of his administration in the Halifax papers. But it was that way even before Nova Scotia turned Conservative with Stanfield. While Henry Hicks was Premier, he too was the apple of their eye." Mr. Daley told us he found that charge "pretty hard to believe." But he didn't offer the Committee any instances of the *Mail-Star* or the *Chronicle-Herald* mounting editorial campaigns against government policies. Nor were our researchers able to discover any.

The Committee was told of many instances where reporters' stories were altered allegedly to fit the Dennis "party line." It is difficult to define exactly the line between "news suppression" and honest disagreements between reporter and editor on matters of taste, emphasis, and presentation. But we think the flatulent nature of the Dennis editorial product supports the view that something very close to news suppression frequently takes place. The interesting thing is that it appears to have happened not to protect the *newspaper's* interests, but to further what the publisher deemed to be the *public* interest. That these interests always seem to coincide with those of the Halifax Establishment recalls a venerable and well-loved piece of English doggerel:

> You cannot hope to bribe or twist
> Thank God! the British journalist.
> But, seeing what the man will do
> Unbribed, there's no occasion to.[2]

We find it ironic, and a little sad, that the *Chronicle-Herald* prides itself on being a direct descendant of the *Novascotian* published by Joseph Howe, the father of Canada's free and responsible press. What would old Joe – a hell-raiser, a crusader, a baiter of Family Compacts – think of the Halifax newspapers today?

Admittedly, these are strong words; our disappointment with the performance of the Halifax newspapers, as one instance of the kind of journalism we deplore, has been expressed in language that some may deem intemperate. It is only fair to point out that two of our own members believe this; of the three Nova Scotia Senators on the Committee, two have asked that they be dissociated from these comments. In the view of Senator J. M. Macdonald and Senator Frank Welch, the *Chronicle-Herald* and the *Mail-Star* are serving their province competently, honestly, and independently in the public interest. They point out that the majority of the Committee, personally unfamiliar with Nova Scotia history and Nova Scotia practice, may apply a yardstick that is inapplicable to Nova Scotia conditions. We respect their position.

We have not singled out the Dennis newspapers because they are especially unique. In fact, they are uncomfortably close to being typical of too many Canadian dailies. The editorial failure of such publications does not stem primarily from "news suppression." It stems, rather, from what Dr. Cameron calls "enforced laziness" – the imposition by newspaper ownerships of an atmosphere in which editorial initiatives are unwelcome. People who want to practise vigorous, independent journalism do not thrive in such an atmosphere. If they're lucky they move on to other news organizations where their initiative will be rewarded instead of subtly penalized. Or else they go into public relations.

We find it remarkable that so few large newspaper chains offer cash incentives to their reporters for distinguished performance – inter-office

---

[2] Humbert Wolfe, 1885-1940.

Pulitzer prizes, if you will. Suppose the Thomson chain were to offer a $2,000 annual award to the Thomson reporter whose work best exemplified the ideal of editorial excellence? We suspect that the improvement in morale, interest, and performance throughout the thirty-newspaper Thomson chain might be quite dramatic. The fact that they haven't indicates to us what should already be obvious from inspecting the product: Thomson doesn't care enough about editorial content, as long as it doesn't interfere with profits.

THE BROADCASTERS

And what of broadcasting? What about *its* function in softening the onslaught of change?

There is a school of thought that would argue that broadcasting in Canada has softened the onslaught of change only to the extent that it has been an anaesthetic, that some day the patient must awake to find his left leg amputated, and that broadcasting will have done nothing to prepare him for his new situation. This, of course, is an overstatement . . . . or is it?

Let us first bear in mind that the broadcaster who wastes his frequency is not just wasting his own property, he is wasting everyone's property. If he does not use his frequency to fulfill his proper role, we are all the poorer. Let us then reflect that the CTV television network devotes just slightly over four per cent of its weekly schedule to regular public-affairs programmes. Let us remember that the only television station in Victoria – capital of British Columbia, population more than 175,000 – has no local news or public-affairs programme. Let us recall the FM radio stations across the country which are simply rebroadcasters of the AM stations that own them.

Clearly, there are programmes other than public-affairs and news programmes that heighten public awareness. The function of broadcasting is to entertain and enlighten, as well as to inform. The potential social relevance of serious and light drama, of humour, music, and sport is not to be denied. But can there be any suggestion that when CKLW-TV, Windsor, elects to broadcast *Sing Along With Mitch* at 11:30 p.m., after the national news, it is offering even entertainment, let alone information or enlightenment? When the same station broadcasts a public-affairs programme (which it does not produce, but obtains from another station) at 1:30 a.m., can it be seriously discharging its public responsibility? Is there, after all, some special need upon the part of insomniacs for information and enlightenment?

What, indeed, are we to make of the fact that the CTV television network has cancelled its only daily programme for children, and shows no inclination to replace it?

People's expectations of radio are not high, it seems. From our research, it appears that radio is expected to provide quick news, and soothing background music, and very little else. In this sense, private radio in Canada may be deemed successful. Radio broadcasters have often gone further. Many now have open-line programmes of some form – an important development in allowing the public some access to broadcasting, and a most welcome one, even though these programmes are at times abused, either by the personalities who moderate them or by those other personalities (often every bit as vivid) who telephone the programmes to become involved in discussions. But with rare exceptions, radio has gone no further than this.

The CBC has tried to maintain a tradition of wide, varied public service through its radio networks, and it has been more successful, perhaps, than an ungrateful public has deserved. It has languished for years in the shadow of CBC television, giving excellent service, receiving little recognition.

Privately owned radio has often been successful in its own terms: profitability, stability, unflagging mediocrity. It has sometimes been successful in developing one skill and exploiting it to the virtual exclusion of all else – as CKNW in New Westminster has done with news. But all too often private radio has set its sights low, and has not worried unduly if even indifferent levels of performance were not attained.

There are signs – very hopeful one – that this will not continue. The possibilities of providing programming more closely attuned to community needs and aspirations are becoming more attractive to private radio stations. And the C.R.T.C.'s action against CJLS in Yarmouth, N.S., for its somewhat casual attitude toward news broadcasts (the licence was not renewed after an admission that such broadcasts had been altered so as not to offend advertisers) has given a number of private radio broadcasters something to think about.

Television is a somewhat different matter. It has been pointed out by critics of Canadian broadcasting that a person who turns the selector dial on his radio seeking different stations can tell almost immediately whether he is listening to a private station or to the CBC. Their programmes are distinctly different. A television viewer, on other hand, would often have difficulty in knowing whether he was watching a public or a private television station, particularly during the prime evening hours. Indeed, he would often be unsure whether he watching a Canadian station. It is a puzzling and possibly unique aspect of Canada that this situation is largely accepted as normal.

This situation is, of course, by no means so pronounced in Quebec. Most television stations broadcasting in French in Canada are either owned by the CBC, or are privately owned CBC affiliates. The independent French-language stations have a hardy programme philosophy of their own.

At times, the viewer of CBC's English-language programmes knows clearly that he is watching the public network. He is most unlikely, after all, to see opera or ballet anywhere else. Likewise, he may generally be unable to tell a CTV public-affairs programme from a CBC public-affairs programme – both networks do them well – until the first commercial rolls onto the screen. At that point, it may occur to him that the CBC does not usually sell commercial time in such programmes, whereas CTV does.

He may, finally, reflect that the CBC does rather more public-affairs programming than CTV. It also does all the serious drama, all the opera, all the ballet, and almost all the serious music, that is ever likely to come his way on Canadian television.

But he knows that a great deal of the prime-time programming of both networks consists of imported programmes from the United States. He knows, too, that these programmes have not been notably successful in preparing the public for social change—he has, after all, the current social anguish of the United States to gaze upon as evidence.

Canada's television networks, and most of Canada's television stations, have the services of broadcasters who very much want to produce programmes of quality, programmes of immediacy, programmes that will genuinely fulfill the central role of broadcasting. But these organizations also feel a very deep obligation to continue their role as the principal medium for advertising soap, cosmetics, and instant coffee. And the competition between the demands of these differing roles is not being resolved in favour of public service or social responsibility.

Neither public nor private broadcasters, it seems to us, have been notably adventurous in developing, not just new programmes, but new *kinds* of programmes. Too often, the imagination of Canadian broadcasters has been directed towards inventing variations on imported formulae. But experiments sometimes succeed wondrously. *Sesame Street* and *The Forsyte Saga* both must have sounded implausible when first proposed. Institutional and commercial support for similarly adventurous ideas in Canada has seldom been forthcoming. One group of Ottawa free-lance broadcasters, for instance, has spent six months developing a programme concept that, just possibly, could revolutionize TV. The idea is to do for broadcasting what *The Whole Earth Catalogue* has done for print: give an urban audience access to the tools and techniques that will help them to function more autonomously in a mass society. Bake your own bread. Recycle your own garbage. Buy a bicycle. Start a neighbourhood nursery school – that sort of thing. The programme would be a multi-media experiment; viewers who saw an item featuring, say, Bobby Hull telling how to set up a pee-wee hockey league would be able to *talk* to Bobby and make their own suggestions on a hot-line radio show broadcast half an hour later; and they'd be able to write for pamphlets if they wanted further information. We think the potential appeal of such a programme could be enormous. And we are disappointed that, apart from a token development grant from the C.R.T.C., neither network has indicated much willingness to support the project.

We have been told, and we believe it is true, that broadcasters – like any good salesmen – have become adept at anticipating the moods and requirements of their customers, the advertisers. We are by no means as sure that they have become adept at anticipating how best their viewers may be served.

2. La Différence

In journalism, as in a great many other things, Quebec is not a province *comme les autres*. The traditions, the audience preferences, the mythologies, the economics of publishing and broadcasting–all are shaped by the French Fact, to the extent that the province's media cannot be viewed simply as one part of the Canadian whole. Thus this chapter is about *la différence*.

It is tempting to define that difference in McLuhanist terms: French-Canadian culture, and the media that help to define it, seem to reflect an oral bias. Ontario, for instance, has forty-eight daily newspapers: Quebec, with about one million fewer people, has only fourteen. The French-speaking population (which is 81 per cent of the total) appears to be less hung-up on print than *les anglais*. In the public-opinion survey commissioned by the Committee, more French-Canadians named TV as their most important news medium than did the English-speaking samples in both Quebec and Ontario.

Simple observation bears this out; there is no other part of Canada where television has become such a tribal medium. Nothing on English-Canadian TV–not even *Seven Days* or *The Forsyte Saga*–has ever achieved the massive impact of *La Rue Des Pignons*. Dozens of Quebec personalities, from René Lévesque to Gilles Vigneault, owe their fame to television.

But the pervasiveness of TV in Quebec is only one aspect of that province's astounding cultural vitality. Quebec has its own Top Forty, its own sex goddesses, its own totem-intellectuals, its own feature-film industry, its own penny-dreadful press, its own little magazines, night talk shows, its own Bob Dylan.[3] Much of this vitality is due to the simple fact of language; Quebec *can't* make do with Johnny Carson and Lawrence Welk. But much more, it seems to us, is due to the French-Canadian genius for being themselves. English-Canadians, after all, import much more of their culture (pop and otherwise) from the U.S. than Quebec does from France. The Quebec media both reflect this vitality and nourish it. We offer some examples.

---

[3] Putting it another way, the U.S. has its own Robert Charlebois.

NEWSPAPERS

Quebec has fewer dailies per capita than most provinces. But French Canada's two great dailies, *La Presse* and *Le Devoir*, enjoy an influence and prestige within their community that perhaps no English-language newspaper can match. Montreal is one of the most competitive newspaper towns in North America—there are six dailies, which is more than you'll find in New York. Montreal and Quebec also share the distinction of being among the very few cities in North America where new dailies have been launched in the past decade or so – and survived.

Pierre Péladeau, president of Québecor Inc., is the man behind that particular miracle. In 1964 he launched *Le Journal de Montreal* hastily during a newspaper strike, saw its circulation leap to 75,000, then fall back to 12,000 when the strike ended at *La Presse*. By ruthless economies, by setting up his own distribution system, by concentrating on local instead of national advertising and, above all, by publishing a *popular* newspaper that emphasized local news and amateur sports, he built *Le Journal* into a money-making daily with a circulation that is now more than 50,000. In 1967 he attempted the same trick in another, smaller city with *Le Journal de Québec*. It began publishing on the day *L'Evénement-Journal* folded. After three years the morning paper is still losing money. But its circulation, almost 12,000, is now twice as large as that of the newspaper it replaced, and Péladeau is confident that it will eventually show a profit.

Péladeau is an almost inspirational figure, for he has demonstrated that it *is* sometimes possible to beat the Media Monopoly Game, by giving the people what they're not already getting. In his brief to the Committee he disagreed with the publisher of the Toronto *Telegram*:

> Contrary to Mr. John Bassett, who recently stated that it is virtually impossible to establish a newspaper in a city where there is one already, we state, and our experience is testimony of it, that it is always possible to do so, and, what is more, to make it profitable.

Could he himself launch a successful paper in Toronto? Yes, he said; he could. One can only applaud such heresy.

It is less easy to applaud Quebec journalism's almost total absorption with Quebec. The Committee reached the conclusion that with the usual exceptions, the news media in English Canada have shown too little initiative in reporting at first hand the story of Quebec in the past decade. We pressed this point, perhaps at tiresome length, in our questioning of English-language publishers. And we apply the same criticism in even greater degree to the French-language press of Quebec, whose newspapers maintain no staff correspondents in the rest of Canada outside of the national capital. Clearly the interests of Canada would be better served by a stronger policy of cultural interpretation in both wings of the national press.

Quebec also has about 170 regional weeklies. Some of them, such as *Progrès-Dimanche* in Chicoutimi, have larger circulations than many Canadian dailies. Controlled-circulation "neighbourhood" weeklies, distributed mostly in the Montreal and Quebec metropolitan areas, have a total distribution of about 200,000. But there is a third class of weekly, unique to Quebec, that represents one of the most remarkable success stories in Canadian publishing. Let's call them the Pop Weeklies.

They are often scorned by the respectable people who read *La Presse* and *Le Devoir,* but they are read faithfully by almost everybody else. They have zippy names like *Allo Police* and *Photo-Vedettes,* and their editorial obsessions are the same ones that have sustained the penny press since the nineteenth century: crime, sports, *le grand monde,* and pretty girls. Most of them are not vulgar newspapers – just popular. And because they're capable of creating fan-mag heroes and heroines from the province's sports and entertainment personalities, their contribution to Quebec's sense of cultural identity has been considerable. As Quebecor Inc. – which publishes eight pop weeklies – expressed it in their brief, these "artistic newspapers" have "contributed, to a very large degree, to the development of a particular taste in things artistic among all French-Canadians, at the same time as they have succeeded in creating a solid attachment between the public and those whose purpose is to brighten their daily lives."

Many lives have been brightened by the pop weeklies. Twenty years ago there were four of them publishing in Quebec, with a total circulation of about 500,000. Today there are about twenty, including two that provide TV listings and two that specialize in photo-stories about crime, the gorier the better. They have a total circulation of close to two million, a large part of it controlled by Péladeau.

If Péladeau is king of the pop weeklies, financier Paul Desmarais is lord of the dailies. Desmarais, Chief Executive Officer of Power Corporation of Canada Limited, controls *La Presse.* Through his 46.6 per cent holding of *Les Journaux Trans-Canada Limitée* (Jean Parisien and Jacques Francoeur have smaller holdings), he also controls a string of daily and weekly newspapers that represent a substantial portion of total newspaper circulation in the province. The holdings of *Les Journaux Trans-Canada Limitée* include three dailies – *La Tribune* in Sherbrooke, *Le Nouvelliste* in Trois-Rivières and *La Voix de l'Est* in Granby – *La Patrie,* one of Quebec's oldest and most influential weeklies, four pop weeklies (*Dimanche-Matin, Le Petit Journal, Photo-Journal* and *Dernière-Heure*) and ten regional weeklies. *Les Journaux Trans-Canada Limitée* also owns two printing companies, a distribution company, and a radio station. Desmarais also has a one-third interest in a company which operates a TV station in Carleton and a radio station in Shawinigan.

These holdings, plus the broadcasting properties that Power Corporation used to control before it sold the assets of Québec Télémedia Inc. to Philippe de Gaspé Beaubien, constituted a formidable concentration of ownership. The Desmarais media holdings, combined with his control of one of the nation's most powerful financial institutions, have caused considerable concern in Quebec. Quebec's Special Committee on Freedom of the Press was established partly in response to this concern, which was articulated for *our* Committee by Claude Ryan, editor of *Le Devoir*. He told us:

> A scant five or six years ago, Quebec had about ten independent dailies, four of them English. Today, more than half of them have been taken over by publishing chains, and at least one of the remainder is presently in very serious financial difficulties. This means that soon there might well be only two or three Quebec dailies that are completely free of any obligation or dependence other than their duty to their public and their journalists.

Mr. Ryan, who is one of Quebec's most respected and influential journalists, sees an inverse relationship between newspaper chains and editorial quality. He told the Committee:

> Insofar as journalistic quality is concerned, the chains we have seen in action in Quebec have tended to do their equalizing downwards rather than upwards. . . . Some newspapers taken over by large chains have succeeded in maintaining their previous vitality, though no one is likely to claim that it has been enhanced by their membership in the chain. In a great many cases, the exact opposite may be observed. Owners and managers like to maintain that the editors of all their member newspapers are completely free to determine the editorial policies of those papers themselves. But it is quite apparent that this freedom may be exercised within certain limits which, for all that they are not strictly defined in writing, are none the less real.

Les Journaux Trans-Canada Limitée, in its brief to the Committee, was somewhat coy on this point. Its 16 weeklies account for more than one third of the total weekly circulation in the province, and its three dailies account for nearly one quarter of total daily circulation. But the company sees itself as holding a "modest position" in the total media picture and they stressed that, although their position is "weak," they regard it as a "sacred" trust.

There is no question that group ownership has conferred some substantial benefits on the newspapers controlled by the Desmarais group. *Les Journaux Trans-Canada Limitée* has provided an administrative input that can only strengthen all members of the chain. It has not only strengthened, but perhaps actually rescued, at least two newspapers – *La Patrie* and *La Voix de l'Est* – and it is one of the few Canadian chains that act as though they were serious about staff training. But it is hard to support the view that chain ownership of *La Presse* or of the three dailies of *Les Journaux Trans-Canada Limitée* has enhanced their editorial quality.

Once again, the case for or against chain ownership is finely balanced. But the fact that a powerful financier could gain control of so many of the province's media in such a relatively short time demonstrated to us the need for governmental authority in this sphere. Maybe the Desmarais acquisitions have been in the public interest. Maybe they haven't. But surely the public should be allowed a say in such matters *before* the acquisitions take place.

PERIODICALS

Whatever you can say about the sickness of the Canadian magazine industry goes double for the magazine industry in Quebec. Foreign competition, a small market, some overflow circulation from France, and the profusion of pop weeklies – all these factors have produced the result we've remarked upon in our chapter on magazines: a gap between the ability to produce good magazines and the ability to make them pay. We quote approvingly from the Québecor Inc. brief, which noted that the problems of Quebec's magazine industry could be dealt with briefly, because "at this stage it is so hopeless that there is practically no problem."

Apart from a few small publications that specialize in such topics as golf or snowmobiling, there is no successful consumer magazine that is independently owned in Quebec. The largest magazine is *Perspectives/Perspectives-Dimanche,* a rotogravure section that is part of the weekend editions of seven Quebec dailies with a total circulation of about 738,000. Next are the French editions of *Reader's Digest* and *Chatelaine,* both with circulations of about 270,000. *Time* also sells about 80,000 copies weekly in Quebec, and *Le Magazine Maclean* about 172,000 monthly.

But any consumer magazine published for Quebeckers, *by* Quebeckers, has proved to be an almost hopeless proposition. There have been a few excellent attempts. *Sept-Jours*, a weekly newsmagazine that has shown real editorial promise, has attained a circulation of 11,000. But as Robert Allard, President of Sept-Jours Inc. put it: "The total losses of *Sept-Jours* have been considerable, somewhere in the neighbourhood of $450,000." In 1970 it was unable to maintain its weekly schedule of publication. *Actualité,* a general-interest monthly, was also encountering serious difficulties.

No other area of Canada enjoys such media diversity, and nowhere else in Canada has so much been done to disprove the notion that the economic imperatives of publishing and broadcasting must lead to a monolithic press. We think the two bodies we have proposed—the Publications Development Loan Fund and the Press Ownership Review Board—should attempt to preserve and encourage this diversity within the province.

3. Freedom

When the Committee was in the preparatory stage of its deliberations, it asked media people across the country for their definition of "freedom of the press." At first glance this may seem like an excessively academic exercise, since the media in a sense "define" their rights every day through their own performance. We thought it was a useful exercise, though, because the term has become debased though an excess of incantation.

Some authorities seem to define the concept mainly in terms of the newspaper's freedom to publish. The Regina *Leader-Post,* for instance, noted that

> If a newspaper's supply of newsprint is cut off, the newspaper's ability to publish is also cut off. If through the imposition of exorbitant truck taxes or through the curtailment of the right to use city streets and highways, the newspaper were unable to operate its vehicles for distribution, then similarly the ability of the newspaper to publish and serve its readers is curtailed and freedom of the press is consequently curtailed.
>
> These are but two ways in which newspapers could be prevented from reaching the public, thus infringing upon the right of freedom of the press.

But most of the authorities we consulted tend to go farther than that. Their notions of press freedom centre around the public's right to be informed, rather than the media's right to retail information. Windsor *Star* Publisher Mark Farrell even argued that the term "freedom of the press" is faintly fraudulent—a shibboleth that can be used by publishers to justify all sorts of mischief. The term, he told us, "is an old whore that should be retired.... it has been prostituted so often that I prefer the expression, 'a free flow of information.' "

Standard Broadcasting Corporation Limited's brief, although it didn't throw around any accusations of easy virtue, took the same line:

> Freedom of the press guarantees to the public that no influence – on the part of government, business, labour or individual – will be allowed to distort, alter or influence the free flow of information. ... And this

> guarantee of a free press should extend equally to the electronic media, as it does to the printed page.

Other briefs also stressed the non-exclusive aspects of press freedom. The Montreal *Star* said:

> We do not think there is such a thing as freedom of the press in Canada. What there is is freedom of speech. We have the rights that all citizens have, with additional responsibilities in that what is said in a newspaper is said to many.

In a similar vein, the Winnipeg *Tribune* noted:

> Freedom of the press is just one facet of the larger freedom of expression and the public's right to know that belongs to us all in a free society. It is not a special privilege given to publishers to print what they like.

Claude Ryan's brief on behalf of *Le Devoir* embellished this idea:

> The right to publish information, isolated from the right to be informed, would be an aristocratic privilege that only a limited class of citizens could enjoy. The right to information, on the contrary, concerns every citizen.

And so did *Le Soleil,* which stressed the danger of state infringement:

> Freedom of the press is the newspaper's right to inform and comment freely, and especially without the possibility of the State's interference, by any censorship measure, with such an activity. It does not constitute a privilege exclusive to journalists. It was rather established in the interest of the public and the readers, who enjoy an imprescriptible right to receive information.

Among all these definitions, there appears to be a consensus on at least two propositions: first, that the press possesses no freedoms that aren't possessed by the public at large; press freedom is simply an extension of freedom of speech; and second, the gravest potential threat to this freedom is interference by government.

Media owners tend to warn against this danger at every possible opportunity. We think they are right to do so. When a government seeks to restrict the freedoms of its citizens, the press is always its first target. And, as R. S. Malone pointed out in the brief of F. P. Publications Limited, such restrictions are invariably justified as being in the public interest. As Mr. Malone expressed it:

> Such restrictive actions are not things of the past, nor confined to non-democratic countries. I am sure you gentlemen are aware of actions taken against the press and newspaper writers in the past few years even in countries such as South Africa, Rhodesia, and Ceylon, because they failed to conform to the prevailing outlook of their government's interpretation of the "national interest."

Lord Devlin, former chairman of the British Press Council, has pointed out an even more insidious danger: restrictions on press freedom can sneak up on you: He remarked:

> If freedom of the Press in Britain perishes, it will not be by sudden death. There will be no great battles in which leader-writers can win

imperishable glory. It will be a long time dying from a debilitating disease caused by a series of erosive measures, each one of which, if examined singly, would have a good deal to be said for it.

We are aware that the very existence of this Committee could be – and has been – interpreted as one such erosive measure. Most media spokesmen welcomed our enquiry as a useful forum for public discussion of an institution that can benefit from outside criticism. Others were worried about it. An executive of Thomson Newspapers, for example, outlined his point this way:

> Any attempt to legislate separately for the press as against industry in general, would be deplorable in that it would strike at the whole principle of an independent press free from special administrative or judicial interference. We believe this to be the case whether the legislation is intended to provide a special benefit to the press, or to regulate or restrict the press or the ownership thereof in any way.

We are also aware that some of our recommendations – especially the Press Ownership Review Board and the Publications Development Loan Fund – will be questioned for these very reasons. They will be seen (to coin a phrase) as the thin edge of the wedge towards a system of government licensing of the press.

We acknowledge the risk involved. There are laws protecting society against press abuses – libel, slander, sedition. Any measure which goes beyond those restrictions, any measure that empowers a government to affect a media corporation's ability to print what it chooses, is a potential danger to press freedom.

The press is hyper-sensitive to this danger for a very good historical reason. Newspapers began as publishing ventures that were licensed by the state. They existed at the pleasure of the King and Commons, and could be shut down whenever they inconvenienced the authorities of the day. It took a long and courageous struggle to end this arrangement. The battle for the freedom to publish thus became an important part of the evolution of freedom of speech. This historic victory makes it understandable that the media's owners should view government intervention as the chief threat to press freedom. But there are others. Unwarranted government secrecy is one such threat. The power of the corporation in modern society is another. The capricious or high-handed actions of police, prosecutors, and judges can also be threats. So can the economic tendencies of the media themselves, for there are places in this country where a few people hold what amounts to an information monopoly; this is not exactly conducive to press freedom. The media have been vigilant in attacking some of these threats. Others they have ignored – especially those instances where their own revenues weren't affected. We're thinking here primarily of official harassment of the "underground" press, a subject we propose to deal with at some length, because of the importance of the issue involved.

There are tens of thousands of people who think Vancouver's underground newspaper, the *Georgia Straight,* is a marvellous publication – provocative, funny, thoughtful, courageous, honest, and joyous. There are probably *hundreds* of thousands of people in Vancouver who, whether or not they've read a copy, think the *Straight* is obscene, immoral, scurrilous, and subversive – an all-round menace to youth. This latter judgement appears to include most of Vancouver's municipal and law-enforcement Establishment, for the *Straight* has been subjected to intimidation and harassment, both legal and extra-legal, that we can only describe as shocking. In 1967, the *Straight's* business licence was suspended by the city's chief licensing inspector for "gross misconduct in or with respect to the licensed premises." In 1969 alone, no fewer than twenty-two charges were laid against the newspaper, its editor, or its employees. Other British Columbia municipalities have refused to license *Georgia Straight* vendors, and police have arrested vendors or confiscated their papers without arrest. New Westminster refused to allow the *Straight* even to *apply* for a business licence, and later passed a special by-law aimed at preventing vendors from distributing the paper in return for "donations."

The harassment of the *Georgia Straight* has also created what we regard as a regrettable legal precedent. The newspaper's lawyers challenged the constitutional validity of the city's action in revoking the newspaper's business license. But the British Columbia Supreme Court approved the city's action, holding that the city's licensing powers come within provincial jurisdiction, under the "property and civil rights" clause [S. 92 (13)] of the B.N.A. Act. This power, the court held,

> is in no way directed to the suppression of free speech or its ancillary right, freedom of the press. It is conceivable of course that in some circumstances the operation of the section could limit the publication or distribution of a newspaper. ... But such an effect would be incidental to the object of the legislation. ...[4]

This judgement was not appealed, which seems to mean that the mayor of Vancouver is now empowered to shut down *any* newspaper which, in his opinion, is guilty of "gross misconduct." We hope the Vancouver *Sun* and *Province* understand that as a result of this decision, they are now under a strong legal obligation to comport themselves as the mayor sees fit.

Other underground newspapers in other cities have received similar treatment. Underground news-vendors have been arrested in Montreal and banned from the Sparks Street Mall in Ottawa – almost within earshot of the Committee's hearings. In 1968, in one Montreal conviction, the judge imposed the maximum fine and commented: "In my opinion, the newspaper in question [*Logos*] is of a revolutionary nature, the purpose of which is to spread dissension and dissent."

---

[4] [*Hlookoff et al v. City of Vancouver et al,* 67 D.L.R. (2d) 119]

When municipalities use their licensing powers, and law-enforcement authorities use their prosecution powers, to suppress unpopular publications, it raises the most basic question of press freedom. Pierre Berton, in his appearance before the Committee, said of the underground press: "This alternative, which is generally in the form of a weekly informal newspaper published by young people, has been subjected to what I can only describe as unbelievable, scandalous, and continual harassment by the municipal authorities and police of several cities in this country."

We concur in his choice of adjectives. It saddens us to report that most daily newspapers have been either lukewarm in their editorial approach to this issue, or have ignored it altogether. We find this reticence strange, especially when the same newspapers are capable of such fire and eloquence on the subject of postal rates. We see no need for additional legislation to prevent this kind of abuse in future. All that is needed, we suggest, is more vigilance on the part of the established media – the same kind of vigilance they display when their own freedoms, and their own revenues, are threatened.

The harassment of the underground press was the most striking instance we found of press freedom being infringed. But it was not the only problem area that was drawn to our attention. We were frequently reminded of the conflict that frequently prevails between the duties of journalism and the duties of law-enforcement. One way of minimizing this conflict, we were told, would be to recognize "newsman's privilege."

It has been argued that the relationship between reporter and informant is one that should be protected in the public interest; and that if a newsman is compelled in a legal proceeding to disclose the sources of his information, the integrity of this relationship could be undermined. Why should people tell reporters anything confidential, the argument runs, if the law says they can be forced to spill their sources in court?

The issue isn't wholly academic. Newsmen have been forced to disclose their sources in legal proceedings, and some who have refused have been imprisoned. One recent case involved a CBC television journalist, John Smith, who in March, 1969, was ordered imprisoned for seven days by the Montreal Fire Commissioner. He had interviewed a young Quebecker who said he had been involved in terrorist fire-bombing incidents. The Fire Commissioner demanded that Smith disclose the interviewee's name. Smith refused – even though police had already identified the man, the interview was never broadcast, and there was evidence that the interviewee wasn't what he purported to be. But Smith chose to go to jail, in defence of the principle that "it is the right and duty of journalists to withhold information given to them in confidence."

Should the state recognize and protect this right? A number of jurisdictions have decided it should. Maryland has protected newsman's privilege since 1898. Today there are fourteen American states where reporters are protected against being forced to disclose their sources. In eight of these jurisdictions, the protection is absolute. In the remaining six, it applies only in cases where the material has been published. There is no similar legislation in Canada, and the few court cases that deal with the issue are inconclusive. But in general it is safe to say that "newsman's privilege" does not exist in Canadian law. Should it?

We don't think so. Communications between lawyers and their clients have been privileged since the sixteenth century, and there are other areas (doctor-patient, priest-communicant, husband-wife) where qualified privilege has been extended. But we can't accept the argument that these relationships are analogous to that between newsman and informant. In the common law, it is generally accepted that four fundamental conditions should be present to justify privilege: first, the communication must originate in a confidence that it will not be disclosed; second, this element of confidentiality must be essential to the full and satisfactory maintenance of the relation; third, the relation must be one which, in the opinion of the community, ought to be sedulously fostered; and, fourth, the injury which would be caused to the relationship by the disclosure of the communication must be greater than the benefit thereby gained for the correct disposal of litigation.

None of these criteria seem to apply to the newsman-informant relationship. In normal privilege, the identity of both parties is known, and it is the communication itself that is protected, not the identity of the informant who made it. Normal privilege is extended for the protection of the informant; but "newsman's privilege" seems designed primarily for the protection of the reporter. Finally, the newsman can assert privilege in connection with *any* information furnished, whether it be confidential or not; traditionally, privilege may be asserted only with respect to confidential communications.

Besides, journalism is a profession where no clearly established professional standards exist; it is hard to see how the public interest could be served by extending this protection when you don't know *whom* you'd be protecting. Our opinion – which we believe is shared by most journalists – is that we should leave things the way they are. If instances arise where reporters feel a personal, moral obligation to go to jail rather than betray their sources, so be it. We believe judicial authorities can be relied upon to apply the law with due regard for the professional sensibilities involved. Besides, if the jail term were short, most newsmen would find the experience refreshing, educational, and possibly even profitable.

We don't believe, in other words, that reporters should enjoy any privilege inside the courtroom that is not shared by other citizens. We think the protection that "newsman's privilege" would extend to the news-gathering process would be outweighed by the possible effects it might have on the judicial process.

Outside the courtroom is something else again. Here we have found numerous and alarming instances of reporters, newspapers, and radio stations being forced or pressured into acting as police informants, in a way that seems to us a genuine danger to freedom of the press. In Haskell Wexler's film, *Medium Cool,* a TV cameraman trying to research a story in a black ghetto is hassled by the inhabitants because they believe he is a police informant. As it turns out, the film's hero *is* an unwitting agent of the police; he accidentally discovers that his station has been furnishing the police with footage he's shot at demonstrations. *Medium Cool* was a fictional exercise, but it happens in real life, as a matter of routine, in Montreal.

Most of the problems arise in connection with street demonstrations. Montreal newsmen—who now wear crash helmets on such occasions—already accept the risk of being beaten up by demonstrators, or by the police, as part of their job. That job isn't made any easier by the fact that the police frequently seize – with or without warrant – tapes, film footage, and photographs made at the demonstrations, to be used in their investigations or as evidence in later prosecutions. Or by the fact that Montreal police officers – according to the brief of *La Fédération professionnelle des journalistes du Québec* – sometimes pose as journalists.

A few examples from this brief:

1. After the 1968 St. Jean-Baptiste riots, Montreal police visited most of the city's newspapers and radio and TV stations and seized all film shot by photographers who had been on duty that evening. The confiscated material was later introduced as evidence in prosecuting the demonstrators.

2. The Montreal *Star,* after noting that its files were being thinned out by constant police requests for demonstration photographs, decided in 1969 not to supply any additional material unless police produced a warrant. The police then started purchasing the same material from the *Star's* subsidiary, Canada Wide, which syndicates material already published in the *Star.*

3. In October, 1969, two officers of the Québec Sûreté and the St.-Léonard police made the rounds of Montreal newspapers and broadcasting stations, apparently collecting evidence for a sedition charge against Raymond Lemieux, who had been active in recent demonstrations at St.-Léonard. One station, CKLM, through vice-president Guy D'Arcy, refused to turn over the relevant tapes. He claimed that, even though the police had a warrant, only the C.R.T.C. had jurisdiction over broadcast production. Mr. D'Arcy was charged with refusing to obey a court order and on February 17, 1970, he was committed for trial.

These three instances – *La Fédération professionnelle des journalistes du Québec* supplied many more – are part of what the *Fédération* describes as a "general condition." Their brief also reports numerous instances of reporters being called to testify for the prosecution, usually to give evidence authenticating material seized as evidence. The brief continues:

> The photos and films confiscated by the police, as well as the tapes and recordings, do not necessarily involve in each case a court appearance of the reporter or the technician. But the fact that this material may be used to complete police files leaves the public under the impression

that the presence of journalists at the scene of an event can serve to incriminate the participants. The journalist thus becomes identified with the police, and therefore risks (1) the permanent loss of information sources (who lose confidence in him), (2) having to censor his own production, thus impeding the free flow of information. Some photographers, for instance, are careful not to take pictures that might incriminate either the demonstrators or the police.

This is an unfortunate and, in some respects, a threatening situation, and it is not restricted to Montreal. It is not caused so much by any excess of zeal on the part of the police as by the fact that violent street demonstrations are becoming an almost routine part of the political process. It seems clear that the public's right to information is threatened when newsmen are dragooned into becoming, in effect, participants in an event they are covering. It seems equally clear that there is no legislative remedy to the situation. Any law that exempted newsmen from testifying about a crime they saw committed, or exempted them from assisting in police investigations of that crime, would be disastrous to the administration of justice.

Our observations regarding "newsman's privilege" seem to be applicable here: special privileges and exemptions seem generally inadvisable — on the broad ground that the press, in our society, enjoys a legal status no different from any citizen's. It seems especially inadvisable in view of the fact that journalism lacks the professional standards that would at least clearly define who is, and is not, entitled to those privileges and exemptions.

We're going to see more street demonstrations in future, and the problem which the Montreal situation exemplifies seems destined to grow more acute. All we can suggest — and we admit it sounds a bit lame — is that police and press in each community attempt to develop the kind of working relationship that will minimize the dangers that such situations present. The legitimate needs of law enforcement don't justify treating the press as though they were unpaid investigators. Neither does the role of a free press justify reporters in acting as though they have no obligations to the judicial process. The best, though imperfect, solution would be a gentlemanly one: the police should resist the temptation to go on routine fishing expeditions, and restrict their demands for evidence to those cases where circumstances justify issuance of a warrant. The press, without being unco-operative, should insist on its rights.

If this has seemed like a rather rambling discussion of press freedom and the dangers that threaten it in Canada, it is because, happily, there isn't too much to write about. All freedoms ultimately depend on a broad social consensus that the people to whom the freedom is extended can be trusted to use it wisely. The press is free by and large in Canada because the press is, by and large, responsible.

Perhaps the nature of the threats that *do* exist will contribute to a definition of what, exactly, is being threatened. We hope our study shows that, apart from the ill-advised (and sometimes illegal) actions of a few isolated officials, governments at all levels understand what the press is for, and why it must be allowed to do its nosy, sometimes unpopular job.

As Stuart Keate, publisher of the Vancouver *Sun,* said: "In newspapering, the name of the game is disclosure." Anything that interferes with that duty is a denial of the public interest — although other, conflicting claims to the public interest often do, and should, take precedence. This notion leads to a definition of press freedom that some publishers have been slow to embrace. It is *not* simply the freedom to publish. It is more than that. It is the public's right of access to information that must be protected. Governments sometimes infringe on that right.

But a more likely source of infringement, we believe, is the economic tendencies of the press itself. If government can legislate to ensure a more "diverse and antagonistic" press, it is not interfering in freedom of the press; it is moving to protect a broader, more basic freedom: the freedom of information. Indeed, the Committee can envision a day when government might have to consider intervening, not to preserve a newspaper's freedom to publish, but to establish a citizen's right to have his views expressed in the mass media. Professor Jerome A. Barron of George Washington Law School, Washington, D.C., has already argued that the first amendment to the U.S. Constitution — the one which forbids Congress to pass any law abridging freedom of the press — could be interpreted *positively,* so as to permit passage of legislation guaranteeing the public's right of access to the media. "My basic premise in these suggestions," Professor Barron writes, "is that a provision preventing government from silencing or dominating opinion should not be confused with an absence of governmental power to require that opinion be voiced."[5]

One American case has already moved towards adoption of this principle.[6] The case stemmed from a broadcast on radio station WGCB in Pennsylvania, in which a super-patriot named Reverend Billy James Hargis accused a journalist named Fred J. Cook of Communist affiliations. Cook asked for, and was denied, time to reply. The appeal to the Supreme Court turned on the issue of whether the Federal Communications Commission's "fairness" regulations violated the First Amendment. The court ruled, resoundingly, that they did not:

> It is the purpose of the First Amendment to preserve an uninhibited marketplace of ideas in which truth will ultimately prevail, rather than to countenance monopolization of that market, whether it be by the Government itself or a private licensee . . . It is the right of the viewers and listeners, not the right of the broadcasters, which is paramount.

There are no similar Canadian precedents. But if <u>freedom of expression</u> means anything at all, it <u>must surely include the right to *disseminate* one's</u>

---

[5] Barron, Jerome A., *Access to the Press—A New First Amendment Right,* 80 Harvard Law Review 1641, 1676 (1967).

[6] *Red Lion Broadcasting Company v. The Federal Communications Commission* [89 S. Ct. 1784 (June 9, 1969)].

views. We think our studies have shown that this right could be threatened by the media's tendency towards a state of natural monopoly. We hope this tendency can be arrested, so that some future Canadian government will not find it necessary to legislate against the possibility of the public being silenced by its own press.

But this is a far-off threat. A much more immediate danger, we believe, is the familiar one of apathy. A public that doesn't care about the media, a public that is given additional reasons every day to be distrustful, resentful or – worst of all – bored by the media, is a public that doesn't prize its freedoms as highly as it should.

4. Press Council

Canada needs a Press Council. We think government should have nothing whatever to do with its formation or operation. We think it should concern itself primarily with the print media—which, in effect, means newspapers—because the C.R.T.C. already is empowered to exercise a similar function for broadcasting. We think many of the problems of the press that this report documents could be alleviated by the existence of a watchdog organization that would monitor the press the way the press monitors society. Public confidence in the press is declining; a press council could help arrest this trend. The media's tendency towards monopoly threatens to restrict the public's access to diverse and antagonistic sources of information; a press council could meet this threat by helping to ensure that media monopolies don't act as though they own the news. Finally, a press council could help to foster a sense of professionalism, and help to develop a set of standards, in an occupation that badly needs them. Even if a press council did nothing whatever, we'd still like to see one set up; because the very act of setting one up would force journalists and publishers, for the first time, to come together on an organized basis to think about what they're doing, how well they're doing it, and why.

During the Committee's research and hearings, we asked publishers and journalists across the country to let us know what they thought of the idea. We weren't conducting a poll; simply inviting expressions of opinion. The response indicated a pretty broad consensus among working journalists that a press council would be desirable. Publishers were less unanimous. Those who supported the idea did so either because they thought it could be a positive, constructive development or because, what the hell, it can't do any harm. Those who opposed the idea thought a press council would be either an invasion of press freedom or simply another useless, do-nothing committee. It was evident that many of those who opposed it had no clear understanding of what a press council is and what it does.

Most of the publishers who saw no need for a press council were from small-town newspapers. They argued that mediation by a press council in a town the size of Woodstock or Fredericton would be slightly ludicrous. If a citizen has a grievance, all he has to do is ring up the editor and tick him off. "We report the activities and opinions of men and women who may well literally be our neighbours," we were told by R. G. Dundas, publisher of the Woodstock *Sentinel-Review*. "Therefore communication is never a problem."

Big-city opposition was expressed by R. S. Malone, president of F. P. Publications Limited, whose brief said:

> I do not believe that any need for a press council has been demonstrated to date in this country or indeed exists. There is, of course, always the risk of the odd lapse but even in such rare instances I do not feel that the present situation warrants the greater risks which are inherent in any body which can exercise any control, pressure or threat over press freedom or the freedom of any editor or writer to express his views or report events without fear of being reported to a press council, or hauled before a board to answer every complaint that was lodged against him. If he has committed a crime the place for him to answer in is our proper courts of law.

And by the Halifax *Chronicle-Herald* and *Mail-Star* submission which advanced the view that "the reading public is a press council in itself. Public opinion and response constitute a stimulus to all newspapers to gain and retain a reputation for accuracy, responsibility, and fairness."

Since these reservations appear to be shared by at least a substantial minority of the people who would have to make a press council work, we'd like to deal with several of the points implicit in their objections:

(a) *A press council could threaten press freedom*. We couldn't agree more, *if* – and only if – government were involved in the project. The idea of empowering a government-appointed tribunal, armed with powers of censure or sanction, to sit in judgement on the press is of course unacceptable, for all the obvious reasons. But what we propose would have nothing to do with the government. A press council should be established by the press itself. Implicit in Mr. Malone's statement, also, is the notion that a press council is primarily a complaint bureau. The kind of press council we'd like to see would be much more than that.

(b) *The law already provides protection against press abuse*. Sure it does, but should people be forced into court every time they're misquoted, harassed, or mistreated by the press? Between the kind of petty grievance that can be redressed by a letter-to-the-editor, and the major complaints that are best adjudicated by the courts, there's a large area of medium-sized problems where a press council would be most effective. Complaints of sensationalism or distortion; of mishandled corrections, apologies, and letters to the editor; of lapses of taste in copy, photographs, and cartoons; of intrusions and invasions of privacy; of unethical or unfair news-gathering methods – all these could be dealt with by a press council.

Britain's Press Council – which we think is an excellent working model – has developed terms of reference that restrict it to this middle ground. The Council won't entertain complaints unless (a) the complainant has already sought satisfaction from the newspaper and failed to obtain it, and (b) the complainant signs a waiver that precludes legal action on the complaint. These excellent rules mean that the council isn't swamped by minor hassles that can and should be settled at the local level. They also tend to give publishers and the aggrieved an additional reason for *not* going through costly and troublesome court proceedings.

(c) *I don't need a press council; if someone's got a beef, my door is always open.* J. C. Preston of the Brantford *Expositor* put his argument this way:

> We feel that the fact that they can call us up, and see our name on the masthead of the paper – they call us up at home; our phone numbers are listed – this gives them a chance to air their beef. ... I mean, we are available. I go down to the curling club; I go down to the golf club. Mr. Pollard does. And we are available to people.

The answer to this objection is contained in the previous paragraph. <u>A press council must not function as a *substitute* for consultation between newspaper and complainant, but as an informal "court of appeal"</u> if the matter can't be resolved locally.

(d) *Press freedom will suffer if every reporter and editor has a "big brother" looking over his shoulder.* This is more or less what Mr. Malone told us, and we think he's trapped himself in his own rhetoric. Obviously, we don't envision an organization that would install a *Gauleiter* in every city-room in the country. But if government benefits from independent scrutiny, then why shouldn't the press? The press has been described as a sort of minefield through which politicians must tippy-toe at their peril. We think one reason for newspapers' declining credibility is the fact that the press has no such minefield.

(e) Which leads to yet another objection: *who needs a press council? A newspaper's readers already constitute the only court of appeal it needs.* This may be true to a limited extent where genuine editorial competition exists. But given the monopolistic conditions that prevail in most Canadian cities today, it's a piece of hollow *laissez-faire* rhetoric. The implication is that if readers aren't satisfied with the way a newspaper is doing its job, well, they can always cancel their subscription. Sure they can – and read *what?* Fly in the New York *Times?* Or quit reading newspapers entirely? We think it is interesting that most of the publishers who advanced this argument come from one-newspaper towns. They know, or ought to know, that if a reader feels his newspaper isn't performing adequately, or if he feels he's been harassed or mistreated by his newspaper, there is practically nothing he can do about it. Dr. Donald Cameron, the University of New Brunswick professor who constitutes a sort of self-appointed one-man press-watcher in the Maritimes, expressed this point admirably in his appearance before the Committee:

> In Fredericton, a good many of us have looked at our daily newspaper, affectionately nicknamed *The Daily Wiener,* and we have judged. We consider the *Gleaner* a dreadful newspaper. So what? No consequences follow from that judgment. There isn't any provision for any consequences to follow. This committee is the first opportunity I can recall for any dissatisfied citizen to do anything meaningful at all about the media. ...

Most of these objections were advanced in Britain in the 1940s, after a Royal Commission recommended the establishment of a press council. It wasn't until 1949, after Parliament considered the report, that British newspaper proprietors got around to considering the proposal themselves. Their deliberations were inconclusive. If there was any enthusiasm for the idea, it was well concealed. But three years later, after a private member's bill to establish a press council *by legislation* had reached second reading in the House of Commons, the industry finally agreed on a draft constitution. The British Press Council came into existence on July 1, 1953.

At first the Council functioned merely as a sort of journalistic grievance committee. Its membership consisted entirely of journalists and publishers. During its first eight years of operation, it dealt solely with complaints from the public. Even then, it hardly constituted a tribunal that, in Mr. Malone's words, would haul a reporter or editor "before a board to answer every complaint that was lodged against him." In fact, during 1967-68, the council disposed of about eighty per cent of the complaints that came to its attention without proceeding to adjudication – either because the complaints were frivolous, malicious or just plain wrong, or because the complainants hadn't first sought redress from the newspaper concerned, or because the complaint was properly a matter for the courts. Its decisions were *voluntarily* publicized by the newspapers concerned. The consensus among journalists and publishers, after eight years, appeared to be that the Council was performing a useful role.

But changes were taking place in the British newspaper scene that made its activities seem somewhat circumscribed and irrelevant. A rash of mergers, takeovers and newspaper closures created the same dangers that prompted the formation of this Committee: that media monopolies were threatening to restrict the public's access to information. In February, 1961, the government appointed a second Royal Commission, under Lord Shawcross, to take another look at the ethics and economics of newspapering. The Shawcross Commission, which reported in 1962, recommended a number of measures to increase the industry's efficiency, in the hope of forestalling future newspaper closures. It also recommended that the Press Council broaden its role – as the first Royal Commission had suggested in 1949 – to become something more than a complaint bureau. The Shawcross Commission accordingly recommended a reformed press council which, in addition to its existing duties, would (1) scrutinize and give publicity to changes in ownership and control of newspapers; (2) publish up-to-date statistics; (3) ensure that newspapers carried the name of the company or individual in ultimate control of its affairs; and (4) hear complaints from journalists of undue influence from advertisers.

The Shawcross recommendations were adopted and in January, 1964, the new council, chaired by Lord Devlin, held its first meeting. Its membership now consists of the chairman, a retired jurist, and a vice-chairman; ten members elected by associations representing British daily and weekly newspapers; two members elected by the Periodical Publishers Association; eight members elected by associations or unions of journalists and editors; and five lay members, appointed by the Council. The Council has a small full-time secretariat headed by Noël Paul and operates on an annual budget of less than $60,000, which includes a stipend of about $10,000 for the chairman.

The Council's constitution spells out its objectives, which are much broader than merely adjudicating complaints:

(i) To preserve the established freedom of the British Press.
(ii) To maintain the character of the British Press in accordance with the highest professional and commercial standards.
(iii) To consider complaints about the conduct of the Press or the conduct of persons and organizations towards the Press; to deal with these complaints in whatever manner might seem practical and appropriate and record resultant action.
(iv) To keep under review developments likely to restrict the supply of information of public interest and importance.
(v) To report publicly on developments that may tend towards greater concentration or monopoly in the Press (including changes in ownership, control and growth of Press undertakings) and to publish statistical information relating thereto.
(vi) To make representations on appropriate occasions to the Government, organs of the United Nations and to Press organizations abroad.
(vii) To publish periodical reports recording the Council's work and to review from time to time developments in the Press and the factors affecting them.

The Council's twenty-seven members meet every two months. Its two main Committees, the Complaints Committee and the General Purposes Committee, each with about ten members, meet every month. Since the establishment in Britain of a government-appointed Monopolies Commission, the Council has spent less time than formerly monitoring economic developments in the newspaper industry. Instead, it has concentrated on adjudicating complaints and – this is important – acting as a sort of self-starting watchdog on press standards and press freedom. The Council can act on its own initiative if it feels a newspaper has departed from accepted journalistic standards, and it has been active in opposing the tendency of various public bodies to exclude reporters from their deliberations. In 1968, the Council on two occasions was approached "to consider allegations of improper exclusion of the Press." It urged stricter compliance with the Public Bodies (Admission to Meetings)

Act, 1960, a statute defining the conditions under which the press and the public can be excluded from the deliberations of such bodies as town-council committees and public-hospital boards.

The Council's procedures for dealing with complaints provide some excellent guidelines for any Canadian similar body. The Council can launch an investigation on its own initiative; it doesn't have to wait until someone from outside complains. Unlike the procedure in a court of law, the complainant needn't have been *personally* damaged or inconvenienced; anyone who feels a newspaper has mishandled a story is entitled to complain.

As we've already noted, complaints aren't entertained unless and until the complainant has sought, and failed to receive, satisfaction from the newspaper concerned. Then he must submit his complaint in writing, with a copy to the editor concerned. Then the staff investigates. A great many complaints don't survive this stage of the process; they're found to be baseless or malicious or just silly. For complaints that do stand up to initial investigation, the staff prepares a fully documented dossier that is presented to the Complaints Committee. This committee makes its decision which is usually – but not always – endorsed by the Council as a whole at its bi-monthly meeting. In its 1968 annual report, the Council recorded that, of the 403 complaints it dealt with during the year, only 114 made it as far as the Complaints Committee. Of these, only 88 were adjudicated by the Council as a whole. And of *these* 88 complaints, the council ruled against the complainant in 53 instances. If a Canadian version operated along similar lines, there would be no reason to fear that the Council would be guilty of capricious harassment of the press.

Britain's Press Council is not the only one in operation. Our research indicates that at least fifty countries have them, and some of these have been operating for several decades. Although in some areas press councils have been used as instruments of suppression, it appears that in many countries these organizations have become an accepted and useful device for promoting press responsibility and press freedom.

The Committee favors establishment of a press council for several reasons. Perhaps the *least* urgent reason, in our view, is the need for a journalistic ombudsman. We don't believe the press is fraught with abuses. We believe that instances of newspapers pushing people around and of distorting the news are quite remarkably rare. This observation is founded on pretty direct experience; since our Committee was formed, a lot of Canadians have written us with complaints about the newspapers in their area. A perusal of these letters indicates to us not only that the public would welcome a press council, but that the press would have nothing to fear from it. The Committee received perhaps two hundred letters dealing with specific complaints. More of them came from the Maritimes than from enywhere else, which may say something about journalistic standards in that part of the country. More interesting still was the fact that, of these complaints, there were fewer than half a dozen that would have earned a slap on the wrist if they'd been presented to the British Press Council. Some were generalized grumbling.

Some amounted to political disagreements. A few letters contained personal grievances that sounded genuine and deserved remedy, and came from the kind of people who would find it too costly to seek redress in the courts. And some of them were plain crazy—like the complaint of the man who wrote to inform us that Harry S. Truman was part of the international Jewish conspiracy. Truman's middle name is actually Solomon, this man informed us, and he wanted to know why his local newspaper was furtively concealing this fact.[7]

The entire experience of this Committee, in fact, suggests that a communications vacuum exists between press and public, and that a press council could help fill it. The most common feedback that members of the Committee have received from non-journalists goes something like this: "Thank God, at *last* there's somebody we can talk to about the media." We're satisfied that there *is* a kind of inchoate concern and awareness abroad in the country about the mass media, plus a lot of goodwill. The very existence of our Committee has demonstrated the need for some structure that can act as a focal point for all this. Much better that the media themselves should create such structures than the government.

But even if this public feeling didn't exist, we'd still favour the idea – because we think it could also provide a stimulus to the development of the permanent organizational structures that the industry so badly needs. Sitting down to help decide how to invent a press council would give the Canadian Managing Editors Conference something meaningful to do. It might help broaden the American Newspaper Guild's horizons beyond the lunchpail level. It might encourage the Canadian Daily Newspaper Publishers Association to think about something other than advertising revenues. It might even encourage those notorious non-joiners, reporters, to join *something* for a change, to advance their own professional interests.

Naturally it's up to the publishers and journalists to work out the terms of reference for a Canadian press council. The British model obviously can't be imported without a number of basic amendments.

By the very nature of our recommendation, it's not up to us to suggest how a press council should function, or what its terms of reference should be. We think that's the industry's business, not ours. Nevertheless, we can't resist making a few observations about the kind of press council we'd like to see. In making them, we're mindful that they'll probably bear very little resemblance to the kind of press council, if any, that actually results:

1. It should be a *national* press council, or at least reflect a national presence. Although the council's ombudsman function could best be handled on a regional basis, its other duties require a country-wide platform. Quebec is

---

[7] The Committee is indebted to Mr. Truman's secretary for the following information: Two of his grand-parents had names starting with S, and his parents couldn't agree on which of these names to give him. And so, in a spirit of compromise that any politician would admire, the parents decided that the initial alone would be the future president's middle name. Sorry about that, all you anti-semites.

already close to the formation of a press council for that province. The daily and weekly newspaper associations, *La Fédération professionnelle des journalistes du Québec, L'Association canadienne de la radio et de la télévision de langue française Inc.*, and several other influential organizations have had intensive consultations on the matter, and have produced a draft constitution. Quebec's special position makes it desirable and inevitable that the province have its own regional organization. We think it is equally desirable that a counterpart organization for English-speaking Canada be formed, and that the two bodies somehow affiliate themselves to form a national body.

We say this because we hope the council will become much more than a complaint bureau. We hope it will take the lead in the evolution and definition of journalistic ethics and standards. We hope it will promote the idea of journalistic training. We hope it will continue what this Committee has attempted – to keep a watching brief on economic developments within the industry, and assess their impact on freedom of information. We hope it will undertake research on matters of professional interest, and work with journalism schools to ensure that the kind of research and development that is routine in most industries becomes routine in the newspaper industry too. We hope it will become a powerful lobby on behalf of press freedom and press responsibility – a sort of journalistic equivalent of the Canadian Association of University Teachers – that will speak out when governments try to push the press around, or when the press tries to push people around, including its own journalists. To do all this, the council would have to be a national body.

2. We have no prescription as to whether the council's ombudsman activities should be organized locally, regionally or nationally. That is a matter for the participants to work out. Perhaps some two-tier system could be devised. This way, most complaints would be adjudicated by regional or provincial press councils. But the national body could provide an informal court of appeal (the lack of such an appeal procedure is one of the most prevalent criticisms of the British Press Council.) With a national body somehow involved in adjudication, it might be possible to evolve, on a case-by-case basis, a set of ethical guidelines that would be applicable across the country. This is the first step towards upgrading journalism from a skilled trade to the status of a profession.

3. Finally, we hope – and we know we're hoping for a lot – that the press council would take the lead in encouraging the formation of community press committees. The idea was outlined for the Committee by Ben H. Bagdikian, national editor of the Washington *Post* and one of the most thoughtful and articulate thinkers in America on the subject of the press. Working with foundation money, Bagdikian stage-managed an experimental program to set up community press councils in six U.S. cities. The object

of the exercise, he told us, was to foster two-way communication between a single community and its media:

> The local press council is concerned with a single community, and the idea is that both parties need to speak to themselves in some other way than the one-way communication of receiving the newspaper on your doorstep every morning and not having a very good method of talking back, or listening to your radio and television and not being able to talk back.

Bagdikian's local groups were *not* vehicles for confrontation. The meetings usually took place once a month at somebody's house after cocktails and dinner. The ground-rules were designed to promote co-operation, not carping. The group represented a cross-section of the community, and was selected by researchers from the local university – *not* by the publisher. The second rule was that the council had no power over the newspaper whatsoever.

Bagdikian's group plans to publish a book on the experiment, which revealed that (a) the publishers didn't know as much about their communities as they thought they did, and (b) the people didn't know as much about newspapers as they thought they did. There aren't many Canadian cities that couldn't benefit from similar experiments.

That's our modest proposal. We're asking the moon – an absolute prodigy of an organization that would single-handed attempt to solve nearly all the problems that trouble the press today in relation to the people it serves. We doubt that a press council could achieve as much as we hope. But we hope it would try. As a former reporter named John F. Kennedy once said: "Let us begin."

A sensible place *to* begin would be at the next annual meeting of the Canadian Daily Newspaper Publishers Association. The better financed such an organization is, the better are its chances for achieving something. We have already noted that Britain's Press Council operates on less than $60,000 per year. We hope the Canadian industry – whose daily-newspaper members in 1968 had total revenues of $295 million – can find it in its heart to do a little better than that.

5. Criteria

> There is, of course, nothing professional about the role of newspaper reporting. As a group reporters have no disciplined academic training in any particular sphere, although they seem prepared to write about almost anything. They do not as an occupational group license themselves, govern their own affairs, or establish their own norms of performance. As Bernard Shaw pointed out so long ago they have no public register. As an occupational group they are not highly paid, nor do they seem to have high prestige. Hence it is unlikely that, as a profession, journalists would have the social standing or professional expertise or group solidarity to offset ownership pressure, although occasionally, as individuals, editors can rise to great prominence.
>
> John Porter[8]

Most working journalists will recognize the uncomfortable acuteness of Professor Porter's observation. Physicians, lawyers, accountants, teachers, and plumbers all insist, in varying degrees, on the right to set the standards under which they perform their work, and to decide who is and who is not qualified to join their occupational ranks. Journalists do not possess this status. They do not appear to have sought it, and their employers assuredly have not encouraged them to seek it.

This wouldn't matter if publishing and broadcasting were just another industry. But the whole thrust of the Committee's thinking is that the media's business is the public's business. The failure of the media, owners and workers alike, to evolve anything approaching professional journalistic standards is thus a matter of public concern. For the plain fact is that only journalists and the people who employ them can achieve this status. Nothing about the media is going to change very much unless and until that starts happening.

The problem has its chicken-and-egg aspects. Professional training won't become the norm until professional status is achieved. Professional status won't be achieved until professional training becomes the norm. Training

---

[8] Porter, John, *The Vertical Mosaic*, University of Toronto Press 1965, p. 485-486.

is, or should be, mainly the employers' concern. Professional status should be the concern of working journalists. The deficiencies in both areas are too apparent.

Let's look first at the area of professional standards – an area that journalists themselves are only just beginning to look at. Almost by definition, journalists are non-joiners. But it is only by organizing that the working press is going to achieve the kind of compensation it deserves, and which the industry can readily afford. But increased bargaining power is not the only reward of professionalism. We think it is significant, and encouraging, that wherever in Canada journalists have organized themselves as professionals, they have begun to win more control over the product they create.

The trend is most pronounced in Quebec, where the relationship between reporter and editor is, on some newspapers, codified as part of the collective-bargaining agreement. At *La Presse,* for instance, the agreement protects journalists against being forced to write advertising copy. Journalists also undertake not to write think-pieces that are "hostile to the Employer or his ideological orientation, nor contrary to good morals and morality." In the event that a change should occur in the owner's ideological orientation "such as to cast a slur on [a journalist's] honour, reputation and moral interests," he can cancel his contract and may demand an indemnity. The agreement also stipulates that the reporter's consent must be obtained by an editor who chops or rewrites an article in such a way as "to change the meaning of the article." The agreement continues: "Should the Employer decide that one or several important changes are essential, and should the author refuse his consent or in case he is not available for his decision, then the Employer must omit the signature."

The agreement on the "professional" clauses of this contract was reached April 25, 1969 after much negotiation. The clauses were effective retroactively to January 1, 1969 and expire December 31, 1971. It is one of the few instances in Canada where a newspaper's management and its editorial staff have sat down and, in a binding agreement, codified the proposition that a journalist is something more than a hired hand. At *Le Soleil* in Quebec City, the collective agreement between the newspaper and the Union of Journalists of Quebec Inc. specifically recognizes "the professional freedom of the reporters," and provides for an elaborate set of mediation and arbitration procedures in cases where this freedom is violated.

Many of the provisions of these contracts, of course, have been common practice for years at many newspapers. Few, if any, publishers will insist that an editorial writer write something with which he disagrees. Many editors, as a matter of routine courtesy and sound practice, consult wherever possible with reporters before slashing their copy. These arrangements have arisen as a matter of mutual trust and respect. But, with a very few exceptions, these arrangements are not protected by any form of written agreement. Nor are they by any means universal.

As far as binding contractual obligations are concerned, a reporter's duty nearly everywhere in Canada is to write what his employers tell him to write. The journalist has no *professional* interest in maintaining or improving the quality of the product he creates.

The basis of professionalism, surely, is that there are certain things a professional will not do, and other things he must do. The recognition and definition of these standards, and the definition of the practitioners to whom they apply, is what separates accountants, teachers, physicians, and lawyers from steamfitters, plumbers, garage mechanics, TV repairmen – and journalists. As a matter of fact, steamfitters, plumbers *et al* have taken a more professional approach to their trade than journalists have; they at least insist on minimum standards of training. Apart from the two cases we've described, there appear to be no other instances where journalists, as a group, assume a collective responsibility for the quality of their product as, for instance, the medical profession takes responsibility for the quality of medical care. We don't think the journalistic environment is going to change very much unless and until journalists start assuming – or demanding – such responsibility.

As we have noted, the process has already begun in Quebec. For the first time in Canada, the principle has been recognized that journalistic standards are as proper a subject of collective bargaining as are salaries and fringe benefits. It is symptomatic of the mood among journalists in that province that they have also organized two professional associations concerned with journalistic standards.

Both organizations are less than two years old, and both were formed at least partially in response to the formation of this Committee, and to the Quebec Legislature's Special Committee on Freedom of the Press. *La Fédération professionnelle des journalistes du Québec* was formed in February, 1969. It is a grouping of some twenty professional associations or unions of journalists with a total membership of about six hundred. According to their brief to the Quebec Special Committee on Freedom of the Press in September 1969, the federation was formed in response to four problems: "the need for professional training and improvement; the proposal for a press council, which could not be seriously examined in the absence of an organization representing the majority of journalists; the professional status of journalists; and concentration of ownership in the mass media in Quebec."

The Association of English-Media Journalists of Quebec, formed in April, 1969, has about sixty-five members, mostly from English-language newspapers and radio stations in and around Montreal. In summarizing its aims in a brief to the Committee, the Association said it "expects to be preoccupied for some time with the twin concerns of ethics and education. There has been far too little discussion of the former; and far too little availability of the latter."

A third group, the Canadian Society of Professional Journalists, was formed in Toronto in 1969 with the aim of ultimately becoming a national association. Its nucleus was a group of newspapermen formerly affiliated with the American journalistic society, Sigma Delta Chi. The role of the Canadian Society of Professional Journalists, which started with about eighty members, was outlined by its president, Frank Drea, in his appearance before the Committee:

> Reporters and editors in Canada's print and electronic media are members of one professional community. That community, to date, has lacked both a forum for discussion and a united voice. The Canadian Society of Professional Journalists was formed to provide such a forum and such a voice.

There should be more groups like these, in all parts of the country. Their task would be to help create a professional consciousness among working journalists. There are very few competent reporters who don't possess that consciousness already. They know, with a surprising degree of unanimity, what is good newspaper practice and what isn't. They spend a good deal of time complaining to each other when these standards aren't adhered to. But until they start dealing collectively with the problems that face them all, they will be powerless to effect any improvements. And that is our parting word to the working press: if you're dissatisfied with the way the news is handled, quit griping and start organizing.

Let us now go on to consider the closely related questions of training and staffing in the media.

TRAINING FOR THE JOB

Concern, as well as candor, compels us to be blunt: the Committee was not greatly impressed by what it learned about the opportunities for professional training available to aspiring journalists in Canada, nor by any evidence that when inexperienced beginners enter the information work force, they are given any kind of organized training on the job.

We have paid some attention to two alternative systems of recruitment operating in other countries. One is the United States, where some 25,000 sudents are enrolled in journalism courses at 120 universities. The other is Great Britain, where about 500 beginners each year are indentured into a three-year working apprenticeship, given time out for prescribed academic courses, and finally examined for a certificate that is the passport to a full professional career. It isn't easy to win the certificate; the failure rate approaches 40 per cent.

Both of these systems have virtues. They afford a recognized route of access to the profession. They weed out most of the potential misfits early, often saving years of economic waste and personal frustration. They provide a corps of beginners who meet accepted standards of basic professional competence.

Canada is so far following, at a great distance and at a lagging pace, the U. S. route. Only three academic programmes exist which could be described as complete courses in journalism; all three are in Ontario, and only two are at degree-granting institutions. Some thirty other universities and colleges offer either abbreviated courses in practical journalism, or studies in what are usually described as "communications arts."

This is not to denigrate any of them. The Big Three—Carleton University, University of Western Ontario, Ryerson Polytechnical Institute—provide courses of proven worth whose graduates are acceptable to the industry. Carleton claims that more than 90 per cent of its graduates go into active journalism (as distinct from public relations and other peripheral fields), and that of the 399 living Carleton journalism graduates, 82.4 per cent are still in positions related to journalism. The largest single group (108) are in public relations; 91 are with newspapers; 40 are with radio and television; 36 are with magazines; and the others are in various occupations ranging from book publishing to journalism education. A roll call of Ryerson graduates has been tabulated: 85 in daily newspapers, 11 in news agencies, seven in consumer magazines, 16 in business magazines, 16 in company publications, 10 in suburban journalism, eight in weekly newspapers, 10 in radio and television news, 27 in public relations, 13 in advertising, 23 in "related fields."

This is a useful contribution, but pitifully small in relation to the need. It remains that the limited output of a scattered handful of academic courses cannot match the demand for writers, editors, programmers and performers in the thousand-odd newspapers, periodicals, and broadcasting stations of Canada.

Some editors (and, regrettably, more publishers) appear to be undisturbed by the disparity between demand and qualified supply. There persists, even within the trade, a pseudo-romantic tradition which holds that journalists are born, not made; that journalism schools are a waste of time, because they devote themselves either to airy-fairy theoretics or to practical techniques which can be better learned in a working newsroom; that some magical process of natural selection operates in journalism, alone among the professions. Senator O'Leary was in this vein when he told us that a man may have "more degrees than a thermometer" and be a journalistic dud.

He was right, of course. The trouble with the theory outlined above is that while it reassures those who have reached the top of the journalistic heap (by assigning them a sort of divine right to be there) it provides no toeholds at the bottom where a disorderly and inefficient scramble persists.

The continuing attitude of scepticism toward academic training, and the lack of generally available training to broadly accepted standards, are among the chief reasons why journalism is not yet a profession. Yet this is an age of professionalism and of increased specialisation. Journalism needs more specialists—labour specialists, health specialists, urban planning specialists, political and economic and social specialists. But they must be specialists *who are also communicators,* and this, in our view, makes a clinching case for an academic discipline which combines the two requirements.

The conditions for establishment of a system on the British model do not yet exist in Canada. The British system was devised by newspapermen. It is controlled by the National Council for the Training of Journalists, which is a body representing all sections of the industry – owners, managers, editors, and working journalists. Each of these component sections has a strong functioning organization able and willing to take a share in the responsibility for training.

In Canada the owners are organized, the rest are not. The owners' groups – Canadian Daily Newspaper Publishers Association, Canadian Association of Broadcasters – are strong and active. But they have displayed no interest whatever in establishing professional standards or in training the people who produce the product they sell. They exist for one purpose – to promote the sale of advertising space and time.

Editors are not organized at all. The Canadian Managing Editors Conference is a loose and informal grouping of news executives who meet once a year to talk shop, but who have no ongoing programme and undertake no responsibilities. On the broadcasting side, the Radio and Television News Directors' Association seems to function more effectively but suffers from the same lack of muscle. The journalists' union is the American Newspaper Guild. It has contracts with about a dozen of Canada's 116 newspapers and with the CBC and two private broadcasters. Its numbers are concentrated in Toronto and Vancouver. Its concerns are pay and working conditions; it has taken no visible initiatives in the direction of improved standards and training.

There is no national equivalent of the Institute of Journalists, the British professional association which is a partner in the training programme. One group, the Canadian Society of Professional Journalists, has recently been established in Toronto. We wish it well, but it is a very long way from achieving a firm local base, let alone a national influence.

The situation is different in Quebec, where both professional groups and union organizations are more firmly entrenched and are making their influence felt, especially in the French-language media. But we repeat: the conditions for establishing a national training plan with participation of the industry and its employees do not now exist.

This means, unless we are content to go along with the present approach to the production of journalistic professionals, that we should strengthen our academic training system. The Committee believes this to be a must, and we have some suggestions for bringing it about. We were aided, in this as in so many other areas, by the willingness of publishers, broadcasters, and working journalists to answer our researcher's questionnaires and provide a factual basis for our recommendations.

We found, to begin with, that the newspapers of Canada alone require new editorial and research staff at the rate of 750 a year. (The total number of jobs is increasing by about 200 a year, but the rate of turnover in newspaper staffs, and the consequent need for replacement, is exceptionally high.) Other kinds of publications – magazines, industrial and business journals, association publications – report an expected demand for 400 recruits each year.

Yet the number of journalism degrees awarded in 1970 was considerably below 100 (precise figures are difficult to establish because of fluid course requirements) and a majority of these included only one year of specific journalism. There were no degrees in Quebec, though Laval University has begun a "communications programme" which is broadly oriented to journalism.

From now to 1974, we calculate there will be more than 7,000 new job openings in print journalism, and the "recognized" schools will turn out about 800 graduates. There will be another 2,500 emerging from one-year, two-year, and three-year courses in the community colleges. Not much more than half of all these will actually go into media jobs.

The figures, supplied by the industry itself, point to a situation of serious and growing scarcity. Our research indicates that about one quarter of those being hired in journalism now have journalistic training, and that the employers would like this proportion to be higher. Specifically, they would like to have access to people with academic degrees plus postgraduate training in journalism.

The Committee therefore recommends that at least four universities which do not now have them should establish full-scale departments of journalism, and that they should consult with representatives of the industry and of working professionals on the design of courses. Tentatively it is our view, supported by the findings of our researchers, that the course content should be about 75 per cent devoted to the academic disciplines – history, English or French, economics, political science, communications theory – and 25 per cent directly applicable to journalism, with the proviso that newsroom mechanics are best learned in the newsroom.

We do not advocate a department of journalism in every university; better a strong, well-rounded programme in each of the regions than a congeries of small ones inadequately staffed. Ontario is probably well enough served with two university departments plus the Ryerson Institute programme. But we should like to see a good school in the Atlantic provinces, one in Quebec, one in the prairie provinces, and one in British Columbia.

What we have said so far relates especially to the print media; we have not forgotten broadcasting, where the same comments apply but where there is a need for additional training of a specialized kind. In broadcasting, journalism becomes show business. A whole range of new elements is added to the basic equipment of the practitioner. Photography, cinematography, speech, music, drama, a knowledge of production values – all these come into the scheme of things.

The need for skilled people, both on and off camera, is even more crucial than in the print media. It is intensified by the C.R.T.C.'s requirement for more

Canadian content in radio and television and for more local programming on cable systems. Operators are literally beating the bushes for production and technical talent; one cable system in Toronto began its community coverage this year using a cameraman who had never held a camera before. The conventional broadcasters are looking for about 800 qualified people annually. There will be at least 650 new jobs each year in the cable systems.

This situation of scarcity has the natural result: a number of so-called schools, described by the Canadian Association of Broadcasters as "fly-by-night or unscrupulous operators," which charge fat fees for courses of little value. A few provincial technical institutes, notably in Alberta and British Columbia, provide acceptable training with a modest academic content. The Ryerson Polytechnical Institute in Toronto has probably the best-developed all-round programme; Carleton, U.B.C., and to a lesser extent Western, have some individual courses directed to television.

This is far from being enough. The Committee recommends, as a matter of urgency, the establishment of university-level programmes in radio and television arts, preferably but not necessarily associated with the regional schools of journalism.

We have one further comment on these journalism-cum-broadcasting schools, which amounts to another recommendation. We believe they should be centres of both research and criticism. To this end they should be staffed partly by communications scholars who are essentially social scientists, and partly by people who have achieved real eminence as mass communicators. Good editors are, almost by definition, good teachers. Detached from the hurly-burly, sitting above the fray, they should hold a watching brief on the conduct of the media, lecture the publishers and broadcasters on their sins, and generally interpret the press to the people. (Our proposal would have the incidental benefit of vacating some places at the top and providing an immediate prospect of upward mobility for a whole generation of young journalists.)

We believe the universities should make an all-out effort to secure the best teachers. And to assist them in the search, we cannot resist offering some nominations of our own. Consider, for example, a faculty that contained these names: Gillis Purcell on news agencies. Patrick Watson and Douglas Leiterman on documentary films. June Callwood on magazine writing. Frank Walker on the role of the press. Stuart Keate and Ross Munro on news organization. Peter Gzowski on interviewing. Bruce Hutchison on ethics. Pat Carney on business writing. Robert Fulford on the arts. Pierre Berton on everything.

In our discussions with working journalists we found, not surprisingly, that they are more concerned about opportunities for continuing education than about training for beginners. We share their view that reporters who are developing themselves as specialists (in education, labour relations, urban planning or whatever) should be able to go back to school for a period of formal study. We commend those publishers who are already supporting this kind of enrichment programme for their staffs – among them, to name a few, the Windsor *Star, Les Journaux Trans-Canada,* and *La Presse.* And many newspapers (like the Calgary *Herald,* the Winnipeg *Tribune,* the London *Free Press,* the Kingston *Whig-Standard*) send editors and reporters to intensive professional seminars at New York's Columbia University, the University of Western Ontario, and the Banff School of Advanced Management.

The Committee believes it would be valuable to have more bursaries like the admirable Southam Fellowships which give recipients a year at the University of Toronto, pursuing the studies of their choice, at full salary. "It is the company's hope," Southam Press Limited told us, "that by enabling journalists to augment their academic qualifications, the general standard of reporting and editing will be raised." Amen. We think it would be appropriate for the Canadian Daily Newspaper Publishers Assoication and the Canadian Association of Broadcasters to demonstrate an interest in raising standards by establishing similar fellowships.

There is a role here for governments too. In the interest of more intelligent reporting and interpretation, we suggest that both federal and provincial governments establish a system of postgraduate scholarships for working journalists.

TRAINING ON THE JOB

Q.—What makes a good reporter?

A.—A good city editor.

This venerable aphorism has as much truth as, though perhaps more relevance than, the one which defines an assistant city editor as a mouse practising to become a rat. It was the substance of many protestations to the Committee about the excellence of the training given to junior staff.

A good editor is in fact a teacher and one of his functions is to develop quality in the people whose work he directs. But it is incidental and secondary to his main job; he carries it out, so to speak, in his spare time. It is easily neglected and all too frequently it is neglected. On this point we heard strikingly different stories from the publishers and from the people they employ.

Item: In Winnipeg, reporters at an informal "bull session" complained that neither of the local newspapers encouraged them to take outside courses on their own time; that they received no close supervision from senior staff during the break-in period; that they were never told whether their efforts were good or bad, or why their stories were altered on the desk.

Item: Junior reporters on the Vancouver *Sun,* discouraged by the same absence of direction, asked management to set up periodic sessions with editors where they would be told what they were doing right and what they were doing wrong. The request was ignored.

Item: When Jim Hume left the Victoria *Colonist,* he gave a month's notice so that his successor might spend some time with him to become familiar with the beat. (He covered municipal affairs and had built up a substantial reference file and many personal contacts.) At Hume's departure, no one had been assigned to learn what Hume could teach him.

We cite these depressing instances not because they are unusual cases of neglect but because they are all too usual. Training, in any meaningful sense, is haphazard or non-existent. We have no statistics on the point, but it is a pretty safe bet that most reporters on Canadian dailies have never seen heir paper's style book – if the paper has a style book. And once again, while this discussion is largely in terms of print journalism, it applies with equal force to broadcasting. Even the CBC, a giant corporation using public funds to support an elaborate news and information structure, confessed in its brief to the Committee that it has no internal journalistic training system. It is one of the few areas in which the private broadcasters follow the CBC's lead.

In fairness, we should reveal our own small honour roll. So far as we are aware, six newspapers have some kind of formal and consistent training plans for people new to the trade. We name them with pleasure and apologize if we've missed one: the Calgary *Herald,* the Sault Ste. Marie *Star,* the North Bay *Nugget,* the Chatham *News,* the Galt *Evening Reporter,* the Toronto *Star.* Two of these belong to the Thomson chain, two to the Southam group. The fact has no particular significance; neither of these groups has a training plan, though Thomson publishes a set of handy tips for reporters and a guide to the dangers of libel. In a survey made three years ago, only two Thomson editors were found to use the company's training materials.

So much for training. In brief, the Committee recommends that the publishers, the broadcasters, and their professional employees should work in concert to define their standards and provide opportunities for training to meet those standards. We suggest that this training should combine some features of the American academic programme and some features of the British model with its stress on technique. And as one instance of the latter, we believe that every reporter who does not use film or a tape recorder should be able to take notes in shorthand. Tests of candidates in the British system have demonstrated that, in the words of the training manual, "reasonably good shorthand and accuracy go hand in hand." In Britain no newspaper reporter gets a job who cannot take 100 words per minute.

KEEPING THEM ON THE JOB

But when the man is trained, what then? After he is equipped for the job and after he has spent a number of years in it, what are the conditions under which he works and what are the inducements to spend the rest of his career in journalism or broadcasting?

We don't intend to deal with the stories we have heard, and the examples we have seen, of overcrowded newsrooms, bleak broadcasting studios, deplorable washrooms, inadequate libraries, lack of such simple necessities as pencils and desk drawers, and antique typewriters (often transferred to the editorial department when they become too decrepit for the business office). These conditions are prevalent enough to distress the outside observer, but squalor and journalism traditionally go together and many journalists, we suspect, would be uncomfortable in surroundings of normal decent housekeeping.

We do intend to talk about salaries. We contend that publishers and broadcasters should be paying more to the people who produce the product they are selling, and that they can well afford to do so. Their employees are, in fact, subsidizing the extraordinary profits which, as we have already shown, are being enjoyed by all but a few publishing and broadcasting enterprises.

As one evidence of what is happening we quote from the Hopkins, Hedlin study which is published as Volume II of this report:

> Reporters have a discernible tendency to desert the business when they approach age 40. There is a high rate of turnover among the university graduates who have entered newspapers in increasing numbers during recent years. It is impossible to measure the effect of salary levels on these personal decisions, but it is true to state that editorial departments in Canada, by and large, lack the stability that accrues to most other organizations.

The cautious researcher could not draw the conclusion that there is a direct relationship between low salaries and high turnover; but we can and do. Let us consider what working journalists in Canada are paid.

The standard industry yardstick for this purpose is the salary paid to a reporter with five years' experience. This is the base from which editorial salary scales go up or down (mostly down) in union contracts, and it is the newspapers with American Newspaper Guild contracts which generally set the pace for the rest.

Currently the highest salary scale prevailing in Canada is in Vancouver, where "top minimum" for a five-year reporter is $10,907. In Victoria the figure is $8,680. In the bigger Prairie cities – Edmonton, Calgary, Winnipeg, Regina – the rate is roughly 10 per cent below Vancouver, and in the smaller Prairie towns it is 10 per cent to 20 per cent below *that,* or between $7,000 and $8,000.

In Toronto, where all three newspapers are unionized, the five-year scale averages $9,620 per year. Hamilton, London, and Windsor are not far behind, but salaries in the rest of the province run as much as 40 per cent below the Toronto level for some salary categories.

In Montreal, French-language journalists are at approximately the Toronto level, English-language journalists slightly below it. Outside the metropolis, salaries again descend to as much as 40 per cent below the Montreal scale.

Major cities in the Maritimes have salaries about 25 per cent below Toronto's. In the rest of the Atlantic region there is another dip of 10 to 30 per cent.

Generally speaking, salaries in broadcasting are about equivalent to newspaper salaries for comparable jobs, except in the TV networks where unionized employees are somewhat better paid than their newspaper counterparts. (We purposely omit magazines and other publications from this discussion. Most of the workers are in newspapers and broadcasting, and that's where the standards are set.)

All this leads up to another cautious conclusion in the Hopkins, Hedlin report: "In Canada the great majority of working newspapermen and women earn from their direct employers less than $9,000 per annum."

Yes. In fact it is painfully apparent that a great many of them earn a great deal less. They earn less than teachers, less than most skilled tradesmen, less than their counterparts in the advertising, circulation and promotion departments, less than they themselves could earn in other pursuits for which their education and training equip them. Is it any wonder that while they are still young enough, so many of them leave for jobs in government or public relations or academia?

No need to labour this. We have already argued that the thrust of modern journalism is in the direction of increasing specialization, and that the specialists it requires must be also skilled communicators—in effect specialists in two fields. This kind of paragon is not going to be attracted and retained for the kind of money he can now command in Canadian communications.

Can the employers pay more? They can. Several publishers told the Committee that newspapers are less profitable than most other businesses. We heard much about the stringencies of the "cost-price squeeze." These myths have been exploded by the Hopkins, Hedlin analysis of industry figures from 1958 to 1968. In that decade, newspaper profits before tax, expressed as a percentage of equity, ranged from 23 to 30 per cent. For 1965 the profit figure was 30.5 per cent as compared with 18 per cent for manufacturing and 15 per cent for industry as a whole.

True, expenditures on wages and salaries grew by 71.5 per cent in that period. But gross returns to capital increased by 95.2 per cent. Salaries, in other words, lagged behind profits.

The story in broadcasting is just as interesting. We have already shown that television and radio, except for the very smallest stations, are vastly profitable (with some television stations showing pre-tax profits of more than 90 per cent in a single year). But we are more interested here in the correspondence, or otherwise, between pay and productivity (that is, the actual value of the employee's contribution to his employer).

Hold your breath. Between 1962 and 1968, wages and salaries in radio increased by 34 per cent while productivity advanced by 47 per cent. In television, pay increased by 39 per cent and productivity went up by 90 per cent.

One further point needs to be made about newspaper salaries. They are, predictably, lowest on the smallest papers, and the predictable reason offered is that the smallest papers are the least able to afford good salaries. For this reason, small newspapers traditionally serve as training grounds for big ones, and readers in small cities get poorer newspapers than those in the metropolitan centres.

In this connection we quote without comment another paragraph from the Hopkins, Hedlin study:

> The largest newspapers (over 100,000) and the smallest newspapers (under 10,000) are the most profitable in terms of returns on equity. Companies publishing newspapers with circulations of over 100,000 and under 10,000 consistently earned before-tax profits in excess of 30 per cent from 1965 onward. In both cases, this profit rate has shown a definite increase in the later years of the ten-year period. This increase was most spectacular for the smaller group, where the rate of return on equity in the early 1960s was less than one-half of the rate in the post-1964 period."

That is all we have to say about salaries.

IV

MEDIA

1. The Daily Miracle

Don't it always seem to go,
That you don't know what you've got
Till it's gone...
—Joni Mitchell: *Big Yellow Taxi*

Because of a labour dispute, the Vancouver *Sun* (circulation: 255,410) and the Vancouver *Province* (circulation: 113,123) suspended publication from February 15, 1970, to May 15, 1970. The shutdown lasted 82 days. Although other media attempted to fill the vacuum, the effects on the city were considerable. With Miss Mitchell's dictum in mind, the Committee commissioned a study by Hopkins, Hedlin Limited, economics and communications consultants, into the effects of the newspaper closure on the community. Limitations on time and money dictated that the study be less complete than the subject deserved. Nevertheless, it served to confirm what most Vancouver residents had already discovered for themselves: if you don't think newspapers are important, try going without them for a while.

Hopkins, Hedlin found that habitual newspaper readers, as a result of the closure, were forced to accept "the frustration of adjusting the daily routine to radio and TV news programming schedules, or unfamiliar out-of-town or weekly papers, or trying to retain news and information that is not written out in black and white."

The restrictions on advertising availability created serious inconvenience, and some hardship. The regional office of the Department of Manpower and Immigration reported that it received an increased number of enquiries from companies seeking employees, and from people seeking jobs, because of the absence of classified advertising. The local entertainment industry suffered too. Night clubs, movie houses, and theatres suffered declines in attendance that were usually in the 20 to 25 per cent range.

Although local department stores turned to radio and TV, and invested heavily in advertising flyers (the Woodward's flyer had a circulation of 300,000), the newspaper closure had a serious effect on most areas of retail sales. The owner of one four-outlet jewelry business reported a 10 per cent drop in sales; one seven-store furniture and appliance chain reported a 40 per cent drop.

Although real-estate sales volume actually increased during the first part of the shutdown, the Vancouver Real Estate Board estimated that telephone enquiries to its agents had decreased by 50 per cent. The absence of classified advertising was felt especially keenly by apartment-hunters.

The effects of a loss of advertising availability were felt most directly. But the effects of a curtailment of news and information service, although less measurable, seem to have been felt just as keenly. Mayor Campbell worried publicly about the effects of the closure on the March 11 municipal referendum on the city's $29.6 million development plan. Both newspapers had supported the plan, and it was feared that the news blackout might influence the vote. It undoubtedly did, but it is impossible to estimate how. There was a 32 per cent turnout at the polls (not too unusual) and the plan was approved by a narrow margin. Radio and TV stations attempted to fill the gap by scheduling longer news programmes and by broadcasting unaccustomed news, such as death notices. Other newspapers, such as the *Columbian* in New Westminster, the dailies in Seattle and Victoria, and the weeklies published in the Vancouver area (including *Georgia Straight*) all experienced a pronounced increase in circulation. *TV Guide's* circulation in Vancouver jumped by 60 per cent. All this happened despite the appearance of the thrice-weekly *Vancouver Express,* produced by the strikers. (In all, 35 issues were printed with an average circulation of 100,000.)

On the face of it, then, the city was well served by competing media. Four dailies from the surrounding area, at least five out-of-town dailies, eighteen weekly (and one bi-weekly) newspapers, four TV stations and twelve radio stations, all moved in to fill the vacuum created by the closure. And yet the effects of the strike were felt directly, keenly, and sometimes painfully, by almost everyone.

Hopkins, Hedlin conducted a poll of 125 Vancouver residents, and its findings are an impressive commentary on the importance of newspapers in the life of any community. More than half the people surveyed felt deprived of news and information as a result of the shutdown. Hopkins, Hedlin asked the 125 respondents what section of their daily newspaper they missed most. The answers are interesting; they are given in Table 20.

TABLE 20. QUESTIONNAIRE: EFFECTS IN THE COMMUNITY OF THE VANCOUVER NEWSPAPER SHUTDOWN

Question 1	One	Both	None	Others
Prior to the newspaper shutdown did you subscribe to one or both of the Vancouver newspapers?................................	92	26	3	23

Question 2	Yes	No
Since the shutdown began have you been receiving any other newspapers on a regular basis?................................	54	72

(a) If yes, which one?...............

Vancouver Express................	31
Seattle Post-Intelligencer.........	5
Seattle Times........................	3
New Westminster Columbian....	13
The Globe and Mail................	7
Victoria Times.......................	2
Richmond Review (bi-weekly)...	8
Citizen (North Vancouver).......	7
Others (weeklies)...................	9

(In some cases more than one paper was listed)

Question 3	Yes	No	n.a.
Have you felt deprived of news and information during the shutdown?............	79	33	13

Question 4

Which sections of the daily newspaper have you missed?........................

Front page general news........	76
Editorial page......................	45
Sports................................	41
Comics...............................	23
Theatre, entertainment..........	23
Advertising.........................	23
Local news.........................	22
Columnists.........................	20
Women's............................	20
TV schedule.......................	10
Vital statistics.....................	8
Letters to the editor.............	7
Bridge...............................	2
Horoscope.........................	1
Crossword.........................	1
None.................................	11

Question 5	Yes	No	n.a.
Have you felt deprived of advertising information during the shutdown?...............	55	63	7

(a) If so, what particular advertising information do you miss?...........

Display...............................	27
Classified............................	19
Theatre, entertainment..........	18

(b) If no, how best are you being served by advertising?................

Flyers................................	25
TV, Radio..........................	4
n.a...................................	96

TABLE 20. QUESTIONNAIRE: EFFECTS IN THE COMMUNITY OF THE VANCOUVER NEWSPAPER SHUTDOWN—Concluded

Question 6
Since the shutdown began on which sources do you rely for news and information?

Radio	110
TV	104
Other (includes out-of-town periodicals, telephone and word of mouth)	21

(a) Do you feel you are being adequately served by these alternate news and information sources?

Yes	No	n.a.
35	75	15

(Of those who added comment, the majority agreed the news reports broadcast by radio and TV were lacking in detail.)

Question 7
Has the absence of the daily newspaper had any impact on your daily routine?

Household	44
Business	20
Leisure	57
No impact	32

Question 8
Would you be prepared to do without a local newspaper on a continuing basis?

Yes	No	Possibly	n.a.
37	72	10	6

Most respondents (110) relied most on radio for news and information; 104 relied mainly on TV. Of the 125 respondents, 75 felt they weren't adequately served by these media ("not enough detail"), and 35 said that they were adequately served.

Seventy-two of the 125 respondents said they would not be prepared to do without a daily newspaper on a continuing basis. Thirty-seven respondents said they would, and ten said they might.

The results seem consonant with those of a similar survey conducted by the American Newspaper Publishers Association's advertising bureau during a newspaper strike in New York. One significant New York finding was that people tend to be satisfied *initially* with electronic news substitutes, but that these prove to be inadequate as a long-term diet. The bureau measured how satisfied people were with radio and TV news at the beginning, in the middle, and at the end of the strike:

	Start	Midpoint	End
Excellent	83%	41%	16%
Satisfactory	11%	37%	16%
Poor	6%	22%	68%

The Committee's researches were admittedly less than conclusive. But they seem to indicate that for the vast majority of people, newspapers *are* important – to their minds, their pocketbooks, and their daily lives. Indeed, it may be that a city without newspapers ceases to *be* a community, and becomes instead a collection of individuals. A sense of community, after all, cannot exist without a body of shared information. The experience in Vancouver, and in other cities where lengthy newspaper strikes have occurred, suggests that no other medium can be an adequate substitute.

Throughout this report the Committee has been critical of newspapers, and especially of the editorial performance that some of them deliver in relation to the profits that many of them earn. So perhaps this is the place to accentuate the positive. Although we have been critical, we have done so in the context of our belief that the daily and weekly newspapers of this country are, in general, doing a praiseworthy job.

In fact, the Committee has developed a certain impatience with the sort of criticism that is usually levelled at Canadian newspapers. They are supposed to be biased, sensational, superficial, beholden to advertisers, and excessively inaccurate. The press has plenty of faults, but we don't think these are among the most prominent.

Let us remember the obvious: newspaper people produce a wholly new product *every day*. Each edition is the result of hundreds of human decisions, each calling for swift judgement, instant clarity, and the fine balancing of other people's perceptions. Journalism, however humble, is a sort of art; there can be very few occupations that are so demanding in terms of speed and judgement. The wonder is that newspapers are as good as they are. They really are a daily miracle.

Much of the criticism that newspapers receive is related to the demand for speed. Newspapers can never know or print as much about *any* subject as does the participant in a news story; and the "depth" in which they can treat a subject is frequently limited by how little the reader wants to know. The marvel is that Canadian newspapers do get so much, and get it so fast, and get it so right.

This marvel would be more apparent, however, if newspapers chose to publish longer headlines. The MAN-BITES-DOG style of headline-writing, a sort of competition in terseness, is a relatively recent journalistic innovation. As Pierre Berton told the Committee, much of the criticism that newspapers receive is based on the headlines rather than the stories beneath them. In fact, the terseness trend may already be reversing itself. Our impression is that as newspapers become less and less dependent on street sales, their headlines are becoming longer, more informative, and more descriptive of the copy underneath.

Before we conclude these few comments on the newspapers, perhaps one aside is in order. As politicians, members of this Committee are accustomed to questions from members of the Parliamentary Press Gallery. So let us anticipate one question: "Why don't you say something about *us*?"

We think we do. While every newsman is not in the Press Gallery, its membership is comprised of newsmen; and their performances is surely what much of this report is about. And besides, we accept the description of the Gallery given us by Charles Lynch in his appearance before the Committee with other members of what he preferred to call the Ottawa press corps:

> The Gallery is a competitive jungle. It is not a boys' club or a cozy place as I am afraid may have been inferred from the report of the Government Task Force on Information. It is very much a competitive milieu and the Gallery as such... has no existence except as a place where we meet from time to time, to do our work individually and to compete with one another.

We think newspapers in general are much better in Canada than they are, in general, in the U.S. We think there are very few economically advanced countries that can boast of a printed press as vigorous, as dedicated, and as responsible as Canada's.

As a demonstration of responsibility, though, there is one thing we wish all of them would do that only some of them do now, and we offer it as an earnest recommendation to newspaper proprietors. We think the masthead of every newspaper should identify its owners, not just carry an unrevealing company title. The people should be told who's talking to them.

2. The Community Press

Canada's first newspaper was the weekly Halifax *Gazette,* established in 1752. The Halifax *Gazette* has long since disappeared but today there are close to 900 – give or take a few each month – weekly newspapers in Canada with an overall circulation around three million. And heaven knows how many readers: probably fewer than the weekly newspapers themselves claim, but more than advertising agencies suspect. Anyway, we're all for them.

Collectively the nation's weekly press represents a national institution in a country which has far too few national institutions.[1] More often than not the nation's weekly press is the first, the most local, the most immediate medium for hundreds of thousands of Canadians. The weekly press complements all other media and in so doing plays a significant community role probably beyond the capability of any other medium.

The retiring president of the Canadian Weekly Newspapers Association presented a rather idealized version of what a weekly does in his retiring speech at the Association's 1970 convention in Winnipeg:

> The role of the weekly newspaper is to mirror, faithfully and conscientiously, the community to the community, to provoke it where necessary, to praise it whenever possible, to defend it faithfully but always to serve it best by penetrating with the local news to a depth not possible with any other media.

But frequently there is an enormous gulf between conventioneering and the very real world of day-to-day publishing. Gerald Craven went on to concede: "There are no perfect weekly newspapers. There are some good ones, some mediocre ones, and too many poor ones." We agree. But good or bad, Canada's weeklies do fill a need that no one else seems to be able to meet. Perhaps only cable television may one day as effectively foster this "sense of community."

---

[1] There still remain 45 pre-Confederation weeklies. Two Fathers of Confederation—Thomas D'Arcy McGee and George Brown—were weekly editors.

The brief which the Committee received from the C.W.N.A. estimated that the typical Canadian weekly contains 65 per cent local news and features, leaving 35 per cent for other material. Ninety per cent of all editorials are based on local themes while national and international issues take up the remaining 10 per cent. The brief also suggested that a weekly on the average would require about 55 per cent advertising content before it could show a profit.

This pronounced emphasis on the local scene is understandably paralleled by a very marked degree of individualism on the part of both publishers and editors (who are usually of course the same person). At the risk of generalizing, Canada's weeklies do represent the more conservative end of the Canadian media spectrum. To be sure, there are a smattering of liberals, but rural weeklies in particular tend to reflect the more conservative leanings of their readership. We are not talking about partisan politics. Editorials, Mr. Craven told us proudly (although for the life of us we don't know why), "seldom take a partisan view of politics."

For all these reasons every weekly editor faces a continuing challenge to be both individual and localized without becoming parochial. The simple fact is that a goodly number don't make it.

Certainly socialism is not one of the weekly editors' longer suits. For example, I.B.M. paid for the C.W.N.A. convention dinner at the 1970 Winnipeg convention. One wonders if this kind of sponsorship is really the route which should be taken by a major league organization? This of course prompts the question whether the C.W.N.A. is a major league organization. But we are getting ahead of ourselves.

Within certain natural confines, weekly editors do have widely divergent views. For example, what motivates someone to move into the business in the first pace? Christina Isabel MacBeth, the publisher of the Milverton, Ontario *Sun,* said that she had gone into journalism "neither for money nor power," but because she wanted to "become involved in community activity." She told the Committee: "I don't think we mirror our society... We are artists who paint pictures of our society." At the same session however, Roy Farran of the North Hill *News* in Calgary indicated that if Mrs. MacBeth was an artist, he was a commercial painter. Farran said that the newspaper "is an economic enterprise whose first duty is to survive." The first requirement of content, according to Mr. Farran, is advertising—next, and only next, comes grassroots "hard news," followed by entertainment, and as a "pour fourth," education.

For most weeklies the truth is somewhere in between Mrs. MacBeth and Mr. Farran. The weekly newspaper can survive only if it has enough advertising; but its survival really isn't very important if its pursuit of advertising becomes an end in itself. In this area it was left to the inimitable Margaret "Ma" Murray, publisher of the Bridge River-Lillooet *News* in

Lillooet, British Columbia, to put things into perspective. She told the Committee that the newspaper business is becoming a racket.

> They're more interested in hearing the jingle of the cash register than in jerking tears or looking after the interests of the people ... You've got to get down on your knees and ask God to give you light so you can look beyond money and pay cheques ... It can't be all money in newspapers ... your job is to help sustain your fellow man. For any publisher of either a weekly or daily that is a Godly mission.

The Committee listened to close to 100 publishers and editors who attended a weekly newspapers forum in Ottawa at a personal sacrifice to themselves. The inescapable conclusion from the panel discussions on revenues and disbursements is that the nation's weeklies are caught in a cost-price squeeze not entirely of their own making. W. E. Dunning of Haney, B. C. argued the need for a Canadian analysis of weekly costs. He pointed out that "1969 was a good year but the net return to an average weekly owner is less than the average bank loan charge with interest rates at 10.5 per cent to 14 per cent."

Rising costs are a problem for all weeklies, but most especially papers whose circulation is under 2,000. Improved production techniques mean rising equipment costs. Attracting young people into the business, staff retraining, and increasing wage demands are part of the same story.

The brief which the Committee received from *Les Hebdos du Canada* put the problem concisely:

> The regional weekly newspapers were the first to adopt the most modern composition and printing techniques. Today, 85 per cent of the regional weeklies represented by our association are produced by the "cold-type" composition and offset printing processes.[2] This is not to say that the cost is any less than that of the traditional method – quite the contrary – but the quality is much better, and the problems are fewer.
>
> While in the past each weekly possessed its own printing shop, today this is no longer true. Owing to the fact that higher investments are needed to acquire and operate an offset press at a profit, we have seen a natural centralization and concentration of the printing works. There is every reason to believe that the same thing will soon happen in the field of composition, with the advent of electronic composition processes.
>
> It is important to bear in mind that the basic composition and printing costs of a newspaper remain the same, whatever its circulation. As a result, the smaller the newspaper, the higher the proportional cost. Consequently, a newspaper must set its advertising rate not in terms of its circulation, but in terms of its basic cost, with the result that the smaller newspapers are handicapped in relation to other more impressive advertising media.

Many weekly publishers complained that distribution costs have skyrocketed because of increasing postal rates. Their criticisms of the poor postal delivery system were loudest. Postal services are discussed elsewhere in this report.

---

[2] The C.W.N.A. estimate for its membership was "over 55%."

About 15 per cent of the weeklies subsidize their operation by doing job printing. Indeed, C.W.N.A. estimates such investment collectively to be worth six million dollars. The problem of course, particularly on smaller papers, is that the job printing side of the operation tends to overwhelm the weekly newspaper which becomes in effect a by-product. Papers like the Cobourg *Sentinel-Star,* to name just one, prove that this need not be the case; but it is enough of a problem to merit consideration.

The biggest source of industry revenue, by far, is advertising, and that phase received our special attention. The past president of the C.W.N.A., A. Y. MacLean, publisher of the Seaforth *Huron Expositor,* informed the Committee that a majority of weeklies charge their readers nearly 3¢ less than the actual cost of the paper. The average weekly's revenue, according to Mr. MacLean, comes 72.5 per cent from advertising, 7 per cent from circulation, 15.5 per cent from printing, and 5 per cent from miscellaneous sources.

Clearly, sagging national advertising revenue is one of the most critical problems faced by the Canadian weekly publisher. Income from national advertising has dwindled to about 12 per cent of all weekly advertising revenue. Any number of reasons, each with some validity, can be advanced for this state of affairs.

The weeklies have a good sales story to tell (they do, after all, reach a readership with spending power) but at best it has been poorly told and more often than not it has not been told at all. This is a critical weakness in the face of competing media which with far greater sales effectiveness speak of their own efficiency and underline, by contrast, the absence of the weeklies' promotional effort.

I. D. Willis of the Alliston *Herald* summed up rather effectively why advertising agencies are reluctant to use the weeklies.

> There are several reasons. (I speak from experience, having been advertising manager for national advertisers and an advertising account executive in advertising agencies for a number of years).
>
> There is the cost of placing advertising in weeklies. The agency works on a 15 per cent commisson basis and placement of advertisements in weeklies is not at all profitable. It may even be a losing proposition. It costs maybe $10 to make out an insertion order, mail it, keep necessary records, check the paper's invoice and tearsheet (and weeklies are notorious for their casualness in invoicing and supplying tearsheets... just ask any agency), prepare the cheque and mail it. Also, there is the cost and work of research to select the right weeklies, selling the advertiser on using weeklies, preparing special advertisements designed for weeklies and so on.
>
> To recover the $10 (not to mention the overhead costs) an advertisement must cost roughly $70. Taking the average weekly national advertising rate at 8 cents a line, this means advertisements of close to 800 lines each or, say, 57 column inches which might be one of 4 columns by 14 inches, which is larger than usually necessary. Actually, advertisements of 300 to 400 lines are ample for most national advertisers. But a 400-line advertisement shows only a revenue of $400 \times 8¢ = \$32$ cost at 15 per cent commission or $4.80 which is a loss to the agency against its operating cost of $10 plus.

Now compare this cumulative loss on advertising in, say, 100 weeklies, to placing one big advertisement in a metropolitan paper at, say, $1.15 a line. The cost of placement is still only $10 and ancillary costs are negligible but the net return on that one advertisement is 1,000 × $1.15 = $1,150, which at 15 per cent brings a profit [i.e., a return] of $172.50. The same is true for national magazines, radio and television.

So is it any wonder that agencies are reluctant to use weeklies, even when they will give good results?

Many weekly publishers are worried about the increasing use by national advertisers of the "flyer" form of presentation. Clearly such advertisers are motivated by cost and profit, with little concern about community needs. So we share the weeklies' point of view. Their concern about public relations releases from various national advertisers, and most especially from the Government of Canada, is a little more difficult to fathom; because clearly they are under no obligation to run such releases. It was pointed out to the Committee, however, that this deluge of "free" material had to come from people who felt the weeklies had some commercial value. So why don't they advertise?

Are there any solutions?

Well, perhaps first of all the weekly publishers should see themselves – and particularly their advertising value – in real perspective. Their first line of commercial attack, it seems to us, should be at the local level where frequently their medium is the only one available for community advertising. Most weeklies try to do an effective job in this area but it is one which can be improved; and perhaps this is the point at which we should underline the wisdom of not allowing cable operators to sell local advertising if a weekly press is to survive.

Many weeklies boast of both the size and value of their classified advertising section. It is perhaps worth noting that at its 1970 convention the C.W.N.A. had a useful forum on improving this phase of its operation.

A decline in national advertising revenue is equally a problem for weeklies in both the United Kingdom and the United States. In both countries the weeklies have concluded that they should redouble their effort at the local level, none of which is to suggest that the weeklies should abandon their quest for national advertising revenue. Quite the reverse.

No advertising agency could be expected to receive 900 separate weekly advertising sales presentations. There must be some grouping of sales effort but the real question is how. There are at least three alternatives. The most obvious is advertising solicitation by the C.W.N.A.; another is by the various provincial associations and still another is by some form of special grouping. Perhaps all of these groups and organizations should pitch in. One of the more effective recent efforts was made by twenty-three weeklies in British Columbia and Alberta combining their sales efforts under the title of Western Regional Newspapers Limited. It seems to us that the C.W.N.A. has some definite responsibility in this area. It was clear, however, that some veteran members of the C.W.N.A. place national advertising sales very low on the C.W.N.A. scale of priorities. Not so Douglas Bassett, vice-president and general manager of Inland Publishing Company Limited, who told the Committee:

> One might expect to get support from the Canadian Weekly Newspapers Association, and also, in our case, the Ontario Weekly Newspapers Association in selling national advertising. In our case, this is not so. In 1969, Inland received one 200-line ad for all our newspapers from CWNA and the OWNA sold two ads for 151 lines for the Newmarket *Era* and seven ads for 1,346 lines for the Stouffville *Tribune*. These associations have not in any way helped our newspapers. There was no communication in 1969 between Inland and either association. We pay an annual membership fee to support these ssociations, but they do nothing to help us secure advertising revenue.
>
> We feel that one of the main functions of these associations should be to help secure advertising lineage for weekly newspapers in Canada.

We think that most weekly publishers, both inside and outside the C.W.N.A., should agree with Mr. Bassett and with C.W.N.A.'s past president Irwin McIntosh, publisher of North Battleford's *News Optimist,* who conceded that "this has been one of the failings of the weekly newspaper industry."

Once the weeklies decide who's going to tell the story they can perhaps turn their attention more directly to the story they are going to tell; and it won't be enough to talk about flexibility, visibility and believability, because advertising agencies understandably require hard facts – even before placing government advertising.

Quite incidentally, another hangup of the publishers is the subsidy received from the government by the Canadian Broadcasting Corporation. Several publishers seem to suggest that in some convoluted way this subsidy comes at the expense of the weekly newspapers. This kind of hand-wringing was frequently linked with a plaintive yearning for more national advertising revenue. There is one way to get it. The weeklies have a story to tell but they had better become more hard-nosed in their approach.

Computerized data and readership studies cost real money—but that should not necessarily be a rub. Surely some of the nation's larger and more affluent weeklies are capable of mounting and leading a concerted and co-operative quest for national advertising revenue.

In any such venture the weeklies will find their own ambivalence about circulation data a real detriment. At the moment an increasing number of weeklies use controlled-circulation methods. Thus papers are distributed free of charge either on a bulk basis to every household, or on a controlled basis to certain selected households. The weeklies then sell advertising agencies on their density of coverage.

But about 80 per cent of all weeklies in Canada still feel it is more profitable in the long run to deal in paid circulation. Two hundred and forty-seven weeklies belong to the Audit Bureau of Circulations, which as its critics point out measures newspaper circulation but not quality. Despite the validity of this argument, the simple fact is that rightly or wrongly, A.B.C. figures mean most to national advertisers.

The bulk of the weeklies provide "sworn" circulation figures—which are just as simple as the weekly publisher actually swearing that a certain number of papers are distributed. More recently the Canadian Weekly Newspapers Association has attracted 153 of its members to participate in a Verified Circulation Figures which purports to be a combination of both the sworn and A.B.C. methods. Weekly circulation data is a confused and confusing picture which must be sorted out in the best interests of all.

One of the great virtues of Canadian weekly newspapers is not only the fact that they are Canadian owned, but that they are traditionally owned right in the community they serve. As *Les Hebdos du Canada* pointed out in their brief: "Since the reader is more familiar with those who are providing him with information, he can more readily make a critical assessment of that information." But the simple fact is that this great tradition is beginning to erode and is in danger of disappearing. Again, *Les Hebdos*:

> We do foresee the disappearance of a large number of regional weekly newspapers within five to ten years. Already, we observe the merging of two or three weeklies in certain towns; in others, one weekly has a clear lead over its competitors, who are ceasing to be profitable; and finally, certain weeklies are becoming too big to remain weeklies.

A marked degree of concentration in the weekly field is beginning to appear in response to these and other pressures, such as urbanization, electronic competition, the cost-price squeeze, and the "territorial imperative" of some daily newspapers. An increasing fact of life in Canadian weekly publishing is corporate ownership, merged regional weeklies and the use of co-operative production facilities which in turn create the climate for further concentration. Indeed, we were told that it makes economic sense for central offset printing plants to serve weekly newspapers within a 150-mile radius.

Already Toronto Star Limited has eleven; Inland Publishing Company Limited (Toronto *Telegram*) has seven and Thomson owns fourteen weekly papers. The box score is not yet overwhelming, but the time to act is now if we are to preserve what Jacques Kayser in his 1955 book *Mort d'une liberté* called the "little newspapers."

Our concern about fewer weekly voices is, however, a two-edged sword. The sad truth is that frequently daily newspaper publishers moving into the weekly field are able to stimulate sluggish national advertising sales as well as to upgrade the paper's overall quality. And so, for example, Inland Publishing Company Limited was able to win no fewer than nine 1970 C.W.N.A. awards including the award for Canada's best weekly newspaper – The Mississauga *News*.

The Committee found the C.W.N.A. executive surprisingly inarticulate when it came to this problem of increased concentration within the weekly publishing industry; and we were bemused to realize that the weekly Thomson papers belong to the C.W.N.A. while their sister daily publications do not belong to the C.D.N.P.A.; indeed virtually all of these weeklies owned by dailies support the C.W.N.A.

We share the concern put forward in a brief from Edith Weber, news editor of the Markham *Economist and Sun:*

> It was interesting to observe the great concern shown by both the *Star* and the *Telegram* for truly independent newspapers. Their attitudes in this respect are hard to reconcile with the unprecedented haste with which both these dailies have been gobbling up weeklies within a thirty-mile radius of Metro.
>
> If it is necessary that daily newspapers remain independent, then it is doubly so for community papers. The Markham *Economist and Sun* is the last of the old weeklies on Metro's fringe to be independently owned and more important, independently operated. There are times when we feel like a mouse surrounded by hungry cats waiting to pounce down and gobble us up.
>
> We've been independent publishers since 1856, and in spite of spiralling postal rates, lousy postal service, screaming wage demands, escalating production costs, we intend to keep going.

We think that kind of spirit, the C.W.N.A. executive notwithstanding, predominates in the weekly newspaper industry. And that spirit, along with the importance to this country of a vibrant weekly press, community owned and operated, deserves our support. That is why we have included weeklies in our proposal for a Press Ownership Review Board, which is discussed elsewhere. In other words, concentration in the weekly newspaper industry would be limited to those instances in which the public interest would be served; meanwhile no one anywhere would be hindered from beginning his own weekly newspaper.

Regrettably, more than a third of the country's English-language weeklies do not belong to the C.W.N.A. Four hundred and thirty-two do – one-third of them from Ontario and more than 50 per cent of them from Western Canada. It is of special concern to the C.W.N.A. that its declining membership is primarily the falling away of smaller newspapers who are not able to meet the Association's minimal fees. It should, however, be possible to subsidize this kind of membership. Fees should not be a deterrent.

It occurs to us that we may seem too critical of the C.W.N.A., especially since its members and leadership are extremely well intentioned. It is useful to remind ourselves that the Association's brief outlined four aims: (a) to elevate the standard of newspaper writing and newspaper publishing; (b) to foster the business and business interests of the members of the Association; (c) to promote a more enlarged and friendly intercourse among its members; (d) to settle differences among its members. But if we have seemed critical we have not been half as critical as were many of the weekly papers who were in touch with the Committee. For example, this from the publisher of an Ontario weekly:

> For a good many years we were members of C.W.N.A. but resigned our membership a year ago when we decided that the Association was not sufficiently interested in the opinions of its members and was inclined to live in an ivory tower.

What more can the C.W.N.A. do? Again, from the same weekly publisher:

> What is needed is *better leadership, more communication, more education* on how to achieve acknowledged purposes, *more information* on such things as costing, selling, office systems and news coverage. However, even if this is done there is no assurance that members will be influenced and, too, it is only members, not the industry which is covered.

The italics are ours. We agree that the C.W.N.A. should think in terms of an industry and not of an association.

Our same weekly publisher added this footnote, to which we subscribe: "We should also mention the good work being done by the *Canadian Weekly Publisher* in the way of information and news of the industry."

The country's so-called suburban weeklies deserve more attention than we were able to give them. They are not quite dailies – not yet at least, nor are they weeklies in the classic sense. Some belong to the C.W.N.A., most do not. It is encouraging to realize that the 1970 C.W.N.A. convention established a committee to take a special interest in the problems of the suburban weeklies. We think any such committee should certainly be affiliated with the C.W.N.A., but it is doubtful if the suburban papers have much to learn from their more traditional brethren. The growth of suburban weeklies – and, of course, community weeklies within urban areas – is an important development. Ken Larone, co-publisher and executive editor of the highly successful *Mirror* newspapers of Scarborough and North York in Metropolitan Toronto, told the Committee: "Without it there could be an information void which would be unhealthy for people living in the sprawling, high-rise megalopolis." We agree.

The relationship between *Les Hebdos* and the C.W.N.A. is to say the least very tentative. This is regrettable because the French-Canadian organization appears to be more sophisticated and advanced than are the English weeklies, although both groups are dealing with essentially the same kind of problems.

If C.W.N.A. membership is trending downward, the reverse is true with *Les Hebdos*:

> Of the 170 weekly newspapers in Quebec listed in Canadian Advertising Rates and Data, 90 are members of *Les Hebdos du Canada*. If we subtract the 30 English-language weeklies, fifteen bi-monthlies and another fifteen metropolitan weeklies devoted exclusively to promotion and advertising, we may conclude that more than 80 per cent of French-language weekly newspapers belong to our Association.

There is as well a scattering of weeklies from Ontario, New Brunswick, and Manitoba. This organization should not be confused with *Hebdos A-1* which is an advertising sales organization whose membership is substantially the same as that of *Les Hebdos du Canada*—and hence fairly effective. This broad membership in the French-language weekly association facilitates a much wider range of services. For example, since 1961 the Quebec Department of Education and *Les Hebdos* have sponsored annual travelling clinics which have concerned themselves with improving both the quality and profitability of regional weeklies.

Newspapering in Quebec is dealt with in more detail elsewhere in the report. Suffice it for our purpose to point out that the fact there are relatively fewer daily newspapers in Quebec than in other provinces has at least partially resulted in Quebec's great weekly newspaper tradition.

Quebec with 28.88 per cent of the national population has only 20.8 per cent of the nation's weeklies but 37 per cent of Canadian weekly circulation. Part of the explanation is to be found in the entertainment weekly phenomenon, but much of it relates to the absence of any marked daily-newspaper tradition which, in turn, created the vacuum into which the weeklies moved.

One result is the relatively greater significance of *Les Hebdos* as compared with their English counterparts whom they could help. The C.W.N.A., for example, is opposed to a press council. *Les Hebdos* on the other hand are about to participate in a press council which is now nearly off the runway. As their brief put it: "The basic object of the Press Council would be to safeguard the right of the people to be informed . . ." Similarly, they exhibited a far greater concern about press concentration generally and within the weekly press in particular. The French-language weeklies share our concern about fewer voices, but also point out that preservation of the French Canadian culture would depend at least in part on the ownership of such vital means of communication as weeklies remaining proportionately – and hence overwhelmingly – in the hands of Quebec's French-speaking majority.

3. The Troubled Magazines

Magazines are special. Magazines constitute the only national press we possess in Canada. Magazines add a journalistic dimension which no other medium can provide – depth and wholeness and texture, plus the visual impact of graphic design. Magazines, because of their freedom from daily deadlines, can aspire to a level of excellence that is seldom attainable in other media. Magazines, in a different way from any other medium, can help foster in Canadians a sense of themselves. In terms of cultural survival, magazines could potentially be as important as railroads, airlines, national broadcasting networks, and national hockey leagues. But Canadian magazines are in trouble. The industry may not be dying, but it is certainly not growing. There are very few Canadian-owned consumer magazines that can claim, with any degree of certainty, that their survival is assured. And if a number of long-established magazines are staring extinction in the face, it is becoming increasingly unlikely that new ones can be launched to replace them. Indeed, during the time since this Committee was established, we have been aware of the possibility that the Committee might outlive some of the magazines it has been studying.

The situation of *Saturday Night* is dangerously close to being typical. For most of its 83-year history, the magazine has fulfilled its founder's promise to make its editorial columns "the most piquant and entertaining of any Canadian paper." Despite an inability to pay its contributors as well as larger magazines, *Saturday Night* has consistently been a showcase for much of the best commentary appearing in print in Canada. Its editorial direction is brilliant. Its circulation is increasing (from 82,732 in July, 1968 to more than 100,000 in June, 1969). On the newsstands, it consistently sells more copies than the combined issues of *Harper's,* the *Atlantic,* and *Saturday Review,* three American publications that occupy roughly the same position on the editorial spectrum. As an editorial product, *Saturday Night* is a *good* magazine. In a rational world, you would suppose, it would also be a sucessful magazine.

But one of the conditions of periodical publishing in this country is that virtue is not necessarily rewarded, and is sometimes actually penalized. Owning a magazine like *Saturday Night,* its publisher informed us, is an exercise in masochism. Competition with TV for advertising revenue has hurt the magazine badly. The effect of increases in second-class and third-class mailing rates, we were told, has been "devastating." The company still owes a substantial sum to Maclean-Hunter, which for a time printed the magazine under a long-term repayment arrangement. (Maclean-Hunter is serious when it says its magazines would benefit from increased competition.) *Saturday Night's* advertising revenues have shown a recent decline. If it weren't for a contra advertising arrangement with a radio station, and the fact that *Time* Magazine chooses to advertise in *Saturday Night,* the magazine and its balance-sheet might be even thinner. The best hope for *Saturday Night's* survival, and for its sister publication *Monday Morning,* appears to lie in subsidizing the magazines through "spinoffs," such as renting their mailing lists to direct-mail advertisers.

Maclean-Hunter's experience with consumer magazines has equally masochistic overtones. The company is Canada's largest publisher of mass magazines; but it is a tribute to the company's determination, its sense of social responsibility – and to the profitability of its business publications – that *Maclean's* and *Chatelaine* continue to survive. Between 1905 and 1960, the company's consumer magazines collected nearly $130 million in revenues, and delivered a total profit, over the 55 year period, of precisely $410,604. As a profit margin that is simply laughable; and during the past decade there has been even less to laugh about. *Chatelaine* and its French-language counterpart, *Châtelaine,* were profitable in some years (notably 1967, the year of Canada's centennial) but not in others. *Maclean's,* despite large circulation increases, was not able to achieve black figures until 1969. The only really profitable decade for the company's consumer magazines, in fact, was the 1940s, when advertising space was rationed, wages and salaries were controlled, and copies sold out on newsstands almost automatically.

The weekend newspaper supplements, which fulfill roughly the same editorial role as large consumer magazines, are experiencing the same sort of difficulty. Between 1954 and 1968, their share of total net advertising revenues declined from 3.4 per cent to 1.8 per cent and during this period a new contender, the *Canadian,* was launched, thus spreading the available revenues even more thinly. In the decade between 1958 and 1968, there were only two years when the weekend supplements recorded significant percentage increases in net advertising revenues. The increases recorded in other years were extremely marginal; and in three of the ten years there were significant decreases.

In the whole country, in fact, there are only four large-circulation consumer magazines whose prospects and financial condition, judged by normal corporate standards, could be described as healthy. They are *Time, Reader's Digest, Miss Chatelaine,* and *Toronto Calendar.* Between them, *Time* and the *Digest* account for more than half the advertising revenue that all major consumer magazines receive in Canada. Moreover, their share of total revenues is on an upward swing; ten years ago, *Time* and the *Digest* accounted for 43 per cent of the total (excluding supplements). In 1969 it was 56 per cent.

Miss Chatelaine, a Maclean-Hunter publication aimed at the teenage fashion market, is fat, sassy, successful, and getting more so; its advertising revenues for the first six months of 1969 were up 132 per cent over the previous year. *Toronto Calendar,* a skillfully edited digest of things to do in Toronto that is distributed free to 120,000 upper-income Torontonians, appears to be firmly on the road to profitability, after less than two years of publication.

All four are good magazines, professionally edited and promoted. But there are more particular reasons for their success. *Time* and the *Digest* enjoy a massive economic advantage over their competitors, because most of their editorial content is supplied by their parent publications in the U.S. They also enjoy protection from other American magazines that might wish to launch similar Canadian editions; Section 12A of the Income Tax Act effectively blocks their entry by declaring that advertising in Canadian editions of foreign magazines cannot be deducted as a business expense – but *Time* and the *Digest* are exempt from this provision.

Miss Chatelaine and *Toronto Calendar* are successful for a different reason: they are the right *kind* of magazines at the right time. General-interest magazines, publications which attempt to appeal to all classes of readers at least some of the time, are in trouble everywhere, not just in Canada. Specialized magazines – those which stake out for themselves a particular segment of a general readership – are experiencing much less difficulty and, in many cases around the world, astonishing success.

We've singled out these two latter cases to indicate that the magazine situation in Canada isn't utterly hopeless. There can't be many industries in this country where the odds are stacked so heavily against success; but it is still possible to beat those odds by publishing the kind of magazine that attracts a class of readers whom advertisers wish to reach, and by being able to spend a lot of money before you start getting it back.

Still, the odds are enormous. They always have been. The magazine industry propagates itself as salmon do, by spawning vast quantities of progeny in the hope that a few will survive. Over the past half-century or so there have been an enormous number of magazine births and a somewhat smaller number of deaths. In the 1920s, some 96 consumer magazines were launched in Canada or were already in existence, and 23 died. Seventy-five were started in the 1930s and 65 died. Ninety-two commenced publication during the 1940s, and 70 died. During the 1950s, 29 new magazines were launched and 50 died. More than 250 magazines were launched between 1960 and 1969, and only 137 died.

An excess of births over deaths, however, should not be taken as an indication of the industry's overall health. The overwhelming majority of these consumer magazines were not, shall we say, very big deals, and never could be. Magazines such as *Town House Magazine's Report on Frozen Food,* the *King Edward Hotel Magazine, Trigger Talk* and *Western Sailing & Jibsheet* – all of which were launched in the 1960s – may fulfill readers' needs, but they can't be said to have constituted a massive contribution to the National Fabric.

Even at the very best of times, the industry has been a weak one, and the evidence suggests that it is growing weaker. Neither circulation nor advertising revenues of all Canadian consumer magazines have grown as fast as the population. In 1954, Canadian magazines (excluding supplements) billed $14,280,000 in net advertising revenue. In 1968 they billed $22 million – but their share of total revenues had declined from 4.2 per cent in 1954 to 2.4 per cent. In 1954, business spent about $3 million more on billboards, posters and signs than was spent on advertising in Canadian consumer magazines. Today advertisers spend about *three times* as much on billboards. The American magazine *Business Week* collects about as much advertising revenue as does the entire Canadian magazine industry. And if advertisers are less than completely sold on magazines as a medium, so are readers; Americans read 60 per cent more magazines per capita than Canadians do.

By far the most important reason for the industry's palsied state is overflow circulation. Unhampered by tariff barriers, by language barriers, or by any form of protective legislation, foreign magazines – mostly American, naturally – pour into the country by the tens of millions, swamping our newsstands and occasionally overloading our postal system. The fact of overflow circulation is of course obvious, but its sheer magnitude is seldom appreciated. *Playboy,* to cite one example, collects about as much money selling its magazine in Canada as do the seventeen largest English-language consumer magazines combined. *Chatelaine,* with a circulation of 980,000, has one of the world's highest per capita penetrations of its available audience; yet *Life* sells more magazines in Canada than *Chatelaine* does. Canadians buy almost twice as many copies of *True Story* as they do of *Saturday Night.* We buy more than sixteen times as many copies of *National Geographic Magazine* as we do of *Canadian Geographic.* We spend more money buying American comic books than we do on the seventeen leading Canadian-owned magazines.

We are also reading fewer magazines. In 1959, we bought 147 million copies of American magazines. Ten years later the total had declined to 130.5 million copies. But the decline for Canadian magazines has been even steeper. In 1959 we bought 45 million copies of Canadian magazines. In 1969 we bought about 33.8 million copies.

There is nothing very surprising about this. American publishing companies can scarcely be blamed for selling their magazines here; since they must meet their costs from U.S. circulation and advertising revenues, their overflow circulation into Canada is almost invariably profitable. Nor can Canadian readers be blamed for buying them. Not only do the Americans produce some excellent magazines; they also produce classes of magazines (true romance, do-it-yourself, and so on) for which there is no Canadian alternative.

It is interesting to note, however, that Canada appears to be one of the few countries in the world which has taken no measures either to discourage overflow circulation or to encourage a domestic periodical industry. In Switzerland, where nearly three quarters of the population speaks German, there is a postal surcharge on foreign periodicals. Austria, also faced with an overflow situation from Germany, imposes a series of taxes which, the O'Leary Commission noted in 1961, are "generally applicable" to foreign periodicals. Both countries, the commission noted, have healthy magazine industries.

Most magazine publishers in Canada don't think of overflow circulation as a primary problem; it is simply part of the environment. What they are painfully aware of, though, is the competition for advertising revenues from other media. It is a scramble between radio, television, newspapers, and magazines for available advertising dollars, and for the attention of audiences – a piggies-at-the-trough situation in which magazines are more and more being shouldered aside.

Between 1954 and 1968, magazines' share of total advertising revenues dropped from 4.2 to 2.4 per cent. The decline in the share of weekend supplements was even steeper. As a matter of fact, *all* the print media – daily and weekly newspapers, farm and business periodicals – have experienced a decline in their shares of total advertising revenue. In the same period, radio's share increased slightly. But the big winner was television, whose share increased from 2.5 per cent in 1954 to 12.9 per cent in 1968. Since most magazines live off national advertising – 80 per cent of television advertising is national – they have felt the pinch far more keenly than the above figures would indicate.

The third factor affecting the odds against the development of a healthy magazine industry in Canada is the presence of *Time* and *Reader's Digest*. We have already noted that these two magazines' share of the total revenues spent in the major consumer magazines has increased from 43 to 56 per cent in the past dozen years. In earlier chapters, we have described how, in the newspaper business, success feeds on itself by lowering unit costs, enabling a large paper to offer lower advertising rates and thus grow larger still.

It seems probable that the same broad principle applies to magazines; and it is reasonable to anticipate that *Time* and *Reader's Digest* will continue to grab off larger and larger proportions of available revenues. The end result, quite conceivably, could be that the only mass magazines serving this country would be the heavily subsidized, heavily protected Canadian editions. O'Leary's rationale was plain: "If there is acceptance of the fact that Canadian periodicals 'contribute to the development of a national identity,' then responsibility must rest upon us all to see to it that such periodicals do not disappear and, least of all, disappear through unfair competition from foreign publications..."

Time and the *Digest* have been publishing Canadian editions since the early 1940s, and the O'Leary findings weren't the first attempt to assault their position. In 1956 the federal government proposed a 20 per cent tax on the value of advertising material in Canadian editions of non-Canadian periodicals. The tax became effective in January, 1957, but was removed by a different administration in June, 1958. (It may be significant to note that while this tax was in force, *Time-Digest* advertising revenues continued to increase, and those of Canadian-owned magazines continued to decline.)

The O'Leary recommendation that advertising costs in Canadian editions of foreign magazines be made non-deductible was not implemented until 1964. But the amendment to the Income Tax Act, although it did not mention the two magazines by name, specifically exempted *Time* and the *Digest*. It did so by limiting the definition of a "non-Canadian" periodical to exclude magazines that "throughout the period of 12 months ending April 26, 1965 ... were being edited in whole or in part in Canada and printed and published in Canada." *Time* and the *Digest* met this requirement. In 1962 – one year after the O'Leary Commission made its report – *Time* had opened an editorial office in Montreal to produce its Canadian section. The *Digest* also had a Canadian editorial staff, and both magazines were printed in Canada.

Since then, both magazines have made earnest attempts to become members in good standing of the Canadian publishing community, and have continued to prosper. The Canadian circulation of the *Digest* and its French-language affiliate, *Sélection du Reader's Digest*, has climbed from 1,068,000 in 1960 to 1,448,000 in 1969. The company's shares are traded on the open market, and about 30 per cent of the stock in the Canadian subsidiary is now held by Canadians. The *Digest's* advertising revenues have risen slightly over the ten-year period, and every year has been profitable. The company has about 450 employees in Canada, including an editorial staff almost as large as that of *Maclean's*.

Time's circulation has increased from 215,000 in 1960 to about 440,000 today. Advertising revenues have almost tripled from $3,946,774 in 1959 to $9,545,752 in 1969. Between 1962 and 1969, Time International of Canada Ltd. spent more than $10 million printing its magazine in Canada, and now splits its press run between Montreal and Evergreen Press in Vancouver. Its marketing and promotion activities incurred expenditures in Canada of about $325,000 last year. The company directly employs fifty-eight full-time staff members and ninety part-time staffers in Canada.

Time and the *Digest* were also instrumental in the creation of the Magazine Advertising Bureau, a research and sales promotion organization which attempts to promote the interests and advertising effectiveness of magazines as a medium. The Magazine Advertising Bureau's members are *Time*, the *Digest's* French and English editions, *Maclean's, Le Magazine Maclean*, the three *Chatelaines*, the *United Church Observer, Actualité, TV Hebdo*, and *Saturday Night. Time* and the *Digest*, on the basis of their share of advertising revenues, pay about half the cost of running the Bureau.

There is no question that both magazines have been good corporate citizens. It is also clear that their financial success is not solely attributable to the competitive advantage they enjoy. Both are excellent products—perhaps the most skillfully edited mass magazines in history. Quite apart from their competitive advantages, *Time* and the *Digest* have prospered because they produce the kind of magazines that a lot of readers and advertisers prefer.

Perhaps the most astonishing indication of their success, however, is the attitude of some of their Canadian competitors. In 1960, when the O'Leary Commission held its hearings, the Canadian magazine industry was unanimous in demanding relief from what they conceived to be the unfair foreign competition. Floyd Chalmers, then president of Maclean-Hunter—then as now the biggest periodical publisher in the country—referred to *Time* and the *Digest* in a tone that was less than effusive. "Quite frankly," he told the Commission, "the parasitical character of these publications suggests that they are not particularly entitled to sympathetic or generous treatment." He pointed out that national policy in the past has been to prevent foreign domination of our financial institutions, our broadcasting, our railroads. "The simple economics of such matters," he said, "have taken second place to broader national considerations. We think there is a strong case for a similar approach with respect to Canadian periodicals."

In its appearance before *this* Committee, Maclean-Hunter's approach was somewhat different. No reference was made in their brief to the O'Leary recommendations because, as a Maclean-Hunter executive explained, "We ask for nothing." R. A. McEachern, then the company's executive vice-president in charge of consumer magazines, said he felt removal of the *Time-Digest* exemptions at this time was unrealistic, and that the competitive situation their presence creates is far from intolerable. "We live with it and make the best of it," he said. "The status quo is something the government created. We are going to make the best of it."

All the Canadian-owned members of the Magazine Advertising Bureau say that they share this view. The rationale appears to be that the Canadian industry's best hope lies in co-operating to promote their medium as a whole. The view has also been expressed that, without *Time* and *Reader's Digest,* Canadian magazines would simply cease to *matter* as a national advertising medium. Without *Time* and *Reader's Digest,* it would be more difficult for an advertiser to obtain maximum coverage through the consumer-magazine medium. Without *Time* and *Reader's Digest,* there would be fewer magazines among which the creative and production costs of advertising could be distributed, thus making the medium as a whole a less attractive buy. "There is considerable importance in Canada [in] having what might be recognized as a magazine industry with status," Mr. McEachern told us. It is plain that MAB member publications feel that, without *Time* and *Reader's Digest,* this status would be reduced[3].

It has also been pointed out that removing the *Time-Digest* exemptions – even if it *did* force those magazines to close up shop in Canada – wouldn't necessarily represent a windfall for the remaining periodicals. Much of the revenue would undoubtedly be diverted to television and newspapers. Some revenue would simply dry up, it has been argued, because there are advertisers who, if they can't buy *Time* or the *Digest,* will stay out of magazines altogether.

Some advertisers, who now advertise in several magazines, might pull out of Canadian-owned publications so they could afford the increased costs of *Time* and *Reader's Digest.* Still other *Time-Digest* advertisers might buy less space in these magazines, but spend the same amount of money to do it. "Thus," comments one publisher, "other Canadian magazines would receive none of the present *Time* expenditures – only the government would. Big deal."

This view was supported by a private survey, which the Committee saw, of Canada's 100 largest advertisers. It indicated that, even if *Time* and *Reader's Digest* folded up their Canadian editions, only 13 per cent of their advertising expenditures would be diverted to other Canadian magazines. (*Time-Digest* revenues in 1969 totalled $14,642,300. Thirteen per cent of *that* amounts to $1,903,500.)

All these scenarios are based on the assumption that *Time* and *Reader's Digest* would cease publication in Canada if their exemptions were removed. But it is possible that, even if the exemptions were repealed, *Time* and *Reader's Digest* would continue to publish here. In 1960, the O'Leary Commission reported, the two magazines earned $1,567,369 in Canada. Taken together, they earn substantially more than that now. With profits of this magnitude at stake – to say nothing of normal human pride – the natural tendency would be to fight rather than run. Besides, Canadian governments have taxed these magazines before, then backtracked. A smart publisher might gamble that if they backtracked once, they can backtrack again.

It is even possible, the Committee was told, that repeal of the exemptions might amount only to a major inconvenience for *Time* and *Reader's Digest.*

---

[3] As far as one distinguished observer is concerned, that status is already pretty marginal. Senator Grattan O'Leary favoured the Committee with his views on what's happened to the magazine industry since he made his report, and concluded that, in his judgement, the existing Canadian magazines have declined in quality. "Were I making my report today," he added, "I would not have been so concerned for those magazines . . . I am not so sure that *Time* magazine today is not the best Canadian magazine we have."

This is because both magazines are heavily dependent on advertising from large international companies. *Time* offers a discount to such companies if they advertise on an international basis. A company which buys space in both the American and Canadian editions of *Time,* for instance, qualifies for a ten per cent discount.

We'll let Richard Ballentine, publisher of *Toronto Calendar* Magazine, pursue the argument from there:

> An examination of the current issue of *Time* (July 20, 1970) shows that out of seventeen pages of advertising almost ten (65%) are international companies who do, or can, buy the Canadian edition from outside Canada, in combination with other international editions and at large discounts from card rates. Thus the elimination of tax exemption would create the following scenario:
> 1. Canadian advertisers including Canadian subsidiaries of U.S. and foreign companies would find their cost of advertising in *Time* increased by 50 per cent.
> 2. Canadian subsidiaries of U.S. or international companies would have to accept the tax disadvantage but such subsidiaries are buying or could buy in Canada at the lower international rates earned by the world-wide advertising contracts of their parent companies and thus their tax penalties would be *less* than for a wholly Canadian-owned company.
> 3. Other companies, largely U.S. and Japanese and German, would still buy at the same, already discounted, international prices and because they have no Canadian corporate identity would pay no tax.
> 4. *Time* would probably lower its rates slightly for wholly Canadian advertisers to offset the tax disadvantages. They might even reapportion the amount of an international contract applied to Canada, lowering it in effect, to reduce the tax liability of the Canadian subsidiaries of foreign firms.
> 5. The effect thus would be to widen the present disparity between, say, a Clairtone and Mitsubishi Electric buying the same space and frequency....
> 6. Thus, as long as *Time* and *Reader's Digest* remained in Canada even after losing their tax exemption, they would be competitively a better advertising buy for outside foreign advertisers and for Canadian subsidiaries of foreign advertisers than they would be for a wholly Canadian company. That seems to me like a strange kind of economic nationalism.

Mr. Ballentine supports the *status quo* because, as he put it, "the removal of a privilege they have enjoyed for years will have drastically different results from *preventing* them from coming into Canada with that privilege in the first place."

He is, however, practically the only publisher outside the Magazine Advertising Bureau who likes things as they are. Last August, a group of non-M.A.B. editors and publishers circulated a statement calling for removal of the exemptions, and urged media people who endorsed the statement to make their views known to the Committee. Some 364 people representing 168 publications did so. They included writers, photographers, art directors, editors, publishers, production people and, gratifyingly enough, three fashion models. They represented or worked for publications as diverse as *Sno-Mo-Go & Outdoor Fun Magazine, Point De Mire* (a separatist journal), the *Fiddlehead,* Southam Business Publications and the Toronto *Star.* Some appended comments, including the editor of *Executive* magazine, who wrote:

> Canada now needs a strong national press as much as it needed the Canadian Pacific Railway in the late 1800s. That press now has the talent, insight and experience necessary to serve the people of Canada in a way that no foreign publications can. But we need the chance to do it – to prove it. Given the amount of advertising dollars now going to *Time* and *Reader's Digest,* it is certain that we'll be given neither the opportunity nor the tools.

It seems clear that what might be called the non-establishment segment of the magazine industry believes, strongly and with near-unanimity, that the exemptions should be repealed. Against that, we must set the possibility that removing them might give foreign advertisers a cost advantage over Canadian companies advertising in the Canadian editions of *Time* and *Reader's Digest;* and that some magazines, instead of benefitting, might actually experience a reduction in their advertising revenues.

There is another reason why a prudent government would hesitate to remove the *Time-Digest* exemptions: the prospect of economic retaliation. Former Finance Minister Walter Gordon has asserted publicly that the exemptions were granted in the first place as a result of severe pressure from Washington. The Americans are said to have intimated to Ottawa that if *Time* and *Reader's Digest* were kicked out of Canada, it might indirectly affect the course of negotiations on the U.S.-Canada auto parts agreement. It is not unreasonable to anticipate similar pressures this time around, and they need not all be at the quasi-diplomatic level. As Mr. McEachern told the Committee:

> Remember that in view of the enormous American penetration of Canada, a great many of the big advertising decisions are not made in Canada, but in head offices in the United States. If the Government of Canada were to go ahead and make a move against the two publications named, this would set off a typhoon of criticism. We would be charged with anti-Americanism and all sorts of things; so certainly for a time we would suffer.

The case against removing the exemptions, in other words, boils down to three propositions: we shouldn't do it because (a) *Time* and *Reader's Digest* would probably continue publishing their Canadian editions; (b) it wouldn't help the Canadian industry very much and, in the short run at least, might even affect their revenues adversely; and (c) the Americans wouldn't like it.

Those three propositions were presented to us as justification for doing nothing. We choose to regard them, however, as a demonstration that something *must be done*. After all, what do these arguments add up to? The exemptions must remain, we were told, because to remove them would mean that two foreign magazines, backed by foreign advertising agencies that are in turn backed by foreign corporations that already control much of our economy, would combine to defeat the intent of the legislation.

Is that true? Are our options truly so limited as that? If they are, if the future of an important – perhaps essential – Canadian industry is already irretrievably mortgaged to *Time, Reader's Digest,* General Motors, Kraft Foods and the State Department, it means that Canadians are much less independent than they like to believe.

We believe that creeping continentalism has proceeded far enough in this country. We believe the present situation of the magazine industry is a perfect example of the dangers of an unexamined acceptance of foreign investment. That is our feeling, and we believe it is shared by most Canadians.

That is why studying the problems of periodicals in Canada can be such a maddening exercise: it embraces, in microcosm, many of the basic contradictions of our nationhood. Geography has made us continentalists, whether we like it or not. Pride and history and the land have made us Canadians – a people who, almost by definition, resist the cold logic of economics in favour of the warmer logic of the heart. Thinking about Canadian magazines is like thinking about Canadians themselves – there is a constant tension between the centralizing, levelling influences of The Market and the inward, wayward pull of our national other-ness. Somewhere, somehow, in all our national deliberations, the line must be drawn between logic and love.

The Committee was extremely conscious of this elusive line when it attempted to shape its magazine recommendations. Like all truly Canadian solutions, our conclusions involve contradiction and compromise. We think they would have gladdened the heart of Mackenzie King himself. We also think they are the *only* recommendations we could in conscience have made.

The logic of love dictates the first conclusion: *somehow, despite the economic pitfalls, a way must be found to create more equitable competitive conditions in the Canadian periodical industry.* The competitive advantage that *Time* and *Reader's Digest* enjoy is greater today than it was when O'Leary made his recommendations in 1961. The consumer magazine segment of the industry is by far the most important segment in terms of our cultural survival. It is also the segment which, because of subsidized foreign competition, faces the greatest difficulties. Whatever the admen say, whatever the economists say, this is a situation we should no longer tolerate.

The O'Leary recommendations were sound when they were made, and the intent behind them is sound today. If Section 12A hadn't been applied when it was, we are certain that Canadian magazines would be a lot sicker than they are. The business press in Canada is a flourishing, profitable segment of the industry. Without O'Leary, today it would be dying – crushed by subsidized foreign competition. Without O'Leary, some of the specialized magazines we referred to earlier in this chapter would not exist. (*Seventeen* Magazine, we are informed, dropped its plans for a Canadian edition when the O'Leary recommendations were implemented. If *Seventeen* had been allowed in, there would be no *Miss Chatelaine* today – and perhaps no *Chatelaine* either.)

We deeply regret that *Time* and *Reader's Digest* were exempted from the O'Leary legislation. It was a bad decision. It really was, as one commentator put it, like locking the foxes in with the chickens. Frankly, we marvel that *any* Canadian mass consumer magazines have survived in such a forbidding climate. It is a tribute to their skill – and to the fact that Canadians obviously *want* Canadian magazines. We are pretty certain that, if Section 12A had been fully applied ten years ago, there would be more Canadian magazines today.

We believe it is important to look at this question in the longer term. What will the effect be five or ten or fifteen years from now – not only on existing magazines, but on new Canadian magazines yet to be born? It seems plain to us that if *Time* and *Reader's Digest* are allowed to maintain their present competitive advantage, it will become increasingly difficult for existing magazines to survive, and for new ones to be launched. We are playing with probabilities here, not certainties; but we are satisfied that the long-term prospects for a Canadian periodical industry – and probably the short-term as well – would be enhanced by removal of subsidized foreign competition.

To believe otherwise is to assume that Canadians aren't capable of producing the kind of magazines that other Canadians prefer to read. We don't believe that. The few Canadian mass magazines (like *Chatelaine, Maclean's* and *Saturday Night*) that do exist have already achieved far higher penetrations of their available audiences than have their American counterparts. The audience is there, and so is the talent. It is simply defeatist to argue that, given more equitable competitive conditions, the Canadian industry couldn't improve its position.

But how can this be arranged in a way that steers a sensible course between love and logic? The Committee considered several options. The first was simply to leave the *status quo* alone, and hope that the massive advantages which *Time* and *Reader's Digest* enjoy could somehow be offset by a network of incentives and subsidies to their Canadian competitors. Although we have, earlier in this report, recommended a mild form of government assistance for periodicals, we have concluded that subsidies, in general, are an unwise alternative. For one thing, it would be too costly; large magazines, when they're losing money, lose a *lot* of money. For another, the subsidy route – as it has in the past – could lead to the perpetuation, at public expense, of ventures which deserve to die because they have outlived their usefulness. Finally, most print publishers say they fear the effects of subsidies on freedom of the press; although it should be noted that they also tend to complain about increases in our subsidized postal rates, usually in the same breath.

Another option was to recommend legislation that would prevent *Time* and *Reader's Digest* from publishing their magazines and accepting advertising in Canada. Kick them out. Send them home. Their American editions would still be available in Canada, but only as overflow circulation. As competitors for Canadian readers, they would be welcome. As competitors for Canadian advertising dollars, they would be expelled.

Blunt as it sounds, this option does at least have the virtue of effectiveness. In the long run, and perhaps in the short run too, it would immeasurably improve the climate for Canadian magazines, living, dying, and unborn.

But the Committee rejected this option too. Singling out for expulsion two corporations that have done business in Canada for nearly three decades, and done it with flair and fairness and excellence, struck us as somehow inconsistent with the Canadian character. We were mindful too of the economic dislocation this could cause. Unemployment in the cause of sociocultural development is a lot more palatable for its proponents than it is for the participants.

That led us to a third option, the one we now recommend. Not surprisingly, it is exactly what O'Leary wanted nine years ago: *we recommend that the exemptions now granted Time and Reader's Digest under Section 12A of the Income Tax Act be repealed, and the sooner the better.*

We think we have fairly presented the arguments against such a move. We found them not wholly persuasive. Even if *Time* and *Reader's Digest* did find it possible to continue publishing their Canadian editions despite removal of the exemptions, they would at least be competing on a more equitable basis than before. The massive cost advantages they enjoy from spillover editorial content would be at least partially offset.

Besides, economic arguments against removing the exemptions are predicated on the here-and-now – on the effects among *existing* advertisers in *existing* magazines. We don't believe the industry is as rigid, or the conditions under which it operates as immutable, as these arguments suggest.

One of the most promising fields of magazine development, for instance, is in the regional and local area. Periodicals such as *Toronto Calendar, Toronto Life,* the late *Vancouver Life, Atlantic Advocate,* and *Atlantic Reporter* (which was in the process of being launched at this writing) can fulfill a genuine need among readers and advertisers, perhaps better than national magazines can. *Time's* regional editions are probably the major obstacle to their growth. (The magazine publishes twelve regional editions on a regular basis, allowing advertisers to buy split-run coverage of such areas as British Columbia, Toronto, Quebec, Ontario, the Prairie provinces, and the Maritimes.) This competition hurts regional magazines, and it seems plain that removing the exemptions would be of enormous benefit to them, even if *Time* and *Reader's Digest* continued publishing. Not many regional and local advertisers are multinational corporations and thus wouldn't be able to evade the intent of the legislation by buying *Time Canada* in the U.S.

The periodical business is so flexible that we feel fairly confident that it would adapt to take advantage of the new competitive situation, loopholes and all. If, as is argued, *Time* and *Reader's Digest* could adapt to the new situation, perhaps their Canadian competitors could too.

Admittedly, we are juggling unknowns. Maybe *Time* and *Reader's Digest* would go home if the exemptions were removed. Maybe they wouldn't. Maybe the large Canadian magazines would suffer a short-term drop in revenues. Most probably, we think, they wouldn't (56 per cent, after all, is a pretty large share of *anything*). Maybe new magazines would find it easier to get started. Maybe they'd find it just as difficult as before. It is impossible to predict the effects of removing the exemptions with much precision. On the other hand, it's easy to predict what will happen if nothing is done: the segment of the magazine business that is subject to subsidized foreign competition will get sicker and sicker. We think the government's wisest course is to remove the exemptions, and see what happens.

We hope we are labouring the obvious when we stress that the measure we propose would *not* limit the right of Canadians to read whatever magazines they choose. *Time* and *Reader's Digest* would still be welcome on Canadian newsstands and in Canadian mailboxes. The proposal implies no restriction whatsoever on their circulation in the country.

We offer a second recommendation which might be implemented after the exemptions were removed, if events warranted it. If it turns out that removal of the exemptions proves ineffective, that the Canadian industry's health does not improve, that *Time* and *Reader's Digest* continue to profit from their cost advantages while Canadian magazines continue to decline, then there is a second step the government could take. *Instead of sending the two magazines home, make them settle here.*

We recommend that if events warrant it, *Time* and *Reader's Digest,* as a condition of publishing their magazines in Canada, be required to sell 75 per cent of the stock in their Canadian subsidiaries to Canadian residents, and that three quarters of their officers and directors be Canadian residents. (*Reader's Digest* is almost halfway there already; 30 per cent of the Canadian subsidiary's stock is held by Canadian residents, and four of its six directors are Canadian.)

There is ample precedent for this approach. The C.R.T.C. has already insisted on 80 per cent Canadian control of broadcasting corporations, a policy which has forced Famous Players Canadian Corporation Ltd. and RKO Distributing Corporation (Canada) Limited to sell their Canadian holdings. The Income Tax Act, in effect, already does the same thing. If an advertisement in a Canadian newspaper or periodical is to be deductible as a business expense, that newspaper or periodical must be 75 per cent Canadian-controlled – *Time* and *Reader's Digest,* of course, being exempted. The government either recently or long ago staked out other key sectors of the economy – uranium, banks, railroads – where Canadian control is regarded as a condition of doing business in Canada.

It also has the virtue of fairness. It involved no wrench of the collective conscience to force Famous Players and RKO to divest themselves of their Canadian assets, because there *were* assets to sell, and Canadians willing to buy them. *Time* and *Reader's Digest* have no such assets. If we simply expelled them, they would have nothing to sell. Their enterprises in Canada are symbiotic; take away their relationship with their American parent and you are left with a few typewriters, a few printing contracts (liabilities, those), a few rented offices. As businesses they are worthless, except in association with their parent magazines in New York.

By requiring 75 per cent Canadian ownership, you would enable the companies to collect very handsomely on an intangible asset. The earnings of both companies – and the profits they have sent home to New York – have ranged from moderate to substantial in recent years. Even in a period of depressed share prices, there can be little doubt that by selling three quarters of their stock to Canadians, through either a public offering or a private sale, the two companies would receive a fair price, in terms of the earnings they generate. Instead of expelling two magazines from Canada, the government would be creating two Canadian magazines.

The big objection, of course, is that by doing this you might be merely substituting unfair Canadian competition for unfair foreign competition. The two magazines, no matter who owned their shares, and despite the fact that they no longer enjoyed the 12A exemptions, would still enjoy the economic advantage of being able to buy most of their editorial content at bargain-basement prices from their American counterparts. (We are presuming here that a condition of the sale would be an undertaking that the names and essential character of the magazines would remain unchanged.)

We think it likely, however, that the American magazines would decide to charge their Canadian counterparts more for their spillover editorial content than they do at present. They would do so, we submit, because they would be foolish not to. The new companies would pay the price because the American editorial content would be essential to their operation. This cost increase could have the effect of encouraging an increase in Canadian editorial content; readers' tastes would be pressing in the same direction. The end result – and, we think, a most probable one – would be two healthy magazines, heavily Canadian in editorial content, overwhelmingly Canadian in ownership. Isn't this what a periodical policy should be trying to achieve in Canada?

The other possibility is that, instead of acquiescing to the 75 per cent requirement, *Time* and *Reader's Digest* would pick up their marbles and go home. That's what we think should have happened ten years ago. If it did happen this time around, it would be the companies' decision, not the government's. We don't think it would take Canadian publishers long to fill the editorial vacuum that such a voluntary withdrawal would create.

At this point we must take note of a dissent – the only one in our entire report. On every other point we were unanimous; the only issue on which the Committee was divided was its recommendation with regard to *Time* and *Reader's Digest*. Fourteen of us agreed. But Senator Louis Beaubien disagreed, and the rest of us respect his right to do so. Indeed we are anxious to have his dissent on our record.

Senator Beaubien is in full accord with the desirability of helping the home-grown industry. He feels, however, that cancelling the exemption under 12A of the Income Tax Act would produce small benefits compared to the economic dislocation to the employees, shareholders, and others connected with both *Time* and *Reader's Digest*.

We admit that what we propose is an imperfect solution. But it seems to us to be the only one that avoids the injustice of expulsion, the pitfalls of subsidy, and the administrative horrors of legislation that attempted to set Canadian editorial content requirements in the print medium.

On the subject of magazines and print in general, a final note of diffidence:

Print is in trouble everywhere. Not because people don't read any more, but because fewer people appear to turn to print for entertainment and enlightenment. The book-publishing industry in Canada – a medium that was beyond our resources to investigate – has problems that are remarkably similar to those of the periodical industry. Could this be because reading, as a pastime, is in a natural state of decline?

We think it is possible. The old literary culture of Shakespeare and Swift and Dafoe and Tennyson and Hemingway and Leacock, and the journalism which is one of its barely legitimate children, may be on the way out. It may be in the process of being replaced by the new electronic sensibility that Marshall McLuhan is so adept at describing.

If that is so, the whole idea of legislative measures to encourage printed communication in Canada may appear in retrospect to have been a profoundly reactionary, profoundly futile exercise.

Maybe it's our linear bias showing, but we persist in believing that print will continue to play a major role in whatever kind of society we may evolve.

4. The Invisible Press

Who needs *Sea Harvest & Ocean Science?* Who has even heard of it? Or *Teaching Aids Digest? Storage and Distribution? Bâtiment? Canadian Pit and Quarry?*

The question is rhetorical. We offer no prizes to those who can correctly identify these magazines. Individually they are well and favourably known to a small, carefully selected list of readers. Collectively they command so little public attention that they might almost be called the invisible press. But the invisible press has a special, and specially valuable, place in the Canadian media mix.

There are 510 periodicals, with a total circulation of 4,400,000, in the publishing category known as the business press. Each is directed to a specific sector of industry, commerce, and the professions. Their function is to assist decision-makers in reaching right decisions. To do this they report and exhort – reporting on trends and developments, on new techniques and new products, on successes in problem-solving; and exhorting governments and industry policy-setters to create the conditions under which everyone can prosper. For the corner merchant or the nation-wide corporation, the name of the game is profit, and profit is what the business press is all about.

The Committee was impressed by the skill and professionalism with which the hundreds of business publications pursue their single-minded objective. They are highly useful, particularly in sifting the flood of technical information with which business and professional men are inundated, and passing on the essentials in a form that can be put to practical purpose.

But they are more than merely informative. Many business editors occupy positions of influence and even leadership in the industries they serve. They see "their" industry as a whole and they work for its material betterment. Many of them have been instrumental in forming industrial associations which serve not only to exchange information but to raise ethical and professional standards.

On occasion they can be crusaders, bringing the light of publicity to bear on abuses and campaigning to have them corrected. We mention only one of many cases in point. The editors of *Canadian Aviation* recognized years ago that traffic controllers at Canadian airports were working under conditions of inadequate salary, with antiquated and unreliable equipment which endangered air passengers. In factual articles and hard-hitting editorials, the magazine warned that a crisis was coming.

At least partly in response to this editorial campaign, a federal inquiry was ordered and the editor of *Canadian Aviation* appeared as a witness with recommendations. Some of these recommendations were adopted, others were not. The magazine continued to prod for action, and its predictions of trouble were borne out in 1969 by a strike of air traffic controllers. No other publication has campaigned so consistently and effectively for safety in the air; no other is so well equipped to do so. Dozens of other members of the business press are doing equally strong jobs in their own areas of concern.

The business press, then, knows where it is going and how to get there. Of all the groups who came before us, the business publishers and editors appeared to have the clearest idea of their role and how to perform it; they are not in need of gratuitous advice and our comments will be brief. They have the three chief prerequisites for publishing success: a clearly understood editorial purpose; a defined and homogeneous readership with common interests; the kind of credibility that wins advertising support.

They have their difficulties, of which we will mention four. One is the fact of overflow circulation, which faces Canadian publishers with a situation unparalleled elsewhere in the world. There are 1,912 American business publications circulating in Canada, and 258 of them have circulations above 10,000. Given the undoubted American leadership in resources, research, and technical sophistication, these are excellent publications and their Canadian counterparts must be of high quality to compete for attention from readers. They can and do compete, because they *are* of high quality and they deal specifically with Canadian conditions as the American magazines do not. But they are hurt in their advertising revenue because many of the potential advertisers in Canada are American companies with Canadian subsidiaries, using the same brand names in both countries, and some of these companies consider that the advertising carried in overflow circulation will do their advertising job in Canada.

Canadian publishers did not complain to us about this situation, which they accept as an inescapable condition of existence in North America. Since 1964, when the Canadian government acted on the advice of the O'Leary Commission, the customs tariff has been used to exclude American publications carrying advertisements directed specifically at Canadians. This averted the most serious threat to the survival of the Canadian industry, which feels it can live with the conditions now existing. We mention it chiefly to explain why the Committee is not exercised about the concentration of ownership in Canadian business publishing.

Most of our important business publications are in the hands of three or four large firms, notably Maclean-Hunter (with sixty-eight) and Southam Business Publications (with seventy-two).[4] We do not see how it could be otherwise. These magazines by their nature have limited circulations and limited advertising revenue; while they are mainly profitable, individual profits are small and it is only in combination that they can afford the research, the graphics, the physical plant, and the staff to make a showing against the glossy American publications.

A second and much publicized problem is the recent imposition of increases in second-class mail rates. The matter is dealt with elsewhere in this report and we will not discuss it here, except to say that we find little solid evidence of any wholesale slaughter attributable to the increases. They probably contributed to the demise of a small number of publications, but they may also have merely hastened the onset of a fate which was inevitable for other reasons. The industry now seems to have adjusted to the new rates. We do not propose that they should be rolled back, but there are some inequities in the present structure which we believe should be removed.

A more serious obstacle to the prosperity of the business press, we suggest, is the aloof stance of the advertising agencies. Advertisers seem to like these publications, which beam directly and economically at a specific market; the agencies don't, and the reason is not far to seek. A full-page advertisement in an industrial magazine may cost $400; in a consumer magazine, perhaps $4,000. It costs the agency as much to prepare and service one advertisement as the other – but the commission in one case is $60, in the other it is $600. The business publications have a strong sales story, but it isn't being heard. Our recommendation to advertisers is that they press their agencies to listen.

Finally, we refer to a problem that is still only incipient but deserves attention before it becomes an entrenched reality. It was brought to our attention by W. B. Glassford, president of the Business Press Editors Association, and we can do no better than quote from his summary:

> Technological developments in the photocopying field and in the development of computer-based information retrieval systems pose major challenges to the business technical press of Canada. In effect, these developments threaten to eliminate the copyright protection needed to ensure that the business press can continue to provide its readers with the information they need, and threaten to deprive the author and publisher of the benefits from their efforts.
>
> Relatively few editors would object to a reader making a photocopy of an article for his own use. But the development of centralized computer-based information retrieval systems adds another dimension to this problem. Such systems (both privately- and government-owned) are, in

---

[4] This figure includes the fourteen publications acquired in August, 1970, by the purchase of National Business Publications Limited.

> effect, providing a commercial information service, using material published in the business press, and supplying this material (without payment to the original author or publisher) to a customer of the system. In effect, this wipes out the value of copyright, and deprives the author of the benefits of his efforts.
>
> This loss of copyright is serious enough, but this type of computer-based system is now going one step further and reassembling information collected from sources such as business publications and issuing them in collected form. These collections are then sold to the subscribers to the service – but the original authors and publishers do not receive payment for this material.

Mr. Glassford pointed out that the machinery for carrying out this piracy already exists in Canada, and that the federal government is one offender. The National Science Library, operated by the National Research Council of Canada, reported that in 1968 it filled 163,000 loan and photocopy requests. This meant a substantial distribution of copyright material for which the authors and publishers received no compensation.

We mention this trend, which of course has implications for others besides the business press, to suggest that it be considered in the review of copyright law which is now under way.

It will be apparent that we admire the performance of the business press, which despite its invisibility is doing an honest, tough, and essential job in the Canadian workaday world. As an incidental by-product, it is doing another job which goes largely unrecognized. We subscribe to the words of James A. Daly, vice-chairman of the board of Southam Business Publications Limited:

> The encouragement of existing business magazines in Canada and the opportunity to create new ones, provide a unique contribution to Canadian unity. There is no other way in which the architect in Vancouver can see what his colleague in Quebec City has done; there is no other way in which the hospital administrator in Regina can learn of a new volume feeding process to improve hospital meals that has been developed in Kingston; there is no other way in which the contractor in the Yukon can learn of a new method of winter concrete pouring in Northern Quebec, and the list of such contributions to Canadian unity and the economy could be endless. Developments that are uniquely Canadian or of interest to Canadian industry and professions are not reported at length in the U.S. magazines.

Our recommendation to the business press: keep doing what you're doing – and give a copy of this to the space cadet.

5. Not for the Family

"We were trying to straddle two sharply divided worlds and we fell in the abyss between."

That's how Peter Hendry, its former editor, explains the death in 1968 of the *Family Herald*. It was a collapse as shocking in its own sphere as the death of the *Saturday Evening Post* a year later. The *Family Herald* too was an institution, the staple family reading of generations of rural Canadians. Even at the end, it had a loyal and nation-wide circulation of more than 400,000. But it died.

Why? The reasons were accurately forecast in the O'Leary Commission report of 1961. Discussing the state of farm publications, it said:

> Their very *raisons d'être* are threatened by the decline in rural population and the urbanization of those who remain – due largely to the impact of TV, radio and other media..... A result of this is the decline in the importance of the farm paper as a vehicle of communication between the advertiser and the farm household, as distinct from that between the advertiser and the farm operator...
>
> In the ten-year period, 1950 to 1959, farm papers' share of print media advertising revenues declined from 4.2 per cent to 2.4 per cent.... The ultimate result of this trend will be a retreat by the farm paper to a less ambitious role as "the farmer's business paper." This may involve the disappearance of some publications... and a severe reduction in the circulation of others.

That's what has happened, and is happening. Since 1959 the farm press's share of advertising dollars spent in all mass media has continued its year-by-year decline, from 1.3 per cent to 0.6 per cent in 1968. And it is noteworthy that the publications in deepest trouble are those which try to serve the needs of the farm *family* rather than the farmer-businessman.

When the *Free Press Weekly* (Canada's biggest rural publication, which took over the *Family Herald* circulation list) asked its farm readers how many owned television sets, ninety per cent said yes. Ninety-three per cent of *La Ferme's* readers have television in their homes. These people no longer rely on the farm magazine to give them entertainment, national and world news, children's features, and home-help hints.

But the specialized farmer who raises cattle or hogs or sugar beets or wheat still wants, needs, and uses the publications that tell him how to produce more at less cost. Three years ago the Ontario Federation of Agriculture asked 3,000 Ontario farmers what was their chief source of practical new ideas and what was their chief source of additional information. To both questions, the farm press led all the rest. Bryan Lyster, preparing a thesis for a degree at Carleton University, surveyed Saskatchewan grain farmers in 1969 and got a similar response.

The strongest farm publications are those, such as the *Holstein-Friesian Journal*, which zero in on a specialty. It is significant too that two of the most popular are distributed by agricultural-implement firms and concentrate on technical information. Recently the federal Department of Agriculture has been making headway with a bulletin called CANADEX, which goes to agricultural extension experts as a way of getting technical information to the industry. There has been some discussion of selling CANADEX to farmers on a subscription basis, probably with regional and specialized editions. This possibility is viewed with some concern; its development would tend to concentrate in a few official hands much of the power to influence agricultural decisions. It seems to us that if farm groups will support their own publications as sources of technical information, they will have more control over the type of information they receive and more influence over the direction of agricultural research.

There are some fifty-five farm publications in Canada now, some in financial distress, some relatively thriving. There is a healthy future, it appears to us, for those which recognize that the farm press is a legitimate branch of the business press.

6. A Job for Journalists

It is a mistake to generalize about the church press; the term embraces too wide a variety of church-sponsored publications ranging from national and regional magazines of high quality and considerable economic stability, to parochial papers dealing with news at the parish-pump level and supported by local gifts. The Committee is concerned with the former – a small group of magazines and newspapers, not more than a score in number, which reach about three million Canadians and can properly be called mass media.

About these, indeed, some generalizations are possible. One is that they share the economic difficulties which affect other branches of the printed press, and in most cases suffer those difficulties in an intensified form.

Another is that their form and content have changed dramatically within the present generation. The message is basically the same, but the church press has become less institutional, more socially oriented. In the words of their joint brief to the Committee: "We see our role as educational, with the hope of humanizing our society rather than acting as the 'house organ' for denominationalism." Or as one church editor put it, the business of the church and of its press is "anything which comes between a man and his God." It is an elastic concept, and the best church editors stretch it to the limit.

They also often stretch their interpretation of their mandates from the churches' governing bodies. A. C. Forrest, of the *United Church Observer,* makes it clear that his paper is not the "official voice" of the United Church of Canada. It is published by authority of the Church's General Council and he is responsible to the Council; but the paper's policies and the opinions it expresses are those of the editor himself. On occasion, the paper finds itself in the role of loyal opposition. This is one of the reasons why it insists on being self-supporting, and refuses to be subsidized from the givings of the faithful who may on occasion deplore its policies.

It is not at all easy for a church publication to be self-supporting; as an economic enterprise, it labours against difficulties which do not affect the secular press. For one thing, religious publications like most others depend in part on revenue from advertising – but advertisers do not measure religious publications by the same demographic and circulation criteria which they apply to others. Church papers are not a natural medium for selling luxury goods; no one looks in the *Presbyterian Record* for limousines, liquor, or cosmetics. Church members travel as much as other Canadians, but church papers do not get travel ads. And advertisers, regardless of the readership figures, tend to look on money spent in church papers as an act of charity. They tell the publishers: "If we advertise with you, we will have to do the same for the other church papers." This is not a yardstick they apply to the lay press.

In circulation, the church press has benefitted from the congregational group-subscription system, but this system has its weaknesses too. It limits the potential market to those already within the church. And church magazines cannot get newsstand exposure. When the *Observer,* an authentic "consumer" magazine and a member of the powerful Magazine Advertising Bureau, attempted to arrange for newsstand distribution, it was turned down by the distributing agency's American head office.

The heaviest recent economic blow to the church press came with the increase in postal rates by the Canadian Post Office. The religious press is distributed entirely by mail. Mailing costs rose by as much as 400 to 500 per cent. Some publications reduced their page size, others cut the number of pages, some reduced the number of issues per year. Most of them suffered a decline in editorial quality.

The whole question of postal rates is discussed elsewhere in this report. We do not advocate a return to the position of special privilege the church press previously enjoyed because of its religious content. We do recommend that there should be no further increase in rates, and we advocate removal of the present minimum charge of two cents per piece, which would materially assist some of the publications which are in serious trouble.

But in essence, we conclude that the church press probably cannot hope ever to be economically self-sufficient. It will have to continue to be subsidized by the donations of church members who see it as a necessary instrument of the church's mission – just as they subsidize a sanctuary for the benefit of those who turn up at only at Christmas and Easter.

For as we see it, the troubles of the church press are in large part the troubles of the church itself: a declining and aging membership, a growing popular distrust of all institutions, a view of the church as an exclusively middle-class movement. In a time when church membership was taken for granted and church attendance was automatic, denominational publications were a sort of fringe benefit. They were afflicted neither by self-doubts nor by worries over survival. As editorial productions, they were often not very good.

They are much better today – as they must be to compete with the multiplying demands for audience attention provided by the lay press, by television and all the other forms of mass communication. The *Observer* is among the best church papers published anywhere. The *Canadian Register,* the *Western Catholic Reporter,* the *Canadian Churchman* are vigorous, provocative, alert to social change, and not narrowly doctrinal.

The church editors believe that people are searching with increasing intensity for meaning to their lives but are seeking it outside the forms of institutional religion. The church press is therefore directing itself outward rather than inward. The submission of the Canadian Church Press phrased it this way:

> Modern man desires belief, but not in a religion that cloaks itself in the spirituality of another age. In keeping with this new mood, we in the Canadian Church Press do not let theological differences obstruct the unity that already exists among us in our efforts to increase the Church's relevance in social and moral issues.

Or as Douglas Roche, editor of the *Western Catholic Reporter,* put it:

> There are two great movements taking place. The first is the movement of the Christian community and the second is the outward commitment and adherence to the social gospel, the application of it in such specific areas as housing, drugs, pollution, Biafra, Indians and so on.

The church editors believe also that the need for a religious press is greater now, in a world of rapidly changing values, than it was in a former age of stability and security. They have scant admiration for the lay press which in their view deals with basic religious issues in superficial terms. Dr. Forrest told an interviewer that if the newspapers covered religion as effectively as they cover sports, "they'd run us out of business. And I'd like to see that happen."

We accept the thesis that the church press is engaged in a job that needs doing. Our study persuades us that those which are most effective are doing it on the principles outlined above. The weakest seem to be those whose own constituents have not fully accepted these principles and still prefer to be served by "house organs of denominationalism." It is for the churches themselves to decide whether they are serious about supporting a press devoted to outreach.

If they are, the one thing we would urge upon them is to provide for more journalistic professionalism. Church papers are invariably understaffed, by people who are grossly underpaid. With one or two notable exceptions, they are visually and editorially inferior to the secular press with which they compete for attention. The exceptions are those which have employed a professional designer and persuaded at least one competent journalist to work for them at a sacrifice.

Throughout North America, the religious press is losing readers. The reason seems to be not that it is dealing with the wrong subjects, but that it is not presenting them in a sufficiently challenging way. Church members will no longer support an inferior publication merely as a part of their religious duty. Our recommendation to the church authorities is that they give practical recognition to the job of religious journalism by turning it over to some able and lively journalists.

7. The Most Mixed Medium

More than three million newcomers have arrived in Canada since the end of World War Two. Their plight was described in the brief submitted to the Committee by *Corriere Canadese,* Toronto's Italian-language daily:

> Most new arrivals are fluent in only the language of their country of origin. They arrive in Canada poorly equipped to take an equal place in our society. Their knowledge of this country is rudimentary. Our way of life is foreign to them, our culture strange. They have made the journey in just a few short hours but the transition will take many years. In some instances it will take a generation.

Clearly these people need help; and luckily they're getting it from Canada's big, disjointed, enthusiastic, loosely organized, well-intentioned ethnic press community. Such leadership in introducing newcomers to Canada is one of the basic functions of the ethnic press. The newcomers buttress an older, established, "new" Canadian community and together with it comprise virtually one third of all Canadians. In other words, one Canadian in three is of neither French nor English origin. More than 100 publications of every shape, size, description, and quality purport to serve this huge polyglot community. They do so with varying degrees of effectiveness. Indeed, with a more unified and united voice the ethnic press might better assist its constituency in developing a voice in the community which more closely approximates its numerical strength.

Ethnic editors conceive their first purpose (although they usually list it farther down their scale of priorities) to be the preservation of the cultural and linguistic heritage of the old land. Paradoxically their parallel purpose is to facilitate the integration of the newcomer into the Canadian mainstream. These may seem contradictory objectives, and it might appear that a highly successful program of integration could reduce the reader's interest in an ethnic publication. But Canadians are fond of talking about a cultural mosaic in which all of us lead fuller, happier lives, at least partially because so many cultures are allowed to survive. The melting-pot, on the other hand, is a peculiarly American institution which seeks to assimilate newcomers. In Canada, the challenge is far more difficult: to facilitate each group's cultural survival without perpetuating ancient political and religious schisms. Unhappily, for a dwindling minority of ethnic editors that is precisely the name of the game.

Each succeeding generation of new arrivals in Canada quickly comes under enormous pressure to integrate. The process is hastened by education, money, the mass media generally, and most especially television. Thus the real challenge for ethnic editors is to evolve "unhyphenated" Canadians who will none the less strive to protect, preserve, and develop their cultural heritage. This can be accomplished only with an ethnic press which strives to relate to and involve its younger readers. This in turn can only happen if the ethnic press becomes more certain of its survival. There are enormous problems, many of which must be solved within the ethnic press itself.

How many people read ethnic publications? Who knows? The brief submitted by the Canada Ethnic Press Federation claimed 2,000,000 readers; but that same morning the Committee received a brief from *Canadian Scene,* a news and feature service for foreign-language media, which spoke of 3,000,000 readers.

What's a million? And who cares? National advertisers, that's who. The August 1969 issue of the Canadian advertising trade paper *Stimulus* said:

> Even a superficial glance at a foreign language Canadian newspaper shows a lack of the more obvious consumer ads. *The proportion of such advertising has no true relation to the very real buying power among foreign language Canadians.*
> Many potential advertisers would like to go after this buying power – and incidentally, to help the ethnic newspapers remain in business. Yet they feel they cannot afford the gamble. *Until the ethnic publications are able to provide meaningful facts about their readership, the dilemna is likely to remain.*

The bulk of advertising in the ethnic press is overwhelmingly local. Only seven papers subscribe to the Audit Bureau of Circulations. The standing offer of free translation simply isn't enough to lure any but a handful of national advertisers – notably banks and breweries – out of their conventional purchasing patterns. Ethnic press leaders like Charles Dojack, the immediate past president of the Canada Ethnic Press Federation, tend to blame the advertising agencies rather than the advertisers. He told the Committee:

> Many of the agencies find it expedient to use the English press rather than the ethnic press. Their rates are higher. The amount of commission is a little more remunerative. There is less production cost; no translation. They know what they are publishing. We often wonder whether it's right or not, but I think they kind of take the easy road out.

There is one national advertiser which does incur the direct wrath of the ethnic press. That advertiser is the Government of Canada. For years now, ethnic editors have trooped to Ottawa in an attempt to unloose a greater flow of government advertising. In March, 1969, such a delegation met Prime Minister Trudeau and came away with the understanding that they could expect an increase in ethnic press advertising which would bring the total amount in the next fiscal year up to about $120,000. The Prime Minister's good intentions notwithstanding, the ethnic editors told the Committee they received "around $64,000." Understandably there was considerable disappointment and no little chagrin. It is perhaps not unnatural that such chagrin tended to manifest itself in the belief that the Government of Canada was under some "obligation" to advertise in the ethnic press.

Clearly, the government does have some considerable obligation to meet the information needs of newcomers. The Canada Ethnic Press Federation brief concluded with a quotation from the report of the Task Force on Government Information:

> Steps should be taken to ensure that Canadian citizens and newly arrived immigrants who have an insufficient understanding of either of the two official languages receive adequate Federal Government information of special interest to them in their own language either directly from the responsible agencies or indirectly through the most appropriate existing media.

We agree.

However, the Committee rejects out of hand the notion that government advertising should be used as an indirect method of subsidizing the ethnic press. Even the Government of Canada resides in a real world in which its various advertising agencies must make their media decisions on the basis of efficiency. This is one more reason why the ethnic press must develop a more effective means of telling its advertising sales story.

Quite aside from improved government information, we think some way should be found in which the government could assist ethnic newspapers. Perhaps before we suggest one method it might be useful to underline the nature of the problem.

With a few notable exceptions, most ethnic publications have a hand-to-mouth existence. Soaring costs, increased postal rates, and lack of advertising revenue frequently mean that publications remain in business only through the support of some organization or the donations of affluent friends. Many papers are turned out on antiquated equipment with little or no research by one man who does everything. Where staffing is financially possible the editor has enormous recruitment problems, made even more difficult by the obvious requirement for bilingualism – English or French, along with the mother tongue. Most ethnic publishers are preoccupied with the marginal nature of their enterprise. No wonder so many newspapers find it difficult to change their approach from immigrant-oriented to citizen-oriented; to replace sentiment with logic. Perhaps such bare-bones resources explain why there is so little apparent concern about editorial quality in the ethnic press.

One of the more compelling presentations the Committee received was from *Canadian Scene*, a non-profit, volunteer organization which was founded in 1950 by two Toronto women seeking to provide newcomers with information about their new country. One year later it became incorporated under the Companies Act of Canada. *Canadian Scene* distributes material about Canadian affairs to foreign-language publications. It has no formal connection with any government or any political or religious group. Indeed, the fact that the organization began with the financial assistance of five major Canadians corporations led the Committee to speculate whether it could be accused of having a big-business bias; but the president, Mrs. Barbara Osler, pointed out that *Canadian Scene* also receives support from the Canadian Labour Congress and distributes, as part of its service, articles dealing directly with labour and labour problems. There is "close co-operation" between *Canadian Scene* annd the Canada Ethnic Press Federation. Indeed, *Canadian Scene*'s services would appear indispensable to the continuing existence of many ethnic publications.

Its releases are produced every second week in the form of an eight-page issue of 4,000 words. Two pages of cutlines for the monthly pictorial service are also prepared. The texts are written in English, translated into fourteen languages, and mimeographed. They are then distributed to the publications free of charge. This service has expanded rapidly from 1951 when it served thirty-one publications until 1969 when it was serving 103 publications. Current costs average about $28,000 annually. Since 1963, *Canadian Scene* has operated at a deficit, its continued operation made possible because of a surplus from earlier years. It is the opinion of the Committee that the government should not only meet this annual deficit but make the kind of grant which would allow *Canadian Scene* to expand and improve its operation.

One of the reasons the ethnic printed word is of such vital consequence is the rather limited access new Canadians have to the electronic media. During the period from September 29 to October 5, 1969, forty-six radio stations in seven provinces carried 117 broadcasts in languages other than English and French. New Brunswick, Newfoundland, and Nova Scotia had no ethnic broadcasts.

The content of this programming covers a wide general range of language, news, and music which tends to be overwhelmed by the comercial nature of the broadcasts. The service element is present but more often than not ethnic broadcasts are brokeraged by the stations concerned to ethnic entrepreneurs. The resultant programming leaves much to be desired. Two radio stations in Canada, CFMB in Montreal and CHIN in Toronto, are licensed to broadcast up to 40 per cent of their total programming in languages other than English or French to cater to the substantial ethnic audience within their coverage areas. *Canadian Scene* provides material to 27 radio stations. Half of this number, plus the CBC International Service, broadcast the translated material.

Ethnic programming on television is almost non-existent although there are occasional Italian presentations on CFCF-TV in Montreal and CHCH-TV in Hamilton. However, it is our view that cablecasting in various languages will fill the vacuum. This is supported by the Committee's research into this area. For example, Ottawa Cablevision Limited and National Cablevision Limited in Montreal invited local Italian communities to prepare programming, and Maclean-Hunter Cable TV Limited informed us that weekly half-hour programmes are carried in Italian, Dutch, and German languages for those groups in Guelph, Ontario. But until cablecasting is more widespread, the Committee believes that the CBC should consider some degree of ethnic programming on radio. We quote from the Royal Commission on Bilingualism and Biculturalism: "We recommend that the CBC recognize the place of languages other than English and French in Canadian life and that the CBC remove its proscription on the use of other languages in broadcasting."[5]

Toronto's 280,000 "Italians," for example, represent more Canadians than live in the cities of Regina and Saskatoon combined. As mentioned, this big community has already spawned Toronto's fourth daily newspaper; and in both its progressive approach to marketing and its lively approach to young people, *Corriere Canadese* may well point the future direction of ethnic publishing.

Canada's ethnic press has a vital role to play in helping to integrate newcomers into the mainstream of Canadian life; but integration is not assimilation. The ethnic press is also needed to preserve and develop an abundance of cultural heritages which enrich us all. It is a significant by-product that in so doing, it provides two thirds of all Canadians with their best insight into how the other third fit into the Canadian mosaic. This will greatly assist to dispel feelings of discrimination and achieve the co-ordination of citizens of all origins in the building of a better Canada.

---

[5] Royal Commission on Bilingualism and Biculturalism, Book IV, The Cultural Contribution of the Other Ethnic Groups, p. 191.

8. The Hotbed Press

The Committee devoted part of its research effort and a full day of its hearings to the student press in Canada. We find it reassuring to report that although the rhetoric surrounding this subject has changed in the past few decades, nothing else has. Canada's best student newspapers are still unprofessional, shrill, scurrilous, radical, tasteless, inaccurate, obscene, and wildly unrepresentative of their campus audience. They always have been. In 1926, A. J. M. Smith wrote a quatrain that is still quoted:

> "Why is The McGill Daily?"
> Asked the pessimist sourly.
> "Thank God," said the optimist gaily,
> "That it isn't hourly!"

The McGill Daily is no better loved now than it was then. Canada's student newspapers continue to be the most deplorable, and the most widely deplored segment of the country's press. Even some staffers on university newspapers are alarmed at the prevailing fashion among student editors to ram SDS ideology down their audience's throats. David Chenoweth, managing editor of *The McGill Daily* at the time of our hearings, told the Committee that members of the student press

> have too often ignored the interests of the general campus audience for the sake of propagandizing along very narrow lines.... The student press has become increasingly ineffective, for it has increasingly alienated its own audience....
> For while the student press has the fewest "external" controls of all the media operating within Canada today, it has internally enslaved itself through politics, immaturity, and an understandable lack of expertise.

Right on, Mr. Chenoweth. But the Committee, which is rich in years and wisdom, cannot recall a time when this was not the case.

As a communications medium, the student press has always been ineffective. But as a training-ground for journalists – Peter Gzowski, Pierre

Berton, Stephen Leacock, Ross Munro, John Dauphinee – it has been unexcelled. Newspapers such as *The Varsity, The McGill Daily* and *The Ubyssey* have a long tradition of editorial freedom, and an equally long tradition of abusing it. It is no coincidence that the student newspapers that publish under the fewest restraints from student councils or university administrations have produced an astonishing number of excellent journalists. These newspapers, as Mr. Chenoweth reminded us, operate with fewer pressures than does any other segment of the media. They are subsidized by their student councils, and thus see no need to "pander to the masses" – that is, give their audience what it wants to read. As a result, a student who has gained control of his university's newspaper may never again find himself in a position of such naked, unrestrained power. Later in his career he may have to worry about audiences and advertisers, payrolls and publishers. But for one sweet season he can print *exactly what he wants,* restrained only by the laws of libel and contempt (which are seldom applied), and the apathy and chronic unreliability of his staff.

This system often results in perfectly dreadful newspapers. But it also subjects its participants to several years of marvellous journalistic training. They mature in an atmosphere of endless controversy and sometimes learn more about the process of social change than they would in six years of postgraduate political science. A lot of concerned Canadians, from Wayne and Shuster to Patrick MacFadden, have gone through this mill. We doubt that the experience caused permanent harm to them or their audiences. In some cultures, it is widely believed that if a man spends a lot of time in bagnios while young, he will be more sensible about sex in his later years. The Committee does not give blanket endorsement to this principle, but we think it has a certain amount of relevance as far as journalistic training is concerned.

And so we have no intention of Viewing the student press With Alarm. Instead, we offer a few observations on current fashions in campus journalism:

*As usual, campus newsrooms are hotbeds of radicalism. But where, in previous generations, this fervour was directed mainly at events within the university community, it is now directed to "outside" events as well. There also seems to be an attempt to present "inside" and "outside" events as part of the same Big Picture – and in years to come this tendency could exercise a salutary influence on professional journalism. George Russell, bureau chief for Canadian University Press in Ottawa, tried to explain it this way:

> We talk about pollution of various kinds rather than the fact that the basis of pollution is a specific relation between man and his environment which is conditioned by specific social relations particular to specific forms of society, such as capitalist society.... We talk about the problems of group ownership of portions of the media rather than the fact that sociologically there is a hegemonic control as a means of mental production in communications by society, by class.

> We see the violence in the streets of Quebec rather than attempting to transmit the interconnection to the psychopathology of oppression which triggers that violence.... All this proceeds from the fundamental assumption that there is no interconductivity of events.

Translation: conventional newspapers present events as isolated happenings, instead of as individual manifestations of an overall condition. Applied rigorously, this is the Soviet view of journalism – that all observed experience must be interpreted in the light of Marxist-Leninist theory. This shouldn't invalidate the technique: as Mr. Russell pointed out, there *is* a connection between two such apparently isolated events as the sinking of the oil tanker *Arrow* and the spendthrift lifestyle of Jackie and Ari Onassis. One of the companies in which Mr. Onassis has interests owned the *Arrow* – although most news accounts described the vessel as simply of Liberian registry – and his extravagance is in part financed by the kind of economy that allowed the *Arrow* to go to sea with almost none of its navigational equipment in serviceable condition. If it violates our prevailing canons of "objectivity" to point out that connection, then there is something wrong with our journalistic assumptions. In a number of Canadian city-rooms, young reporters who are alumni of "radical" student newspapers are dismaying their elders by demanding a reassessment of "objectivity." We think the reassessment is long overdue, and we acknowledge the role of the student press in bringing the issue to the fore.

*Student newspapers are becoming a light industry. There are fifty-five of them publishing, they collect about $600,000 annually in advertising revenue, and they have a readership that must be almost as large as the Canadian university population – about 300,000 in 1969-70. Canadian University Press, the Ottawa-based organization that operates a news service for fifty members, has recently attempted to form a national advertising sales bureau. We hope they succeed, because the more advertising student newspapers attract, the less dependent they are likely to be on student councils and university administrations.

*The University of British Columbia, York University, University of Waterloo, and McGill publish administration-sponsored newspapers. This appears to be due to the administration view that the student newspapers on these campuses are doing a rotten job of informing their audiences. Some of these publications are excellent, and more are likely to appear in future. Again we approve. Competition never hurt anybody, even on campus.

9. Down but not Out

> The extraordinary thing about this new consciousness is that it has emerged from the machine-made environment of the corporate state, like flowers pushing up through a concrete pavement. For those who were almost convinced that it was necessary to accept ugliness and evil, that it was necessary to be a miser of dreams, it is an invitation to cry or to laugh. For those who thought the world was irretrievably encased in metal and plastic and sterile stone, it seems a veritable greening of America.
> —Charles A. Reich[6]

We sometimes feel that way when we contemplate those house-organs of the New Consciousness, the underground press in Canada. Set against the ocean of official statements, ponderous editorials, reports on zoning by-law debates, and other turgidities that make up so much of the content of conventional journalism, the underground papers sometimes provide a delightful contrast; and beautiful, alive, funny, green, and free.

It shouldn't be necessary to elaborate what the underground press stands for. Weekly newspapers like *Logos* in Montreal, *Georgia Straight* in Vancouver, *Harbinger* in Toronto and *Octopus* in Ottawa are for: love, peace, bicycles, dogs, macrobiotic diets, communal living, grass (for lolling upon or for smoking), nude-ins, sit-ins, lie-ins, love-ins, power to the people, Huey P. Newton, nearly all rock music, and Leonard Cohen. They are against: policemen, armies, authoritarianism, pavement, pulp companies, parents, pollution, the Mayor of Vancouver, Lawrence Welk, hypocrisy, drudgery, cars, Mace, depilatory creams, and everything made out of plastic except Frisbees.

We wish all the underground newspapers were as good as the *Georgia Straight* often is. We wish they would do more digging into Canadian issues from the vantage-point of their own lifestyle, and less automatic reprinting

---

[6] Reich, Charles A., *Reflections: The Greening of America,* The New Yorker, September 26, 1970, p. 111.

of the latest manifesto from Chicago or San Francisco. We wish they wouldn't call policemen "pigs" quite so much. Sometimes we even wish they weren't quite so dirty.

But mostly we wish them well. We've already described in another chapter how underground newspapers have been harassed in several Canadian cities. We hope their editors will see this persecution for what it is: a kind of accolade. Most of the freedoms the press now enjoys were won by editors and journalists who were not out to win popularity contests. Joseph Howe, Etienne Parent, Louis Joseph Papineau and George Brown were some of the great men of Canadian journalism. In their day they were despised and deplored by some of the Very Best People. We think some of the best underground newspapers have earned the right to be included in this pantheon of the disreputable.

We're also mindful that the underground newspapers can have, and in some cases have had, a beneficial influence on their established counterparts. They are continually challenging the commercial newspapers' versions of local events, covering scenes that the commercial newspapers don't bother to cover, and occasionally breaking stories that the larger newspapers wish they'd had first. They can also have a more subtle influence, by demonstrating new directions in newspaper layout and in personalized reporting.

Unfortunately, everything we've said so far applies only to the best issues of the best underground newspapers. There is much less to admire in the norm. Underground newspapers are too often guilty of distortion, parochialism, unresearched non-exposés, and dullness – psychedelic versions of the same failings they condemn in the "straight" press. No underground newspaper in Canada is one-tenth as good as *Rolling Stone,* the American rock-music journal.

Crass as it may sound, we suspect that many of these failings can be attributed to a lack of funds. Underground newspapers are heavily dependent on volunteer labour, which is fine only up to a point. You can't put out a newspaper indefinitely on love alone.

This may be interpreted as a subtle attempt at co-option: but it occurs to us that no underground newspaper is likely to become a true "alternative" unless it becomes financially sound. Some editors argue that *any* form of profit-seeking would undermine their newspapers' liberated character.

As *Georgia Straight's* editor Dan McLeod told the Committee: "We are wary of depending on advertising to support the paper, as that could lead to pressure groups or pressure from the advertisers." Some editors, however, don't recoil from the idea of economic viability. *Octopus* co-editor Stephen Harris said: "We do want to get bigger. We want to come out more often and at a more professional level. We are attempting to increase our circulation and our advertising in order to put together a more commercial paper."

It's up to individual editors to decide whether they're capable of living off advertising *and* maintaining the character of their newspapers. But there's another route, too: living off circulation income by charging an unusually high price for the product, and hoping readers will be loyal enough to pay it.

Either route seems chancy under present circumstances. But without some reasonably assured source of income, without some guarantee of a reasonably regular wage for the people who produce them, we can't see how underground newspapers can hope to rise above their present level of jolly amateurism. Our recommendation, then, is: get businesslike, but don't let it show in your pages.

10. Broadcasting

THE BEAST OF BURDEN

Television is the most believed and most important medium for international news, and for Canadian news of national importance. Television commercials are believed by Canadians to be more influential than advertisements in other media. Radio is the most immediate medium, the medium to which Canadians would turn first in an emergency, but it is also a soothing, relaxing background. Television is the medium for the whole family. And television is the most sensational of the media.

These are some of the things turned up in research done for this Committee, research aimed at discovering how Canadians perceive the elements in their lives that perceive them most: the mass media.

Broadcasters who came before the Committee made it clear that they were tired of being publicly scrutinized; that they had been royal-commissioned, special-committeed, and federally regulated to the edge of endurance and perhaps beyond. They were weary of being x-rayed, cross-examined, and prodded in sensitive areas, like charity patients in a teaching hospital populated by singularly tiresome medical students.

This Committee is not a royal commission on broadcasting, or even some adjunct to the Canadian Radio-Television Commission. It is an enquiry into Canada's mass media, and that enquiry would be incomplete if it did not seek to analyze the relationship of broadcasting to the rest of the mass media in this country.

The problems that trouble the mass media generally in this country also afflict broadcasting. The areas of concern – freedom of the press, training of personnel, credibility – are as much areas of concern in broadcasting as they are in other portions of the media spectrum. Some of the concerns, because of the special nature of broadcasting and the special demands made of it, are even more acute in radio and television than they are in newspapers and magazines.

Broadcasting, the most recent arrival on the mass-media scene, is held in many ways to be the most vital and effective form of communication. This is particularly true of television, which many Canadians feel is one of the greatest influences on their lives.

Great faith is put in broadcasting, by its practitioners as well as its audience, and consequently it is, in communications, the Beast of Burden. It must lighten our drab little lives, sell the soaps or instant puddings we manufacture, bring war into our living rooms, present politicians before us with unretouched warts, amuse the baby, enlighten the mother, show us the increasingly insane and violent world around us, and then reassure us that nothing like that could ever happen to us in our wonderful world of frozen dinners, aphrodisiac shampoos, and deodorant soaps.

Indeed, broadcasting is so much a beast of burden that we have saddled it with responsibility for holding the country and our Canadian culture intact. No other communications medium has this charge laid upon it by Act of Parliament: "to safeguard, enrich and strengthen the cultural, political, social and economic fabric of Canada." We rely for this on the same medium that is the principal advertising mainstay of the soap industry.

We rely on it, and we expect broadcasters to shoulder the burden cheerfully. After all, the other shoulder is often employed in carrying quite heavy bags of money to the bank.

Cultural survival is perhaps the most critical problem our generation of Canadians will have to face, and it may be that it can be achieved only by using all the means at our command. It appears that it may have to be achieved in spite of frequent insistence that broadcasting is an industry and not a service, in spite of the belief that whoever produces Canadian television programmes, it should not be the private Canadian broadcaster.

Broadcasting began in this country more than fifty years ago. It began as private radio in Montreal, with the station that is now CFCF. It spread across the country, it grew into networks through the energy of the railways. And it was seen from the start as a powerful instrument for national unity, potentially a more binding force even than the railways.

There was, initially, a belief that all Canadian broadcasting should be nationalized, that the country should be blanketed with a series of powerful radio transmitters, and that where private stations existed they should be bought, and closed down. A start on this was even made.

But the economic circumstances of the 1930s and the determined resistance of private broadcasters put an end to this policy. Private and public broadcasting began to grow side by side, and a concept grew up which still persists: local service by a relatively large number of stations, rather than a few powerful nationally owned transmitters. That concept is now one of the cornerstones of Canadian broadcasting.

In the Canadian Broadcasting Corporation, from the late 1930s onward, Canada saw the development of a broadcasting agency unique in the world – publicly owned, broadcasting domestically in two languages, using the facilities of private broadcasters to transmit programmes beyond the ability of a small local broadcaster to produce. The CBC is still unique, although its founders had something very different in mind from what exists today.

In 1968, Canada had a new Broadcasting Act, which for the first time articulated clearly what Canadians had, over the decades, come to agree on: that broadcasters used public property in transmitting their signals through the air, and that Canadians had a right to expect that broadcasters would use that public property to strengthen our culture, rather than dilute it.

This Committee supports the Broadcasting Act. It supports the process by which the Canadian Radio-Television Commission has evolved from the regulatory agencies preceding it.

This Committee supports the Canadian broadcasting system, with its public and private elements in unique symbiosis. It knows that the strength of the system is more than equal to the burden.

THE PUBLIC SERVICE

Every consideration of Canadian broadcasting, every analysis of the mass media in this country, must contain a reference to the Canadian Broadcasting Corporation, because it is so great a factor in Canadian communications. And every time the CBC is scrutinized, faults will be noted, because it is a very large and complex organization, and it is not in the nature of such organizations to achieve perfection.

Unfortunately, sniping at the CBC has become a national pastime that ranks with watching National Hockey League games and thinking deeply about the reform of the Senate.

The CBC is a national communications medium in a country that has no national newspaper. It is the only truly national broadcasting enterprise in Canada, offering service to all but a tiny minority of Canadians in both official languages. It has striven to develop Canadian talent, to reveal Canadians to one another, to strengthen the fabric of Canadian society – and for all these things we can only be grateful to the CBC as an entity quite unlike any other in the world. But there are faults, and they have in some cases been noted before, and they have not all been remedied.

Fault-finders contemplating the CBC can usually be divided into professionals and those who still retain amateur status. It seems to be a characteristic of the professional that he considers commercial policy to be the CBC's principal vulnerability, while the amateur tends to feel that the CBC can most easily be faulted on programme policy. This Committee would not consider that it has become a body of professional fault-finders, but nevertheless we shall consider the CBC's commercial policy first.

The view of many private broadcasters (and of some public idealists) is that the CBC should not have a commercial policy at all. It should produce high-quality Canadian programmes, and perhaps be allowed to broadcast them, but the art of accepting money from advertisers should be left to those with a more natural bent for that kind of thing. Since the CBC primarily operates on public money, they say, let it operate entirely on public money, and stop being some kind of hybrid. Their position is that for a public broadcaster to take private money is somehow against nature.

Some 20 per cent of the CBC's operating budget derives from its advertising revenue. It is tempting to feel that if the CBC got out of the commercial business, we would all be better off. Television viewers could then find at least one channel carrying programmes uncluttered by commercials. The cost of maintaining commercial sales and commercial acceptance departments would disappear. Perhaps there would be less tendency to purchase foreign programmes, more opportunity for television producers who wouldn't have to worry about structuring their works for the requisite number of commercial breaks.

There are certainly some attractive aspects to the idea, and the Committee gave the matter intensive thought. But there are other aspects that are not as attractive.

When the government produced the White Paper on broadcasting in 1966, it indicated that the CBC would be financed by five-year grants – an arrangement similar to that enjoyed by the British Broadcasting Corporation. This system has never been introduced, and the CBC still derives an operating grant from Parliament each year.

Not only does this prevent the CBC from doing any effective long-range planning, it throws the public broadcasting organization even more firmly into the arms of the advertiser. The CBC is like a housewife, obliged to pay the costs of running the home but never certain how much her husband will give her out of the pay packet each week. She knows that costs are always going up, but she does not know how or if she will be able to meet them. In such circumstances, she may be obliged to take in washing – to get her hands on revenue that may be small, in terms of her overall household needs, but at least is there, and is something the old man can't get his hands on.

The CBC made it plain in its appearance before this Committee that the year-to-year reliance on Parliament for operating grants leads to difficulties. For one thing, as the CBC points out, it has to repay capital loans from the government out of its operating grant from Parliament – an unusual, possibly unique situation which in the 1970-71 fiscal year will take $14,700,-000 of the CBC's operations budget. The current freeze on the CBC's operating budget therefore means that allocations of funds within that budget must be changed, and the viewer is not necessarily better off for it. Also, the CBC has collective agreements with many trade unions. It has other commitments which extend over several years, and must be met regardless of a frozen budget.

In its appearance before the Committee, the CBC did not indicate where the money would be made up, but clearly the cuts have to be made in areas where exact sums are not committed, and it would be surprising if programming were not one of them; perhaps the major one.

There are other possible consequences. The CBC is required by Canadian Radio-Television Commission regulations to increase its Canadian programming, both over the whole day and during prime time. Canadian programming costs more than procured programming, in much the way that it would cost more to build your own car from the ground up than to purchase one that just rolled off the assembly line.

In its 1970-71 English-network schedule, the CBC has several new Canadian programmes, and it is to be commended for having found the resources, despite a budget freeze, to produce them. Among them are *Luncheon Date, 55 North Maple, Theatre Canada,* the *Mike Neun Show,* and *Zut.*

These programmes, however, are not for the most part in what the CBC refers to somewhat cryptically as its *option* or *available* programming; rather, they are designated as *metronet* programs. Briefly, option programmes are those that the CBC's private affiliates are required to broadcast, and available programmes are those that the affiliates can add to their schedules without paying programme costs. Metronet programmes are for sale, and they are sold through United Program Purchasing, an organization set up to serve the CBC and its private affiliates by obtaining programmes at group rates.

Many of the new programmes that the CBC has designated as metronet programmes are designed to carry commercials. A private broadcaster striving to build up his Canadian content is attracted to them, because of the possibility of deriving some revenue. Since he must increase his own local production if he is to comply with the Canadian Radio-Television Commission's requirements, he has a greater need for revenue.

But when the private broadcaster knows that U.P.P. takes a commission on each sale, though it does not even arrange for distribution (since the private broadcaster simply plugs into the CBC microwave feed for the programme), he tends to feel the price is too high, and he therefore resists buying. Besides, there is a feeling that programming produced with the taxpayers' money should not be disposed of in quite the same way as commercially produced programming.

The end effect is that the CBC and U.P.P. realize some income, that the private broadcaster feels he pays too much (and that, possibly, he should not pay at all), and that even while relations between the CBC and its private affiliates are weakened, the service to audiences of those private affiliates is diminished.

Undoubtedly, one of the sources of pressure upon the CBC comes about because of the Corporation's record in collective bargaining. The CBC seems to have been rather less successful than other employers in resisting wage demands, with the result that it faces an unavoidable and rising bill for labour costs. The relationship between the CBC and the unions with which it has agreements should be carefully examined, we believe, and the collective agreements involved should be compared with agreements between the same organizations and other employers. This would, we believe, give the CBC some indications of where it should resist firmly further wage demands beyond the levels suggested by the federal government.

Again, we urge strongly that the CBC be financed by five-year grants. Its commercial revenue is a needed buffer between it and Parliament, but responsible planning is rendered enormously difficult under the current system of an annual dole.

In considering whether the CBC should stay in the commercial field, the Committee was particularly struck by an argument put forward by the CBC's president, Dr. George F. Davidson, who had himself expressed misgivings about the effects upon programming of relying too heavily on commercial revenue. Dr. Davidson told us:

> I would myself not wish to see the Corporation entirely remove itself from the commercial side of the operation partly because I think it helps to keep us in touch with the real world in a way we might not if we were off on cloud nine programming without any regard whatever to the community and the practical tastes and interests of the community which we are supposed to be serving...

The CBC, he argued, was driven into the commercial field by "the sheer necessity of receiving additional funds to meet the obligations we feel we have to meet." Dr. Davidson said his personal preference would be for a more limited participation in the commercial field, and he made a comment we found most significant: "My personal belief is that we are excessively dependent on commercial advertising now. It is showing signs of affecting the quality and nature of our programming in prime time."

Possibly no more ominous words could be spoken about a public broadcasting agency. They were spoken by its chief, who can hardly have been pleased about having to voice them.

We repeat: the CBC, whatever its faults, performs a unique public service, and has special obligations laid upon it by the Broadcasting Act. It must be financed in such a way that the head of the CBC need never say something like that again.

At the time of the 1966 White Paper on broadcasting, the government instructed the CBC to undertake no increase in commercial programming. Further, it instructed the CBC to seek to maintain its 25 per cent share of Canada's television advertising revenue, and its four per cent share of the country's radio advertising revenue.

The CBC has been unable to maintain these percentages levels, although it has attempted a more vigorous sales policy. Its share of television advertising revenue had slipped to 23.9 per cent by 1968, and its share of radio advertising revenue – 1.8 per cent – was so small that Dr. Davidson admitted he had considered taking CBC radio out of the commercial field entirely.

It is worth noting that the instructions described above were exactly counter to the thinking and recommendations of the CBC management of the day. While the two top officers of the CBC have changed, and while Dr. Davidson told us that he had received extensive co-operation since becoming head of the CBC, it is interesting to speculate whether the government's instructions could be wholeheartedly carried out if substantial numbers of upper and middle management disagreed with them.

We may also note with curiosity that the value of programme time available for advertising but unused for that purpose was $26,935,000 in 1965, but had increased to $31,177,000 by 1969. This, too, may reflect the diligence with which the CBC sought to abide by the government's instructions.

Our impression of the effectiveness of the CBC's commercial sales department is that there is considerable potential for improvement. We also feel that the commercial acceptance department has not succeeded in substantially reducing the offensiveness of commercials, although it appears to have held back the CBC's sales efforts to some extent. However, we were pleased to note that the CBC had managed in 1969-70 to increase its advertising revenue by some 20 per cent while holding the increase in selling expense to some 12 per cent.

Various representations were made to the Committee about the CBC's commercial rates, the private broadcasters generally holding that they were too low, and in effect constituted a subsidy to the advertiser and unfair competition for the private broadcasters. This view, not unnaturally, was denied by Dr. Davidson.

One instance, however, is memorable. The Committee was informed that at a point when the 60-second commercial rate for CFTM was $700, the equivalent rate for CBFT was $350. Both these stations serve the metropolitan Montreal area, with very similar coverage patterns; both broadcast in the French language. While CFTM's audience is very large indeed, it is clearly not so immense as to justify this relative difference between this private station's commercial rate and that of the CBC's French-language owned-and-operated station in Montreal. Serious consideration must be given to the charge, made publicly by CFTM, that something akin to economic warfare may be going on here, a thing quite different from the competition between private and public broadcaster which exists elsewhere in this country.

We note, however, that this gap has been partly closed, at least to the extent that the CBFT/CFTM 60-second commercial ratio is now $425/$750. Neither this, nor the $290/$500 ratio for CBMT/CFCF, seems to us to reflect fairly the CBC's competitive position in Montreal against the private broadcasters. In Toronto, for example, comparative CBLT/CFTO ratio is $475/$550. In Vancouver, CBUT and CHAN are equal, at $300/$300.

Certain measures have been taken by the CBC to increase its level of commercial revenue, including an increase in the number of commercial minutes per hour it is willing to sell, and some slight movement towards selling spot advertising time, rather than what it is pleased to call participating sponsorships.

A sponsor in the classical sense paid all the costs of producing a programme, and then paid a broadcaster for the time it took to have the programme delivered through the airwaves to the public. Where it was a network programme, he also paid the transmission costs. This concept of sponsorship has virtually disappeared in North America, except for National Hockey League game broadcasts in Canada, and certain specials. The CBC does not seek to recover all (or even most of) the programme costs for Canadian programmes. It does specify a charge for connecting its stations for network advertisers.

A participating sponsor is one who, with other advertisers, shares in the available commercial time in the programme. He might as well be buying time by the minute, since this is the way he normally buys time; but the CBC insists on its own terminology. The CBC's reluctance to abandon the sponsorship concept is most difficult to understand, considering that every other major broadcasting system in North America has found it worthwhile to concentrate instead on the sale of spot time.

We feel that the CBC should consider carefully its rate structure with a view to upward adjustment where warranted; that the commercial sales department could be improved, and that the function and philosophy of the commercial acceptance department needs careful examination.

Our consideration of the CBC's commercial activities deals, in Fowler's celebrated phrase, with the housekeeping aspects of the Corporation. We also have some few words to say about the programme aspects. Dr. Davidson summed up one area of concern very nicely:

> I believe Canadians are getting a disproportionately small amount of Canadian programming to balance off against the very rich variety of American programming that is available to them, and I think that this should require the Canadian Broadcasting Corporation to review the extent to which it is carrying American programming in its programme schedules, and this is what we are doing at the present time.

His explanation for the CBC's seeming preoccupation with United States news – indeed, all aspects of life in the United States – was similarly forthright: "When you stand in the shadow of a giant, you become preoccupied with the shadow of the giant, if not with the giant himself, and I have offered the same criticism to the Corporation."

Sadly, it seems inevitable that until advertisers can be convinced that United States programmes are not necessarily always the best buy on Canadian television, Canadian broadcasters will rely on these programmes for an important part of their revenue.

While we reject the Canadian Association of Broadcasters' position that the CBC should get out of broadcasting and instead produce Canadian programmes for free supply to private broadcasters, we feel that the CBC has a special role to play in developing new and better Canadian programmes that can attract and hold large audiences. This is congruent with our view that Canadians do not have true alternative service when what they are offered is the same kind of programming on two different Canadian channels.

Alternative television service in Canada really means alternative *programme* service – something like a genuine choice. It is encouraging that the CBC seems to feel somewhat the same way, even if the *Ed Sullivan Show* is still a fixture in its Sunday-night schedule. When the two English-language Canadian television networks, and what we hope will soon be the two French-language Canadian television networks, can offer equal but complementary service, Canadian television audiences can be said to have genuinely alternative television service.

It should not be construed from this that we feel that Canadian television broadcasters should schedule nothing but Canadian programmes. Our view is that we are 100 per cent behind Canadian content, but that we do not favour 100 per cent *of* Canadian content. We have been pleased by the efforts of Canadian broadcasters to obtain the best in television programming from the rest of the world. We accept the argument of E. S. Hallman, head of the CBC's English service, that television productions from the rest of the world may merit broadcast in Canada, and that the CBC may have to provide for such broadcasting where the programme material is not suitable as an advertising medium – as with Sir Kenneth Clark's series on Civilization.

Mr. Hallman told us: "I think to make us exclusively and narrowly Canadian would really be detrimental to the services we should provide to the Canadian people." And we agree. The CBC should become a great two-way showcase, displaying to Canadians and to the world just how great is the potential of this most involving of media.

If the CBC is to do this, it will have to overcome two difficulties which we simply note briefly here in passing. One is its dollar efficiency in producing programmes; the other is its preoccupation with the major production centres in Toronto and Montreal.

Because so many of the Canadians served by the CBC's French network are in the Montreal area, it is perhaps inevitable that the network's programme should reflect the Montreal scene to a great extent. But there *are* French-speaking Canadians living elsewhere in this country, even though this fact is hardly apparent from French-network programming. We must, however, acknowledge the excellent work of the CBC's French network in developing Canadian programmes that draw very large audiences indeed. The fact that the four most popular television programmes – *Moi et L'Autre, Quelle Famille, Rue des Pignons,* and *Les Belles Histoires* – are all produced by the network is a tribute to the energy and imagination of those involved.

We do not feel that the success of these Canadian programmes is entirely due to their serving a French-speaking population surrounded by Anglophones, a view frequently expressed by private broadcasters. It was interesting that when the Canadian Association of Broadcasters appeared before this Committee, its president, Raymond Crépault, also felt that the ghetto theory for explaining the success of Canadian broadcasting in Quebec was inadequate.

The situation is rather less excusable when it comes to the English network's Toronto orientation, because there are very large English-speaking centres in this country other than Toronto. It is heartening to know that, as a result of the increased emphasis on Canadian programmes, the CBC is turning to some of these other centres for programme ideas and programme production. This process must continue, and production centres must be developed outside Toronto, if the rest of the country is not to be continually drained of its television talent.

For one thing, we must face the reality that if the most talented Canadians are drawn to Toronto, there is also a flow in the other direction; and the misfits and obstructionists of head office are likely to be shipped out to the regional centres – which, being devoid of creative production anyway, are all too likely to be thought of as punishment camps.

We are aware that certain television programmes are produced by the CBC at very low cost. Some benefit by economy, and look pleasantly taut; others just look cheap. When Pierre Berton appeared before this Committee, he made the point that editing videotape is time-consuming and expensive, as well as being often unnecessary if appropriate preparation is done. It is not our intention to instruct broadcasters in the details of their business, but we accept the view of Mr. Berton and others that some economies might well be considered, and that the kind of editing practices he described are harmful to the production, misleading to the viewer, and ultimately expensive to the taxpayer.

Out of an operating budget of approximately $200 million, programme expenses – radio, television, and international service – account for some $108 million, or about 54 per cent. While the overhead costs of operating a 9,000-person organization must necessarily be high, we wonder about the cost efficiency of a broadcasting organization which needs a dollar of input to produce 54 cents worth of programme.

This Committee feels strongly that the CBC can take most pride in its radio service. It has, we know, been called the Ugly Service by cynics within the Corporation who assert that the beautiful people go to television. It has been suggested that AM radio is the orphan of the CBC, and that the FM service is the orphan of the orphan. As we have noted elsewhere, the CBC's radio service is the one broadcasting organization in Canada to which one can tune in and know at once that it is Canadian, and that it is public broadcasting.

There is a tendency in radio today to become community-involved, to narrow the programming focus. We welcome this trend among private broadcasters, as a relief from their years of regarding radio as some species of perpetual Wurlitzer. But we would hesitate to endorse a similar approach on the part of the CBC.

Network radio, as a private concept, is largely dead. Its passing, if the result is community service where little existed before, is not much to be mourned. Public network radio is, we feel, still a vital element of the Canadian broadcasting system, and we urge the CBC not to be hasty to abandon it. The success of the news programmes *The World at Six* and *The World at Eight* are examples of fine network radio service.

We know the audiences are small, the commercial revenue is pitiful. But network radio permits experimentation where network television, because of the higher costs and the higher risks in terms of public reaction, permits far less innovation. Some steps could be taken to remedy the audience situation, and perhaps the revenue situation, as a consequence. It seems incredible that the CBC uses its television service so sparingly to promote its radio service, and that indeed the money available to promote radio through any means is so niggardly.

As we have noted before, the CBC is a national institution in a country that lacks national institutions, a national medium in a country unable to support a truly national press. CBC radio may have been called the Ugly Service; but it has been a needed counterweight to television, which has all too often been the empty-headed service. Considering how much it gives for its relatively small slice of the CBC budget, we feel it should not be tampered with wantonly because of the trend among private broadcasters. The CBC need not play their game.

Dennis Braithwaite, a Toronto journalist who used to strike terror into the hearts of CBC executives in the days when he wrote a television column, once said that he had heard for years of people who planned to reform the CBC into the great institution it could be, and that none of them had ever achieved it. His conclusion, upon reflection, was that the CBC is fundamentally unfixable. Our view is that it needs some work here and there, and these few halting words have been prepared in the hope that the work can be done.

One thing that stays firmly in our minds as a result of our explorations of Canada's mass media is that the CBC is so fundamentally a part of Canada's communications that it could not be removed or substantially weakened without a very wide ring of repercussions through the rest of the media, and through our society.

We are faced with the fact that if the CBC did not exist, we would have to invent it.

THE PRIVATE INDUSTRY

For many years, the Canadian Association of Broadcasters has been the voice of private broadcasting in Canada, and we were particularly interested in what this organization had to contribute to our study of broadcasting and its place in the fabric of Canada's mass media. With reluctance, we were driven to conclude that the private broadcasters, no matter how sophisticated their individual thought, seem by group interaction to achieve a level perhaps best described as neanderthal.

The C.A.B.'s appearance in front of this Committee was a truly remarkable performance. Equally remarkable was the C.A.B.'s action in sending the Committee a telegram reproving us for hearing Nicholas Johnson, Federal Communications Commissioner, a student of broadcasting whose refreshing views have done much to strengthen the concept of broadcasting as something other than a form of strip-mining.

There was a certain irony in being chastised by the C.A.B. for listening to a citizen of the United States, considering the extent to which private broadcasters have procured programming for Canadian stations from the United States, and the frequency with which they have held up the American broadcasting as a model.

We might consider four of the positions taken by the C.A.B. before this Committee.

On the question of concentration of ownership of broadcasting media, we were told by the C.A.B. that this is inevitable, that broadcasting in this country will be in the hands of a dozen or so groups within five years, because of the operational efficiency of this kind of ownership. One is struck in considering this position that it reflects a belief we have encountered before: the belief that operational efficiency must be served at all costs, that the system must be strengthened and perpetuated regardless of human needs or values, that the machine's needs must be satisfied. The idea that the public might not be best served by having all Canadian broadcasting owned by about a dozen groups seems simply to be considered irrelevant. The notion that some regulatory agency might refuse to allow this to happen is apparently held to be no more than proof that regulatory agencies are hopelessly out of touch with reality.

No less remarkable is the C.A.B.'s considered opinion of the Canadian Broadcasting Corporation. In the C.A.B.'s view, the CBC should get out of broadcasting – which it presumably does not understand – and instead become a production agency which would supply the private broadcasters with Canadian programmes, thereby relieving them of the responsibilities of production.

A certain proportion of these Canadian programmes would be carried by the private broadcasters – who, indeed, would be the only broadcasters – as a condition of licence. This basic service apparently would be available to the private broadcasters at no cost, since the question of their somehow paying for this Canadian content is only raised in connection with obtaining *additional* programme material.

This position is held to be the basis of Canada's having both public and private elements in its broadcasting structure, a truly unusual view expressed by the C.A.B.'s president, Raymond Crépault, to the Committee as follows:

> This is why we are one of the very few countries, perhaps the only one maybe, that has this kind of double structure, precisely in order to ensure that our cultural heritage would be safeguarded, maintained and encouraged and developed through public funds.

The notion that a private broadcaster might spend some of his *own* funds for these purposes just doesn't seem to be even thinkable.

Much as the C.A.B. likes this idea that the CBC would cease competing with the private broadcasters and simply donate programmes to them instead, it seems resigned to this not happening, and it has a fall-back position. The position the C.A.B. would accept, albeit under protest as unfair, is that the CBC stop selling commercial time, and therefore stop competing with the private broadcasters for advertising revenue.

The idea that the CBC should get out of commercial activities has some appeal at first glance. We have considered it, and it is discussed at length elsewhere. Suffice it to say that while it would undoubtedly represent an improved financial situation for private broadcasters, it would harm the CBC, and we do not recommend it.

The C.A.B.'s opinion of the Canadian-content regulations governing the broadcasting service is that the levels set are impossible and unobtainable, that they will result in bad programming, and that they are ill thought out, since they are what the C.A.B. calls "tonnage" requirements rather than requirements that high-quality programmes be made.

This Committee accepts the goals of the C.R.T.C. and its regulations. We feel there is simply not a shred of evidence to support the C.A.B.'s protestation that the private broadcasters, if left to their own devices, would produce plenty of high-quality Canadian programmes. Some private broadcasters have produced high-quality Canadian programmes. We feel this country should recognize them for what they are: persons so exceptional in the private broadcasting world as to be virtually of another species.

In private television, we have seen the accomplishments of such stations as CJOH in Ottawa, CFTO in Toronto, CFTM in Montreal, and CFPL in London, Ontario. Private radio has seen CKNW in Vancouver develop a very strong news service, CFRB in Toronto its news and public affairs, CJAD in Montreal its news service, and CFPL its general programming.

But the fact is that the vast majority of private broadcasters have done the minimum required of them by law, and no more. They have been content to let the networks fill the prime-time hours with imported programmes; they have been happy to take whatever the networks would supply free; they have filled the rest of their hours with as much syndicated material as possible, producing themselves as little as possible. They have been content, as one of the exceptions once noted, to "sit at the end of the pipe and suck."

Private broadcasting is, for the most part, quite profitable in this country. Some sections of private broadcasting are immensely profitable. One reason it is so profitable is that broadcasters have been protected by successive regulatory agencies against competition. Mr. Crépault told us of three United

States television stations that went bankrupt in one month, because of the rather different licensing policy of the Federal Communications Commission. He did not tell us of any Canadian television station going bankrupt; the fact is that none ever has.

The C.A.B. was unable to convince this Committee that there is any reason at all why some of the healthy profits of private broadcasting might not be turned into something more than the legal minimum of Canadian programmes.

The C.A.B. was unable to convince this Committee that there is any reason at all why private broadcasting's profits should be made even larger by removing the commercial competition, or the broadcasting competition, of the CBC.

The C.A.B. was unable to convince this Committee of the validity of a fourth position taken by the Association: that private broadcasters have done more for Canadian talent than the CBC. And a comparative glance at the schedules for a private television station and a CBC owned and operated station make it clear that this alleged superior aid to Canadian performers is not reflected in programmes.

Perhaps the C.A.B. feels genuinely that commercials, which earn extra income for performers, represent the finest flowering of the television art – it would be consistent with another of their representations to us. But we don't feel many performers would agree, and we are sure that almost all viewers would disagree.

The matter of commercials was the subject of a curious remark during the C.A.B.'s appearance before this Committee, a remark so odd that it was diligently pursued in the discussion since at first blush it was hard to believe that it was seriously meant. The C.A.B. believes that the more commercials there are in a programme, the more the audience likes it. This is quite distinct from the notion that a station with popular programmes will have many commercials, because it attracts audience and therefore advertisers. The C.A.B. seemed to hold that the presence or absence of commercials has a direct effect on the number of viewers.

W. D. McGregor, who since the C.A.B. appeared before us has become its president, articulated the idea. "When the station quite deliberately removes all commercials from a programme, the audience goes down," he told the Committee. Asked to produce figures to back this up, he answered by making another assertion. "What we have done, and a number of stations have done this and among them my own, is quite deliberately to put additional commercials into a programme – that is a programme that wasn't carrying or didn't have the popularity to attract advertisers, we have put commercials into those programmes in an effort to see what would happen, and the audience went up."

The Committee has research indicating something rather different: that the primary public complaint about television is about the commercials, both their content and their timing. The commercials are seen by the public as irritating interruptions in the programmes, and it is quite difficult to understand why the majority of television viewers would consider them in any other way, when they fall within a programme.

Perhaps the view expressed by Mr. McGregor is, for private broadcasters, an article of faith. Is it a closed equation? If freed of regulation, would they fill an entire programme hour with commercials, and thus achieve the most popular programme of all time? Mercifully, we may never know.

We may reflect, however, that if commercials are not the finest flowering of the television art, they at least represent one kind of pinnacle. They are, for the most part, the ultimate in presenting a totally false picture of reality. We are all familiar with examples: the toothpaste that makes people blow kisses to you; the hair oil that makes the gals pursue you; the tonic that transforms your wife from apathetic drudge to a hot-eyed temptress; the constantly screamed message that if you will only *consume* something, your pimples will vanish, your stomach and head and feet and back will cease to ache, your sexual life would be the envy of Haroun al-Raschid.

All our ills are *not* cured by consuming. Our lives are not, by consuming, transformed into a single uninterrupted flow of bliss. We have had it painfully brought home to us in recent years – and the signs were there long before that – that consumption of some things may be very bad for us; and for all our neighbours and all our descendants. The social consequences of advertising, particularly on radio and television, deserve some thoughtful study, and it may well be that the Canadian Association of Broadcasters would be a logical group to do such a study, or at least to sponsor it.

For we believe that the c.a.b., despite its current state, is potentially a most useful organization – and in ways beyond its function as a lobbyist. There is nothing wrong with the c.a.b.'s acting as a lobbyist, although its spectacular lack of success in this function of late has much to do with the organization's dwindled and depressing condition today.

Its inept attempt to bully the Canadian Radio-Television Commission led directly to the c.a.b.'s losing the membership of two of this country's most powerful and respected broadcasters, and also to its losing the support of a third private broadcaster, who decided to retain membership in the c.a.b. while dissenting from the organization's campaign against the Canadian Radio-Television Commission.

It may be that in making its attack on the regulatory agency, the c.a.b. was reflecting a belief that this Committee certainly noted among small private broadcasters: the notion that every broadcaster's licence is in jeopardy every day from the whims of an all-powerful Canadian Radio-Television Commission. We were told – by the officers of Countryside Holdings Limited, for example, and by others – that no broadcaster would dare criticize publicly the policies or proposed regulations of the c.r.t.c., because of the risk of losing his broadcasting licence. That intelligent men could be under this delusion is proof in itself that the C.A.B. has failed in its duties towards its own membership.

The lot of the small private broadcaster may be a difficult one, as he sees the best of his staff leaving for larger cities, as he realizes that the ability of his station to generate profits cannot possibly match that of the larger stations to which the best talent tends to be drawn.

We have noted, in studying Canada's newspaper world, that <u>the small newspapers do a poorer journalistic job than the large papers</u>. We have also noted that their relative performance is not simply proportionate to size, and that the smaller newspapers do a poorer job than one could expect, even taking their relative smallness into account. In broadcasting, this phenomenon is even more pronounced. <u>The smaller stations offer a much lower level of service than seems reasonable</u>, even granted that they find good staff hard to keep.

We found in our research that while broadcasting in Canada is highly profitable, profitability and size are closely related. It matters little what measure of profit is used: <u>the bigger the station, the higher the rate of profit</u>. In 1968, for example, there were 221 radio stations operating in Canada independently of television stations, and only 22 of these (8.4 per cent) had gross revenues of one million dollars or more. But these same 22 stations accounted for just over 68 per cent of the total net operating revenue for all 221 stations.

In television, the size-profitability relationship is even more striking. In that same year, 1968, there were 29 television stations operating independently of radio stations. Eight of them — 27.6 per cent of the total — had gross revenues of $1.5 million or more, but these eight accounted for 92 per cent of the total net operating revenue of the 29 stations in the group.

One reason why larger stations are more profitable is that they tend to be located in larger communities, where the absolute demand for advertising time is higher than in the smaller centres. Also, the larger audiences enable the big stations to maintain very high advertising rates while simultaneously offering advertisers a relatively low cost-per-thousand; so that an advertising rate that would discourage advertisers from utilizing a small station would not discourage them from buying commercial time from a very large one.

Particularly with television, the demand for advertising time on the very large stations is so strong as to constitute a forceful argument for the legal restriction of the number of advertising minutes a station may schedule in its day. Otherwise, the temptation to satisfy the demand for advertising time might lead to a sharply decreased level of service to the viewer, as programme minutes yielded to advertising minutes.

Legally limiting commercial time, however, leads in turn to an argument for licensing second and third stations, as necessary, in major centres. The consequence of not licensing such second or third stations, while at the same time limiting commercial time, is to encourage the first station to set a very high advertising rate, since he can be certain of selling all his time. The consequent revenue will not necessarily be reflected in the quality of service to the viewer, and the less affluent advertiser will be driven away.

It is noteworthy in all this discussion, however, that profitability in broadcasting is generally higher than profitability in manufacturing, which in turn is higher than the business average.

There is one area in which we feel some financial inequity is being worked upon Canadian broadcasters. It will be recalled that Section 12A of the Income Tax Act provides that Canadian advertisers may not write off as a business expense any money spent on buying space in U.S.-owned publications, a provision designed to give a measure of protection to Canadian magazines faced with the dumping of editorial material in "Canadian editions" of American magazines.

Canadian broadcasters, particularly television broadcasters, are also faced with competition from across the border. In some fairly notorious cases, the competition comes from stations deliberately created to live off Canadian advertising, and not designed to provide any service to the United States communities in which they are nominally licensed. It has been argued, and we believe correctly, that without the existence of KVOS in Bellingham, Washington, Vancouver could support a third television station. The situation with KCND in Pembina, North Dakota (population: 600) which covers the Winnipeg area is less clear; its proprietors profess to be losing money. There is also substantial penetration of the Hamilton-Toronto area by the three commercial Buffalo stations – WGR, WBEN, and WKBW – as well as the situation in Windsor, Ontario, where there are five commercial U.S. television signals available – WJBK, WKBD, WWJ, WXON, and WXYZ – from transmitters directly across the river, in Detroit.

It seems, in any case, that the growth of Canadian television service in areas penetrated by U.S. television signals is likely to be impeded unless Canadian advertisers are given some motivation to keep their money in Canada. Also, it may be noted that certain Canadian laws or regulations – those dealing with food, drugs and alcoholic beverages, for example – may be avoided if advertisements are placed with American rather than Canadian stations, a practice we feel is not in the public interest. We recommend the extension of Section 12A to cover Canadian advertising placed with American broadcasting stations.

We do not consider that, as the head of one group of radio stations told us, owning a radio station is merely a way of getting into the advertising business. We do not consider that television viewers derive pleasure and comfort from knowing that a programme contains commercials. We do believe that private broadcasters and public broadcasters alike have an interest in knowing more about the commercials that help pay for programme service, and that they are entitled to reasonable income tax provisions, and we believe the C.A.B. could be an effective instrument in research and in responsible lobbying.

This will not take place while the C.A.B. has its present constitution and its present structure. The organization needs to be overhauled. It needs to stop thinking of its role as simply that of staving off regulation, and to start developing a positive, creative policy of information and research. It will not be able to do this without the participation of the major broadcasters, because an association of small broadcasters cannot generate the funds or the influence needed.

There can be no doubt of the need for an organization to do some intelligent research in broadcasting, to help the small broadcaster keep abreast of developments, to make the large broadcaster aware of his position in the national broadcasting system. Research aimed at something other than inducing advertisers to buy time might not only yield valuable information, it might persuade broadcasters to start thinking of the audiences they serve as people or communities, rather than as "markets" – the term invariably used by broadcasters appearing before us in describing their operations.

It will be a pity if the C.A.B. declines this opportunity.

AIRING THE NEWS

People are not consistent in their ideas about the mass media. This is one of the more obvious conclusions to be drawn from our studies.

Their relationship with the media is an emotional thing, shifting, unresting, sometimes uncertain. Their attitudes to news broadcasting point this up very well. Canadians, we found, put a great deal of faith in television for national and international news, but they feel television is more likely to reflect government ideas than any other mass medium. Many feel the television camera can distort reality, but this does not much concern them; they feel they can trust the integrity of the broadcasters.

Despite this widespread faith in the integrity of broadcasters, about half the people seem to feel that television may contribute to a breakdown in moral standards and a disrespect for religion – although no one seems to feel that radio contributes to these ends.

Indeed, although radio is held to be the most immediate medium – the natural place to turn during time of crisis – it seems to be considered for the most part as simply background sound, a non-involving interior decorating for the mind, best suited to housewives and teenagers.

It is tempting to conclude from our studies that the one thing people fear most about television is that it might report news so accurately as to shake their beliefs about their lives. They recognize its ability to present news clearly, to bring stories to life – and they fear the stories it might bring, and the new reality it might expose.

For the most part, people do not seem to realize how news broadcasting comes about. It would be harder for them to hold some of the opinions they do if they knew more about it.

Radio and television really occupy opposite ends of the news spectrum. Radio can bring news faster than any other mass communications medium, while television – except in the most fortuitous or the most planned circumstances – brings it very slowly.

Many radio stations in Canada have found in recent years that they can build an audience by providing thorough local news coverage, and some stations have built well-deserved reputations for their news-gathering ability. CKNW, CJAD, CFRB are examples. Oddly, despite the enormous followings built by Gordon Sinclair, Jack Dennett, and a few other highly individual newscasters, the public seems unimpressed, preferring newspapers for local news and television for national and international news.

The key perhaps lies in the presentation of material that the public does not necessarily think of as local news – weather reports, traffic conditions – but which it seeks through radio.

Television's technology, and the curious consequences of living in a country 4,000 miles wide, lead to television being a relatively slow way of discovering the news of the day. Television news without some kind of pictures to support it – film, or at least graphics – is considered by the broadcasters an unworthy use of the medium. But film takes hours to process and edit, and in many cases is quite impossible to obtain, due to the persistent habit of news events to take place without prior warning.

Where news events occur *with* prior warning, there is a suspicion that they have been staged especially for the benefit of the television cameras, as indeed they often are.

Professor Daniel Boorstin, and others, have suggested that in this case they are pseudo-events; although it seems illogical to conclude that something that happens simply because its perpetrators wish to attract attention should therefore go unreported. Rather, the attention-seeking aspect should be made clear, and the occurrence described simply for its news value, where it has any.

Although some broadcasters have been very diligent and very successful in developing their news-gathering techniques, news remains for both radio and television a sideline. Their principal activity is not to purvey information; no matter how one considers it, their principal activity is entertaining.

It can be argued that a newspaper's principal activity is making money through advertising, but newspapers, however far from the high journalistic standards we might wish, cling to the tradition of filling the space between the advertisements mostly with news.

The CTV television network, which mounts a very creditable national news programme every evening, devotes a little over four per cent of its schedule to news. On its owned-and-operated stations, the CBC broadcasts more news, but the total amount of time involved is not an impressive portion of its schedule. Most local stations produce one or two news wrap-ups a day, and some – like the Victoria station, CHEK, which has been mentioned elsewhere – do rather less than that.

Because news is for the most part a sideline for broadcasters, the great bulk of news-gathering in this country is done by newspapers, and the bulk of distribution of news is undertaken by their co-operative wire service, the Canadian Press. CP has a division, Broadcast News, which supplies a wire service to broadcasters. Much of it is rewritten from the newspaper wire, although CP and BN buy stories from radio stations as well. The BN wire carries a handy summary of the news every hour, regional as well as national and international, and this is the standard fare for many news broadcasts.

When Charles B. Edwards, the general manager of Broadcast News, appeared before this Committee, mention was made to him of two stations in the same town which broadcast exactly the same news stories, word for word. "I would regret that that is the case if it is so," he said, "but we don't encourage them to do that."

It is hard to know what BN can do about it, if the broadcasters are satisfied simply to tear stories off the wire and read them in their summarized form without exercising even a minimum of enterprise. The remedy must lie with the broadcasters, not with BN.

For the work of Broadcast News, we have mostly respect. It provides a good basic service at modest cost, and every news broadcasting operation relies upon it at least to some extent.

We have noted with interest the development in recent times of Canadian news services other than BN, which distribute voice reports on a group basis. Contemporary News and Standard Broadcast News are examples. These services contribute to a diversity of viewpoint that is most welcome in news broadcasts, and is equally welcome in the related area of public-affairs features of the Berton-Templeton discussion type. They help in the cross-fertilization of radio information programming.

They also represent a different kind of networking, a silent kind (since the broadcast takes place after the actual transmission), which may well be the way of the future for private radio in Canada.

But we repeat: Broadcast News is the basic service, and Broadcast News is largely built on the news stories turned up by newspapers rather than by broadcasters. By the time a local news story has been transmitted from one end of the country to the other, or even to the middle, it has become a national news story. People seem to feel that television is a more reliable source of national news, yet the chances are that the television station and the local newspaper both obtained that story from the same place, CP/BN, and it is not inconceivable that the same CP man wrote them both.

The CBC is able to maintain correspondents in major centres in Canada, and in some international bureaux, and it can draw upon the resources of its owned-and-operated stations for news coverage. CTV has rather less to work with, relying on staff in Ottawa and Toronto, and also drawing upon the news operations of its affiliated stations.

Both mount creditable news broadcasts, although the CBC's overseas staff seems to contribute relatively little considering the numbers involved. Both rely on the very large news operations of the American networks to supply actuality footage that can be edited into the appropriate form for Canadian consumption. We feel that the news service of both organizations could be improved. Network news broadcasts have to be prepared in Toronto or Montreal, where the best facilities are. There are problems, necessarily, with time zones and sheer distance in trying to cover adequately a country as large as Canada.

The news and public-affairs function of these networks, however, is one of their most important functions. It should be considered as being at least as important as entertaining the population.

While no broadcaster has said he considers news unimportant – although few seemed to feel it was a primary function – we are left feeling that many broadcasters wish they did not have to be concerned with it.

Both CBC and CTV have their news operations in the hands of competent and respected newsmen, but there can be no question that there are conflicting pressures. We believe both networks should consider carefully how best to ensure that the news function is not sacrificed to something that may be more profitable but less in the public interest.

THE CABLE CONUNDRUM

Perhaps no area of Canadian broadcasting is as confusing, as variously represented, as devoid of real data, as the peculiar world of cable television. It is represented as the destroyer and as the saviour of conventional television; as the force that splits audiences while enlarging them; as the bringer-in of distant television stations and the last hope for local television programming. What makes consideration of cable television so exhausting is that all these ideas, and many more, have an element of truth to them.

In considering radio and television, we are dealing with technologies that are fairly well known and understood. We are dealing with social effects which, if not understood, have at least been described over a period of years. There is a body of knowledge upon which we can draw, even if we wish there were more research, more information. When the technology is known, and the goals are more or less clear, and the abilities of the medium – well, the basic abilities, at least – are defined, consideration of policy and performance is relatively simple.

So many things are possible with cable, so many ends could be effectively pursued by its use, so many methods involving cable can be adopted, so many levels of service could arbitrarily be declared to be basic, that cable policy has to be considered in terms of picking a way through many possible interweaving paths, rather than as finding the correct highway and then following it.

The situation in Canada has not been helped by the reluctance of government before the Broadcasting Act of 1968 to attempt realistic regulation of cable television. Nor can we look to the United States for guidance, since the Federal Communications Commission has been even more reluctant to regulate cable, has entered the field more recently, and has had to deal with an industry in a less developed stage. We realize that the Canadian Radio-Television Commission and the Department of Communications, whose jurisdiction in cable is contiguous with the bulk of responsibility being the Commission's, have had difficulties in their work to date; and we will discuss it at some length later in this section.

More than one million Canadian households are connected to co-axial cable. The rate of growth continues to be high, with a single British Columbia enterprise wiring up new subscribers at the rate of 400 per week. Relatively to population, Canada seems to be the most wired-up nation in the world.

There are insufficient data to make authoritative statements, but it seems clear that where cable television systems have been established for some years, they are (except for the smallest systems) very profitable, even though the entrepreneur must normally expect to go without much revenue while laying out substantial amounts during the initial period of wiring.

It seems fair to suggest that cable television damages the operation of a television station to the extent that it offers viewers more channels than they can receive off the air, and in so doing fragments the audience. Equally, it is fair to suggest that where cable television artificially extends the reach of a television signal beyond the station's local market, it tends to increase the size of the audience, and therefore is a benefit to the broadcaster and the advertiser. One of the major problems of cable television policy has its solution in the discovery of the extent to which these effects neutralize each other.

Another puzzling area involves the possible uses of cable television, other than as a means of delivering clear, steady television signals taken from the air. Many uses have been proposed: home computer terminals; newspaper delivery; electronic mail delivery; security surveillance; shopping by cable as a step along the road to a cashless society; dial-a-program; machine-aided teaching; and a great many others. It has been suggested that only the cautious policies of the federal agencies stand between the Canadian public and some sort of cable-assisted information millennium.

It might, in this context, be worthwhile to recall the somewhat despairing remark made before this Committee by Israel Switzer, chief technical officer of Maclean-Hunter Cable TV Limited, a major group in Canadian cable television. He told us plaintively: "I am the person in this organization who actually has to go out and do these things that other people dream of and speculate on." He went on to tell us:

> I do not see the large-scale implementation of many of the technical developments of which cable television is possible, things like 20-channel systems and switch systems which use cable for access to computers.
> I could have a computer terminal in my home right now. I could call up General Electric – they have a time-sharing among other users there – the Bell has a line into my house and I could run a computer right from my house from my telephone line right now. But I don't feel the need for a computer in my home. I frankly don't, and I think the marketability of many of these services has been drastically overrated.

It seems a fair question to ask whether any of us really want a computer terminal nestled next to the telephone table, desirable as some of the other services might be.

However, at a time when Toronto cable systems are undergoing a distinct feeling of crowding because of the number of television signals they must try to distribute through existing twelve-channel systems, it is difficult to understand how the current limitation to twelve channels can last much longer; we urge that it should not.

Cable policy in Canada, as it has evolved to date, seems to have five major elements: the widest possible direct community ownership; a ban on networks; a ban on advertising; a requirement that cable systems provide community and educational channels; and protection of the conventional broadcasters.

We agree strongly with the principle of the widest possible direct community ownership, but we are concerned that it does not seem to be fully working out in practice. Too many licences are being granted to major groups which already control several cable television systems or have interests in other media. Granted that the licensing agency, the Canadian Radio-Television Commission, must feel an obligation to ensure that a licensee will provide continuous service, it still seems to us that granting licences to newcomers is in the interest of building cable television into what we feel it should be: a new medium.

We are pleased that the Canadian Radio-Television Commission has, for the most part, moved to keep television broadcasters out of cable (as when it curbed the imperial dream of Bushnell Communications Limited), although one can wonder about the extent to which the Maclean-Hunter interests are involved in all phases of broadcasting. But we feel the Canadian Radio-Television Commission must be willing to give imaginative newcomers more of a chance. And they should be genuine representatives of the community, not carpetbaggers who have managed to rent a token local citizen especially to front for them during their licence application.

The question of networking, like so many aspects of cable television, is not simple. But we feel that networking has a place in cable television, particularly where a large urban area is divided among several cable systems; and we are pleased that the C.R.T.C. has made some provision for networking in such cases, even if the cable operators themselves have not been swift to take up the idea.

We agree, too, with the ban on advertising. The cable television operator obtains the bulk of his programming by taking it from the air, paying no one for it. He has an obligation to provide a community channel, but there is no reason to believe that its costs cannot be convered (at least in the case of medium-to-large systems) by subscribers' payments – and the benefit of the community channel, after all, is to the system's subscribers, not to the public at large.

The development of community programmes on cable television srikes us as a most welcome addition to the mass media in Canada, a new dimension that can dramatically improve the quality of life in our country.

One of the obstructions to true public access to the broadcasting media has been the reluctance of the broadcaster to turn over, if only very briefly, his one signal to any member of the public, except under conditions of very strict control. He has, after all, only one frequency; granting too free an access could cost him his audience, his income, and his licence.

The cable operator is in quite a different situation. He has not entered just a single horse in the race and staked his life savings on it; rather, he owns the race track, and it is the only one in town. A television viewer who is bored or irritated with his community channel can watch a variety programme or a drama instead, but he is still using the cable system, and the system's subscribers have not diminished if some of them elect not to watch the community channel. The subscriber is unlikely to cancel simply because he doesn't like the community channel. He would, after all, be losing all those other channels, and in any case it is a much greater effort to cancel the service than it is just to turn the switch.

The cable operator may be in legal difficulty, or in difficulty with the C.R.T.C., if he is wantonly perverse in his method of granting the community access to the community channel; but in granting public access, he is in a much safer position than the conventional broadcaster.

Two groups have developed ideas for easing the cable operator of some of his responsibility in this matter. Town Talk, in Thunder Bay, Ontario and Intercom, in Toronto, have suggested that responsibility for at least part of the programming on community channels might be taken over by community-based production groups, of which they are the prototypes. Intercom has suggested that, since it would link up adjacent cable systems in Toronto, it would be licensed by the C.R.T.C. as a cable network, and would therefore be answerable to the regulatory agency for the programming is distributed. These proposals are open to several objections but they seem to us to be at least worthy of study, and we urge the Commission to consider them.

It seems to us that two things are needed in connection with community programmes on cable. One is some form of regulation to encourage the cautious cable operator to grant access fairly freely – some indication that his responsibility to grant access should not be overshadowed by his responsibility for every word that is uttered on the channel. The other is some indication of the size of system that is expected to originate community programmes.

Systems in Canada vary greatly in size, from those with a few dozen subscribers to those with many thousands – the largest, Canadian Wirevision of Vancouver, having more than 100,000. To attempt to equate the financial ability of the cable giants with that of tiny operations is futile, even though the Canadian Radio-Television Commission's policy on the matter at present is simply that each system must have a channel available for community programmes.

When one considers that the minimum annual cost of community programming is in the order of $20,000, that setting up the most basic studio is in the order of $10,000, the inability of systems with a hundred or so subscribers to undertake these ventures is obvious.

Again, the cable giants tend to operate in the very large urban centres where the need for more than one community channel is clear. The C.R.T.C. has provided for this to the extent that it may require a second community channel if there is a need for programming in both official languages, but it would seem reasonable that where profitability is high and profits are substantial, a higher level of community programming – both in quality and quantity – should be demanded.

The Federal Communications Commission has established that cable systems of 3,500 subscribers or more must originate a channel, but there is not the same emphasis on community programmes with the consequent production costs. We feel that the Canadian Radio-Television Commission should state the point at which a cable system is large enough that community programming may be expected.

The whole question of protecting the conventional broadcaster seems to us an exceptionally difficult problem with which the C.R.T.C. has not, to date, been successful in dealing. For one thing, as noted earlier, it is unclear to what extent the broadcaster really needs protection. The Canadian Association of Broadcasters, following its customary solipsist philosophy, feels that the broadcaster needs protection so greatly that he should own the cable system. This Committee, considering what it has learned of concentration of ownership, has no difficulty in rejecting that idea.

There are no instances of television stations in Canada going bankrupt because of cable systems, or indeed for any other reason, although some cetrainly are losing money. Further, a recent study in the London market by the Television Bureau of Canada Inc., a creature of the private broadcasters themselves, indicated that the effects of cable television are not necessarily lethal.

The report presents four conclusions: that cable television does not significantly impair the ability of the home station to provide advertisers with total coverage of the market; that the homes lost by the home station are partially recovered by other Canadian stations; that the reach of most schedules purchased on the home station will be higher than usually anticipated; and that the audience to a community channel is not large enough to be a factor that the advertiser should consider. This report has been challenged, but so far it has not been refuted.

We feel also that even if the danger to conventional broadcasters were clear and undisputed, the techniques indicated by the Canadian Radio-Television Commission in its cable television guidelines of April 10, 1969, are not necessarily the best ones, and indeed that they contain inconsistencies and anomalies that make their effectiveness doubtful.

The Commission has chosen to suggest a restriction on the number of commercial United States signals which might be carried by a cable system, and also a requirement that a cable operator must black out on the American channel any program that is carried by a Canadian channel either at the same time, or within seven days before or after.

The difficulties for a cable operator in administering these guidelines appear to us to be considerable, and it is not surprising that the cable operators themselves, while agreeing that nothing should be done to destroy conventional broadcasting, have said they will resist these restrictions with all the means at their command.

If, as the C.R.T.C. has indicated, a primary factor in its consideration was the ability of cable television to lengthen the commercial reach of American television stations and networks, perhaps some thought might be given to blacking out the commercials rather than the programmes. This is simple to do and our research indicates that the public, despite the Canadian Association of Broadcasters' opinion to the contrary, is not fundamentally in love with commercials.

As suggested earlier, we feel there are many possible ways and combinations of ways to deal with this problem, and we urge the C.R.T.C. to continue to explore as many of these paths as possible. In particular, we would deplore the imposition of blackouts. Blacking out a programme on an American channel simply because it is also on a Canadian channel only guarantees that when the Canadian channel is broadcasting American programmes, those programmes will get all the audience; but when the Canadian channel is carrying Canadian programmes, the audience will have an alternative, non-Canadian channel to watch. We can't see how this benefits anyone.

Some thought might be given to requiring the cable system to black out programmes only at the request of the local station which claims to be affected – which would put at least some of the onus on the protected party to ascertain just what programmes really damage his position.

We have noted also the proposal that cable operators be prevented from relaying non-Canadian television signals containing programmes or commercials that are contrary to Canadian law or regulation. In off-prime time, U.S. stations carry up to sixteen minutes per hour of advertising, as well as additional messages – public service announcements or promotional announcements – which under Canadian regulations are classed as advertisements. Does the C.R.T.C. seriously expect the cable operator to monitor his non-Canadian signals constantly to make them conform with the Commission's regulation of not more than twelve minutes per hour of all such material? Is the cable operator to monitor also for possible infractions in commercials of provincial laws on alcoholic beverages, or federal regulations regarding food and drugs? This would be a massive and necessarily constant editing job.

Again, we feel that the C.R.T.C. is evolving policy as it goes along, and that its task has been very difficult. But we also feel that it must strive to make its cable television policy rather more realistic. And it must move to do this soon, because development of cable television in Canada cannot be delayed.

We must emphasize that we believe the Commission has tried very hard to bring order out of chaos. We simply feel that the cable television situation can be dealt with better, and we trust that the C.R.T.C. has not decided that it need develop its policy no further.

An aspect of cable television that has much vexed this Committee is the extent to which telephone companies are entangled in it. The vast majority of cable television operations involve leasing a portion of cable from the telephone companies. Some few cable operators have been able to make arrangements with electric utilities companies or local public utilities commissions, but most of them have had to deal with telephone companies which have stipulated that the cable operators may not own the main cable, but must simply lease a portion of it from the telephone companies.

We are uneasy about the possible effects of this. For one thing, it means that far too much of the physical plant of Canada's cable television systems is owned by one giant company: Bell Canada.

But there are other implications, complex and far-reaching, of the involvement with common carriers that give cause for concern, and at the risk of appearing to pile Ossa on Pelion we propose to consider them at some length. For some of the decisions still to be made, and urgently required, are crucial to the whole future pattern of Canadian communications.

To begin with the basics: common carriers are regulated by the Department of Communications and have been assigned the responsibility of providing, for compensation, telecommunications services to those who seek them by means of any appropriate facility or apparatus. The federal government has favoured ownership of such facilities by the common carriers because it has recognized the need for a high standard of telecommunications equipment and because systems so owned may be rented to more than one user without unnecessary duplication.

This is a reasonable philosophy, but in practice it is causing problems, and in some cases hardship, to the broadcasting system of Canada. It works this way:

Microwave systems which connect cities or span long distances are installed, maintained, and owned by the common carrier. If a broadcaster wishes to use part of an *existing* service, usually an equitable rental can be established. But if no microwave service exists, problems can arise.

Technical standards set by the Department of Communications require the installation of an elaborate system, with duplicate service in case of breakdown, with excess capacity for rent to potential future customers, and capable of delivering a very high quality signal at the receiving end. The system far exceeds the needs of most broadcasters and cablecasters, but they are compelled to use it if they wish to extend their service or to receive distant signals at their head ends. As we will explain, the broadcaster often ends by paying a rent for his use of part of the system which resembles a gift of capital to the common carrier.

Involvement with the common carrier is not confined to inter-city communication. Cable operators must hang their coaxial cables on poles or insert them in conduits owned by telephone or public utilities companies. In most provinces (there is no general rule because the carriers have not established a standard policy) the common carriers insist on owning the coaxial cable. Contracts between cable operators and common carriers call for payment of a large initial fee – often equal to the full cost of materials and construction – and then an annual rental for use of the poles or conduits.

Let us consider an imaginary but representative example, with figures based on actual experience. A cable system requires 100 miles of coaxial cable. The initial payment to the common carrier will be in the neighbourhood of $450,000, and the annual rental approximately $20,000. The service contract is for ten years, with means the cable operator's total expenditure will be $650,000. But the increase in his tangible assets will be zero. The cable operator has paid for the system, but the common carrier owns it.

If there is any kind of logic in this arrangement, it can only be in the Pickwickian sense. What makes it even more difficult to construe is that the cable operator could purchase and install the coaxial cable himself for about $350,000. He would still have to pay rental for poles or conduits, but he would own the cable and he would have a physical asset on which he could borrow money.

As we have suggested, we think the common carriers ought by now to have established a standard policy on ownership and rates for cable systems. Equally, we question the rigidity of the Department of Communications' regulations. For one thing, we wonder if it is really essential in all cases to insist on "gold-plated" systems. The likelihood of multiple requests for microwave service in northern Ontario, for example, or between Halifax and Sydney, is remote. Shouldn't the need of the public for broadcasting service in such areas override the technical equipment standards currently laid down? In these cases less costly equipment would suffice. If the common carriers and the Department of Communications find it difficult to accept responsibility for lower standards, there is an alternative. The broadcasters undoubtedly would be happy to install and maintain the system, and the Canadian Radio-Television Commission through its licensing power is able to govern the quality of signal reception.

Even if, in the end, the common carriers must own the facilities, we suggest that broadcasters and cable operators should not be charged for what they do not need and do not use. They should be charged for the share of capacity which they use, and on the basis of the value of a system which would be adequate to their needs.

One of the reasons this problem has not yet been resolved is that it lies in the hazy area of overlapping jurisdictions. We therefore recommend the creation of a joint committee, equally representative of the Department of Communications and the Canadian Radio-Television Commission but chaired by a D.O.C. member, before which the responsible common carrier and the broadcaster or cablecaster would appear. The committee's responsibility would be to recommend to the Department of Communications who should own the facilities required and, if the common carrier should be directed to own the equipment, to establish an equitable rental charge.

In the case of cable systems, we see no reason why rate standards cannot be set for head end antennas, coaxial cables, amplifiers, poles, tap units, and drop wires. This matter also could be referred to the joint committee, since the interests of both the carriers and the broadcasters must be considered.

We support the concept, which appears to be also the C.R.T.C.'s concept that cable operators should own at least part of their systems. Otherwise the common carrier could rent out spare channels for use by closed-circuit systems. We are concerned about the total lack of regulation over the kind of programming that may be used on closed-circuit systems. We would oppose, for example, the use of cable as a data retrieval system if the operator's selection of data sources was not regulated as to variety, quality, and Canadian content.

The Committee is aware, for example, of a theatre in Toronto which, by using films that have been converted onto videotape and then displaying these productions on television monitors, has successfully avoided regulation by the Ontario film censor. Since the theatre cannot be said to be a broadcasting undertaking – having neither transmitter nor head end, and being limited to paying customers – it is not regulated by the Canadian Radio-Television Commission, either.

Another example is the educational information retrieval system for schools that has been developed in Ottawa as an undertaking among the school boards, Bell Canada, and the Ontario Institute for Studies in Education. It involves a central library of some 2,500 films and videotapes, upon which the classroom teacher can draw either by spontaneous request or advance booking. These are displayed on classroom television monitors.

While education is, of course, within the jurisdiction of the provinces, it seems to us that there is an unregulated area here. It is our belief that this unregulated area should be regulated, and that this should be done through the C.R.T.C. The necessary jurisdiction could be established through an amendment to the Broadcasting Act.

We feel that the future for cable television in Canada is a bright one. We do not agree with the broadcaster who told us he considers that cable will be obsolete before long. We repeat that it will be difficult to pick the correct path from the interweaving possibilities presented by cable television, but we feel that this matter must be pursued, and that although finding a solution may be difficult, it is nonetheless possible.

THE REGULATOR

This is a report on the Canadian mass media, not on the agencies of government which deal with them. The operation of the Canadian Radio-Television Commission therefore lies in a sense outside the Committee's terms of reference. But it is patently impossible to consider the role and performance of broadcasting in this country apart from the powerful influence of the C.R.T.C., and we therefore venture some few brief comments on the part the Commission plays.

It was established by the Broadcasting Act of 1968 and given sweeping new powers to license and regulate all Canadian broadcasting, public and private. Its mandate was simple in concept – to carry out the intent of Parliament that the national broadcasting system should serve the national purpose – but frighteningly complex in interpretation and execution. (Example: the same act which gave the Commission its total authority to regulate, laid down in law the principle that "the right to freedom of expression .... is unquestioned.") The new agency inherited some thorny problems of jurisdiction, of earlier conflicts unresolved, and of urgently needed policy decisions which had remained undetermined while Parliament pondered its own action. This was particularly true in the burgeoning business of cablecasting, which proliferated without regulation before the regulatory body was established.

Let us say at the outset that while we have some suggestions to offer in the hope that they will prove helpful, our admiration for the Commission's performance is almost unbounded and our agreement with the principles it has enunciated for Canadian broadcasting is total. In little more than two years, grappling with issues of a complexity which few laymen (and not even all newspaper critics) can appreciate, the C.R.T.C. has produced considerable order out of considerable chaos. It has enunciated clear, consistent, coherent goals. Using suasion by preference and constraint when necessary, it has begun to move the broadcasting system into the channels defined by Parliament. With the exception of a few areas where the limiting factor has been time to research and formulate policy, broadcasters know where they stand.

The Commission could still be assisted by a little help from above in the form of more explicit legislative direction. The Committee has noted three areas in which this applies. One is the question of concentration of ownership, where the trend toward larger and larger economic groupings has already been noted. The C.R.T.C. in our view has been dealing with the pressures intelligently and properly, but it would undoubtedly be more certain and comfortable in its decisions if it had clearer guidelines to follow. This Committee would not recommend the adoption of any rigid mathematical formula; the American practice here is not applicable to Canadian conditions. Each case should be dealt with separately. Elsewhere in this report we have described the guidelines we would apply to media ownership generally (above all, the preservation of the public interest). We believe it would be useful to incorporate these guidelines in the Broadcasting Act.

A second area where clarification would be helpful is that of jurisdiction. The C.R.T.C. authority is now clear over cable systems which take signals from the air, but it is not clear that any supervision is currently possible over closed-circuit systems and information retrieval systems which select and distribute programmes. This is touchy ground (such systems do not use the public airwaves) and the Committee does not propose to tread it; but we believe the competent authorities should study first, whether these operations should come under regulation, and second whether they should, as programmers, be under the wing of the C.R.T.C.

There is also the question of where authority should be divided between the C.R.T.C. and the Department of Communications, when the interests of broadcasters collide with those of the common carriers. This subject has been touched on in the previous section; it needs to be resolved.

Finally, there is the tangled jungle of copyright law which currently bewilders and distresses everyone involved – broadcasters, writers, composers, performers, and inevitably the C.R.T.C. The Committee is aware of certain options in connection with cable policy which were considered closed because of uncertainty over copyright. We did not attempt to enter this highly technical maze because a governmental study is already under way.

Given the additional tools just outlined, we believe the C.R.T.C. will be fully equipped to discharge its mandate. It is already admirably constituted with a dedicated, firm and resourceful chairman; a vice-chairman long recognized as one of Canada's most imaginative broadcasters; a group of commissioners who contribute wide experience and varied talents; and an able staff. The Commission is notorious in Ottawa for its 16-hour working days and for the economy of its operation (less than $3,000,000 in 1969-70).

Having said this, we proceed with some temerity to suggest where it might do better.

We think the C.R.T.C. would be advised to establish, on a personal basis, closer relationships with the country's broadcasters – by which we do not mean the owners of broadcasting enterprises. (The owners are constantly on the Commission's doorstep now; it is interesting to note that many of those who complain most loudly of the C.R.T.C.'s interference in their affairs are to be seen most frequently visiting its offices unsummoned.) Whatever the owners may decree, it is the producers and directors who give us the programmes we see and hear. It is our impression that these programmers are generally sympathetic to the C.R.T.C.'s thinking, and would be most encouraged to have the Commission listen to *them*. Since the Commission chooses to work by persuasion rather than by fiat, cultivation of these people should be fruitful. What we are really urging, then, is a cunning kind of counter-lobby.

Which is not to decry consultation with the broadcast owners. We have already said that individually the broadcasters are mainly sincere and public-spirited; it is only in their collective groupings that they display the woolly-minded irrationality of the herd. We think the Commission would do well to include in its inner councils a representation of people with a background in the business of private broadcasting.

We think the Commission could improve its public relations on several fronts. In the first place, it could do more to bring the public into discussions of policy. While it protests that concerned citizens are invited, and indeed welcomed, to participate in its various hearings, that word is not really abroad and something more active will have to be done to promote public attendance. We concede that a deterrent until now has been sheer pressure of business, but as the Commission clears its decks we hope it will make room for the people.

Second, we think the C.R.T.C. could explain its decisions better, and at the same time improve the machinery by which it makes those decisions known. If some of the public debate on C.R.T.C. policies has been ill-informed, a share of the responsibility must lie with the Commission itself. There is probably no need to labour this; in the wake of the fiasco of the CHIN and CKPM announcements, we would be surprised if the subject were not already high on the C.R.T.C. agenda.

We think the C.R.T.C. could expand its research more widely into the social implications of all phases of broadcasting. This, after all, is or should be the basis of all policy. We mention two examples of the kind of research we mean. First: it would be immediately valuable to have a determination, using tested sociological methods, of the readiness of community groups (especially minority-interest groups) to engage in programming on local cable channels, of the kinds of programming that might win acceptance in the community, and of the material and human resources which the cable operators are able and ready to commit. This is at least as important as the economic considerations involved, which are what we chiefly hear about. Second: What are the effects on children of TV violence generally, and of consumption-oriented children's programming? We were told by several organizations – the Canadian Association of Consumers, the Canadian Home and School and Parent-Teachers Federation – that this information is urgently needed. No one is assembling it; we are left to the usual resort of importing American studies and hoping that they will apply in Canada.

We are aware of one small piece of volunteer research. A group of concerned people from two church congregations in Montreal monitored CBC, CTV, and CBS programmes over a 64-hour period. They found that on all channels, the prime time for killing is 10:30 a.m. to 12:30 p.m. on Saturday – the Children's Hour. In that period, there was a killing every 11.4 minutes and an act of violence every 3.4 minutes. What is *that* doing to the kids?

It may be that the C.R.T.C. has done, or is doing, research in both these areas. If so, it reinforces our conclusion that its public relations could be improved.

These are incidental criticisms. The Commission is already aware of some weaknesses in its administrative structure and is dealing with them. We endorse its interpretation of its mandate, and the combination of toughness and understanding with which it seeks to carry it out. In particular, we support its developing policy on ownership concentration and its determination to forge a broadcasting system with a truly Canadian character. We quote the eloquent words of the chairman, Pierre Juneau, when he spoke to us on March 5, 1970:

> It is like an individual, how he sees his life, how he imagines what he is driving at, where he is going.... It is the image he has of himself, the image he develops as to what he wants to make of himself....
>
> Unless you decide what you are going to do, unless you have a somewhat precise image of what you want to do, it is no use thinking that you are going to get up in the morning and do something. To get up in the morning and just do what you did the morning before, continue in a sort of pragmatic down-to-earth way – I am not saying that you are not achieving things this way; you are, but you have no hope of going very far....
>
> If a country doesn't have a lively, vital and active communications system, if all the talk, all the movement of views, ideas and opinions, and all the images come from outside, then I suggest that after a while you have no common purpose, and if you have no common purpose it is like an individual who has no personal purpose...
>
> Of course, if we think of broadcasting as a pipe system to transport goods, that is another matter altogether.... But that is not why my colleagues and myself have accepted the responsibility of this Commission, and I don't think that is why Parliament has taken all the trouble of developing this Act. If you read it carefully there are much broader and fortunately much more intelligent expectations in this Act than just providing canned entertainment.

In the view of the Committee, we can safely entrust the development of the Canadian broadcasting system to a Commission with that kind of vision.

V

SUPPORTS

1. (CP)

Think of news agencies, and you think of Canadian Press. This is only natural: the familiar (CP) logotype speckles the pages of Canada's newspapers like raindrops on a pond, and the breathless bulletins of the half-hourly newcasts could not go on without a ceaseless flow of flimsy from the CP tickers.

Canadian Press pervades the news scene so completely that it has become endowed with a kind of semi-official status as an arm of the public service, like the Post Office and Air Canada. Even politicians trust it. Nor is CP itself inclined to be unduly modest about its place in the scheme of things. With a fine disregard for its own tradition of objectivity, CP described itself in a Centennial-year pamphlet as "the finest news service in the world." And staffers have been heard to claim that if a news event was not reported by CP, it didn't happen.

There are, in fact, other agencies that serve the press of Canada. United Press International, with a smaller budget and fewer people, attempts to compete with CP by using more hustle and more flair. It is a commercial service, not a co-operative. Southam News Services provides a distinctive and intelligent daily file for the eleven members of its newspaper group, supplementing rather than duplicating the CP report. It is especially useful for its coverage of Ottawa, Quebec City, and foreign capitals.

A Dow Jones wire carries business news into newspaper offices. Most Canadian papers subscribe to one or more of the services, both domestic and foreign, that offer news and feature material by either mail or teletype: the syndicates of the Montreal *Star,* the Toronto *Star,* and the Toronto *Telegram;* the London *Observer,* the *Guardian,* and the *Times;* the New York *Times;* the Washington *Post*-Los Angeles *Times;* Publishers Hall; Miller Services; Religious News Service; Gallup Poll; and dozens of others. There are even public relations services (Telbec, Canadian News Wire) which pump in their offerings by teletype.

But these are frills. It is Canadian Press that carries the news load, and the newspapers could not live without it. Of Canada's 116 dailies, 103 are members of CP; the only sizeable absentee is *Montreal-Matin,* which subscribes to UPI but concentrates heavily on local news. More than 70 papers rely on CP for *all* the news they publish beyond what is written locally by their own staffs.

They get a comprehensive world news report. CP has bureaux in New York and London, and staff writers in Washington and Paris; but the bulk of its international news comes through its access to the world-wide networks of Associated Press, Reuters, and Agence France-Presse. These agencies funnel some 250,000 words a day into CP's New York office, where a staff of nine editors select and condense to produce perhaps 60,000 words for transmission on the Canadian circuit. On a big news day CP might deliver 175 columns of news over its 40,000 miles of leased wires, and 100 columns of this would be Canadian news. Even the biggest newspapers, if they published nothing else but the CP file, could carry only a portion of this volume.

Its total coverage and overwhelming indispensability give CP a clout beyond all proportion to its numbers (a mere 180 editors and writers). Its stories go into most composing rooms (79 of the 103) by teletypesetter, which virtually precludes local editing. CP standards tend to become the standards of Canadian journalism; the CP style book is the style book of the industry. Professionally, the child rules the parent.

For it is often forgotten what Canadian Press is, and why it was established. It is a non-profit co-operative owned by the members it serves. It was set up not to originate its own news coverage but to *exchange* news between papers within Canada. It does a good deal of original reporting now (notably in Ottawa and the provincial legislatures) but its primary function remains the same. CP is the Canadian news clearing house.

It does this job supremely well. Serving 103 masters, it supplies a daily news report that is fast, comprehensive, reliable, tough, and more colorful than it is often given credit for. It is kept on its toes by a steady bombardment of demands, complaints, and comments from its customers, and there are regular sessions with newspapers editors in all the regions where CP's performance is ruthlessly dissected.

The performance is in two languages. In this, and in its basic job of information exchange between the regions, CP is a strong force for national unity. By its relationship with AP, Reuters, and Agence France-Presse, it is also the main channel by which news of Canada reaches the rest of the world.

Inevitably, the Committee heard some criticisms of CP. One of these we wish to discuss at some length, but the rest can be dealt with briefly because they are for the most part inaccurate or inapplicable.

The first of these is the feeling, held by some publishers, that CP's rate structure is unfair to smaller newspapers. (Rates are set by a complicated formula based roughly on circulation, except in cities with competing newspapers where part of the charge is split evenly and the remainder pro-rated.)

The case can in fact be made that small papers pay a disproportionate share of the total. The Thomson group, for example, points out that it has only eight per cent of the total daily circulation but pays fourteen per cent of the cost of maintaining CP. We have only two comments. One is that if the smaller papers do feel unfairly treated, the remedy is in their own hands. The co-operative is governed on the basis of one paper, one vote, and there are more small papers than big ones. The second comment is that small papers need CP the most, and benefit the most from it. The point was made most clearly by J. R. H. Sutherland, publisher of the New Glasgow *News* which has a circulation under 10,000:

> Because of CP, and only because of CP, the New Glasgow *News* can have the same news report as is provided for much larger papers in Sydney and Halifax and Saint John and Moncton and Quebec and Montreal, and so on across Canada.

A second criticism is that CP is an exclusive club which keeps out prospective competitors either by black-balling or by making the cost of entry prohibitively high. We could find no evidence that this is the case, though it may have been close to the truth in former years. There is no entry fee, only a charge for service delivered. Until 1969 the assessment in a new member's first year was 25 per cent above the prevailing rate, dropping by five per cent in each of the first five years. In 1970 this provision was dropped. As a protection against financial instability, the new member must pay his first year's assessment in advance, but the advance is recoverable, with interest, over the next three years.

CP still reserves the right to refuse service if it calculates that the applicant has no solid prospect of being able to stay in business. But it appears to be extremely chary of exercising this right; although CP correctly forecast that the Vancouver *Times* would not survive, it granted service. "No applicant for membership has been turned down in the last 35 years," notes the Canadian Press brief.

We come now to complaints about the actual quality of CP service, one of which is that its very universality and vacuum-cleaner thoroughness produce a drab uniformity of newspaper reading across the country, each paper being a carbon copy of every other. We think we have made it clear that we're all for diversity, but we can't be much disturbed about this criticism. If CP does a competent job, as we believe it does, why should it not be as available to the reader in Saskatchewan as the one in Nova Scotia? Should CP be expected to write 103 versions of every news story? Most people read just one newspaper anyway; they aren't likely to be bored by reiteration. In any case, it is a criticism that should be directed to the newspapers themselves; if diversity is desirable, let them supply it.

We are somewhat more sympathetic to the argument that CP is weak in its attention to the arts and cultural matters, and to the currents of social change. We think it is somewhat too slavishly attached to the hard-news, who-what-where-why-when tradition of journalism and too little concerned with interpretation, imagination, and the stirrings of the spirit.

But we're sympathetic to CP in this too. Its assignment is to run the record and to run it complete. It is surely up to the newspapers themselves to build on that bedrock job.

There are nine CP subscribers who can fairly claim that they receive a service that is inferior to all the rest. These are the papers – seven in Quebec, one in Ontario, one in New Brunswick – which publish in French. Claude Ryan of *Le Devoir* put the case succinctly:

> Canadian Press... supplies at least twice as much material in English as in French. Parliament, for example, gets daily coverage by at least ten professional CP journalists producing copy in English, compared with the two or three who write in French. Similarly, the network of English-speaking CP journalists criss-crosses the whole of Canada. There are only a few groups of French-speaking correspondents. This means that the French-language papers must either (i) be satisfied with the synthetic fare offered daily in French by the CP, which hardly leaves any room for originality; or (ii) make their own translations and adaptations of the Canadian coverage that comes to them in English over the CP wire service, which is generally fresher and more complete than that available in French.

Quite frankly, we see no quick solution to this typically Canadian problem, and we commend CP for its determined efforts to give adequate service to its French-language members. Service in French was established in 1951 with a staff of six editor-translators in Montreal. It now has twenty-two staffers – twelve in Montreal, six in Quebec City, three in Ottawa, one in Toronto, and one in Paris. In 1964, the world news service of Agence France-Presse was brought in to supplement the sources available in English.

The French-language papers still receive a substantially smaller daily file than the English-language members, and they suffer from the time lag involved in translation. But as Mr. Ryan acknowledged, the difficulty involved is the harsh one of economics. "It is already felt," he observed, "that the CP's French service is subsidized to an abnormal extent in relation to the contributions of the French-language members alone."

On the plus side, CP's French subscribers do receive a balanced budget of Canadian and world news, day and night, in French. It is the world's only French-language news service delivered for automatic typesetting. The best measurement of its utility is that its subscribers believe CP is doing everything it can to meet their needs. So do we.

A glance through the preceding pages will probably persuade the reader that we hold a pretty high opinion of Canadian Press. Right; we do. It might suggest that we have no fault at all to find with the agency. Wrong; we have. We come now to an area of operation in which we think CP could be, and should be, doing a better job for the people of Canada. We think it should have more staffers abroad, reporting the world scene *as Canadians speaking to Canadians.*

In this, we may as well confess that we are going against some of the evidence. CP itself does not admit the necessity for a view of world events through Canadian eyes. (Why, then, does it put Canadian staff men in Washington, the United Nations, New York, London, and Paris?) Most of the publishers we questioned think the news we get from three foreign agencies via CP is jim-dandy. And when we asked the Canadian people, in the survey published in Volume III of this report, we appeared to get a similar response.

Seventy-two per cent of the people said they thought the balance of local and international news was good. Sixty-eight per cent are satisfied with the amount of news they are getting; twenty-nine per cent would like to see more, and two per cent want less. Of those who would like more, thirty-five per cent want more national news, thirty per cent want more local news, twenty-nine per cent want more international news.

We also commissioned a study, by Professor T. Joseph Scanlon of Ottawa's Carleton University, of the actual news content of thirty representative Canadian newspapers over a period of three months. The breakdown showed that they gave 67.1 per cent of their space to Canadian news, and 32.9 per cent to news from the rest of the world.

In terms of relative volume, this seems to us to be not a bad score. But it brings us to the heart of our very real concern: not how to get *more* international news, but how to increase its "Canadian content." In the words of John Holmes, director-general of the Canadian Institute of International Affairs, we are pleading for more and better information on international affairs in the Canadian mass media – but with "heavy emphasis on better rather than more."

By better, in this context, we simply mean more Canadian. We do not suggest that the Associated Press, for example, is not a fine news service. It is. But it is an American news service, and no amount of tinkering with AP copy in CP's New York office will give it a Canadian character. An American reporter, writing for an American audience, writes in the American idiom, which is not yet the Canadian idiom. He writes from a background of American experience and American national interest, which are not the Canadian experience and the Canadian interest. He uses American illustrations which are not Canadian illustrations, and he draws on a literature, a history, and a political tradition which are his and not ours.

To an importer of widgets, the nationality and allegiance of his supplier are not especially important. To an importer of news they are crucial.

Every reporter has a bias. We think it is immensely important that the reporters who give us our picture of the world should reflect the kind of bias that Canadians tend to share, rather than the bias that Americans or

Frenchmen or Englishmen tend to share. We think there should be more Canadian reporters abroad.

The best newspapers (is it a coincidence that they include the most prosperous?) obviously share our view. The Montreal *Star, La Presse,* and the three papers in Toronto have staff reporters stationed abroad. The Southam group has its own corps of correspondents. We find it disappointing that the Thomson chain, with thirty newspapers, cannot field a single reporter in Europe or Asia, and that the F.P. group, with the largest total circulation in Canada, has only three – who in fact belong to the *Globe and Mail,* not to the group.

It is mainly a matter of cost, of course, and this places the burden on Canadian Press where costs can be shared. Our researches put the price tag on a full-time reporter stationed in Europe at upwards of $25,000 a year.

Considerably upwards, in some cases. The cost to *La Presse* of a staff correspondent in Paris is $38,000 a year, including salary. His expenses break down like this:

Travel	$ 3,000
Entertainment	650
Telephone equipment	250
Telephone tolls	390
Subscriptions to papers, magazines, etc.	780
Cable tolls	3,029
Rent (office and toward house)	11,000
Miscellaneous	520
	19,629

The correspondent assumes the cost of his children's education in Paris. The cost of moving him and his family to Paris, borne by *La Presse,* was $2,548.

The Toronto *Star*'s men abroad, according to a *Star* executive, run from $50,000 to $80,000 each, "depending on their amenities and the travelling they do." *Star* men travel widely, and in some style. Other Canadian foreign-correspondent costs are more typical: a man based in Washington, $36,000 last year; a man in London with a local assistant, $40,000. The External Affairs department sets levels of foreign allowances for its people which are often more generous than the correspondents enjoy.

Canadian Press operates more modestly. Its budget for the Paris staffer is about $25,000 a year. He stays close to Paris. Two men in Washington cost about $25,000 each, and four in London (three of whom are Canadians) operate at a total cost of about $100,000. The CP man abroad is usually not as senior, and not as highly paid, as the newspaper staff men; he travels less and entertains less.

CP's own current view of its function in a foreign bureau is that it should provide a basic and comprehensive spot-news report from the area: in other words, that it should compete on the main news with the international agencies. It does not feel obliged to provide for all its Canadian members the kind of analytical and situational "special" writing that only the biggest papers are getting from Canadian reporters now. This limited view of the job of the national wire service means that CP men abroad spend their time watching and rewriting local news-agency files and newspapers so as to keep abreast of everything.

CP last year withdrew its Moscow correspondent on the basis that he was restricted to writing "specials" and could not really compete on the hard news with AP and Reuters. This was considered to be $25,000 a year wasted—although those "specials" may have told readers a lot more about Russia and eastern Europe than reports of diplomatic comings and goings, or the managed news announcements rewritten from TASS. For the same reasons, CP does not intend to put a man in Peking where Canada and China have succeeded in establishing diplomatic relations.

We hope CP will reconsider its policy on the kind of reporting it wants from abroad, and that the newspapers which provide it with funds will take another look at the figures. We think it would make more sense to rely on the basic news file of the international agencies and provide all Canadian papers, large and small, with more thoughtful reviews and analysis. As John Holmes pointed out, we don't really need a daily head-count from Vietnam; our understanding might be better served by a considered summary once a week. Some publishers (Mark Farrell of the Windsor *Star,* for one) told us they would be willing to pay an extra charge for this kind of service. We do not advocate, certainly, that it should be done by paring down CP's domestic service.

Let us suppose, for example, that CP added just six men to its foreign string and that each of them, travelling fairly extensively, cost the agency $40,000. If our calculations are correct this would add about $10,000 to the annual assessment of the Toronto dailies. It would add about $3,800 a year to the charge on a paper with 50,000 circulation and $1,200 to the smallest papers with 10,000 circulation. So for $100 a month, one quarter of the cost of a local reporter, every small-town newspaper in Canada would acquire six writers of international stature, explaining for its readers the trend of affairs in the world's news centres. A bargain.

We think some such programme is not only desirable but essential to Canadian understanding of the world we live in. But we really don't presume to tell the media barons how much of their money they should spend. If six men are too many, why not begin with three? Only let us begin.

2. Postal Rates

> Recent research in political science has suggested that the cohesiveness of a national community depends to a large extent on the number of messages that circulate within its borders. In a country such as Canada, where a combination of small population and vast distances makes intercommunication both harder and more necessary, the government must do all in its power to facilitate the process.
>
> In this light, the curtailment of postal services in general, and the increase in periodical rates in particular, can have only a bad effect. If, for example, the post office department must pay its own way, by the same token so should all other systems of transportation and communication. Assuming that the preservation of Canada is a valid goal, such a principle falls of its own weight. Communications are expensive, and so is the country. If the latter is to survive, the former must have constant aid. Any government action that compromises for financial reasons communications between Canadians, in print or otherwise, is to say the least short-sighted.

We subscribe to these words of Tom Sloan, who addressed the Committee as chairman of the communications program at Laval University. We regard the freest possible flow of printed information and opinion as being vital to the national unity of Canada. We regret the recent imposition of increases in postal rates on newspapers and periodicals, and the concurrent elimination of Saturday urban delivery. We have evidence that these measures have resulted in the death of a few publications, and have caused reductions in the size, frequency, and quality of many more. Whatever the accounts of the Post Office may show, we believe Canada is the poorer.

The Honourable Eric Kierans, appearing before the Committee as Postmaster-General, forecast that in 1969-70 the Post Office would lose $24,000,000 on its handling of Canadian publications. It seems a large sum (in fact, it *is* a large sum) but it also seems reasonable to compare it with the $166,000,000 which Canadian taxpayers contributed in 1969 to the operation of the CBC. And the Post Office deficit is incurred in the carrying of literally hundreds of millions of copies of newspapers, weeklies, magazines, business papers, religious and farm journals, scientific and medical bulletins, and a host of other publications both commercial and non-commercial.

We do not regard a Post Office deficit as a subsidy to publishers. Ralph Costello, publisher of the Saint John *Telegraph-Journal* and president of the Canadian Daily Newspaper Publishers Association, forcefully made the point that it is a subsidy to readers. The Post Office has argued that second-class rates were last increased in 1951 and that the current increases can be passed on to subscribers; in most cases it is a few cents per copy. But there seems to be a point, and some Canadian publications have now encountered it, beyond which subscribers will not go, at which they will refuse to pay an extra price however slight and legitimate. When that happens, communication suffers.

It is our view that printed communication should continue to be subsidized and that postal rates for publications should be set high enough not to attract a host of merely frivolous free-loaders but not so high as to deter a publication that serves a readers' need.

If this means a continuing loss on the carriage of second-class mail, so be it. We can think of no better way to invest $24,000,000. And if the Post Office is required to break even on its operations, the remedy is simple. Let the deficit be met by an annual grant from Parliament (which is essentially what happens anyway) and let the Post Office balance its books. This, incidentally, is the principle now adopted in the United States, and is substantially what Mr. Kierans himself suggested.

An objection to this simplistic proposal is that the Post Office does not enjoy, in the words of Mr. Kierans, "playing God to the publishers" by determining what rates they should pay on any other basis than the cost of service. But someone will have to do this, and the Post Office is the only organization with a hundred years of quite successful experience in the field. Mr. Kierans suggested some sort of committee representing the publishers and the government. We see little prospect that this could be effective: the interests of the two groups in this matter are fundamentally opposed, and the committee could be only advisory, not decisive. Nor is any committee needed to elicit the publishers' views; they will be freely offered, as they always have been.

The setting of postal rates for publications is a complex and sophisticated exercise calling for resources which this Committee was not able to command. It involves the making of social judgements as well as accounting calculations. For example, should a newspaper pay the same rate as a religious magazine if the Post Office's cost of handling them is the same? Should a publication which is paid for by subscribers be charged on the same basis as one which is circulated free? Should a magazine supported by advertising, and published for profit, pay the same postage as one which goes to members of a professional association and is paid for by their fees?

When the Post Office raised its rates in 1968 under Bill C-116, it made many judgements of this kind. It reclassified some publications to different and higher rate bases within second-class, and shifted others into third-class where they pay still higher rates. It excluded from the second-class statutory category publications circulated free, and periodicals distributed by associations, unions, co-operatives, and church congregations. The result of the rate increase plus the reclassification, plus a new minimum charge per piece of mail and other provisions, was to face some publications – small weekly newspapers, for example – with mailing costs 400 to 500 per cent higher than they had previously paid.

This Committee does not profess the competence to analyse the intricate rate structure and attempt a detailed overhaul. But our research has been sufficient to suggest two general propositions. One is that further rate increases would be severely damaging to the dissemination of news and ideas in Canada. (We do not suggest a general roll-back to the *status quo ante*. Publications which survived the 1968 increases have in the main adjusted, and the damage done will not be undone. The *United Church Observer*, for example, which reduced its frequency from 24 to 12 issues per year, would not revert even if the previous rates were restored.)

The other proposition is that some individual rates are nevertheless too high, and that there are inequities within the present structure that could be removed. We shall deal as briefly as possible with the revisions we consider most urgent.

First, it is evident that the minimum charge of two cents per piece of mail, instituted in April, 1969, works a particular hardship on the publications least able to withstand it.

Let us consider the case of a weekly newspaper with a circulation of 9,000, weighing four ounces. At the old rate of three cents per pound, it paid .75 cents per copy to mail. At the new rate of five cents per pound it would pay 1.25 cents; but under the imposed minimum it pays in fact two cents.

Suppose the same newspaper weighs 6.4 ounces. At the old rate it paid 1.2 cents; at the new rate, its weight just brings it to the minimum charge of two cents.

Now consider a weekly with 50,000 circulation, weighing four ounces per copy. The old rate was five cents per pound, the mailing charge 1.25 cents. The new rate is still five cents per pound, but again the minimum two-cents charge applies.

These examples are given to illustrate two points. First, because of the two-cents minimum, the rate increase has been relatively stiffer for light-weight publications than for heavier ones. But the lighter ones are usually those with less advertising revenue and hence less ability to absorb the higher charge. Second, the increase has been relatively higher for publications with small circulations; they have lost the favoured position they enjoyed under the previous system. But again, the low-circulation publications tend to be the least profitable and the least able to pay. And it should be noted that while we have used weekly newspapers as examples, the same point applies to *all* printed publications.

We therefore advocate removal of the two-cents-per-piece minimum charge, as a measure of assistance to those who need it most.

In the area of rates, our other major recommendation is that the complex system of categories should be simplified, and in a way that involves certain reductions below the present scale. In particular, it seems to us that publications operating on the "qualified circulation" system – that is, circulated free to a selected readership – are excessively penalized in the present rate structure as against those with paying subscribers. An argument for the present discrimination – and we concede its validity – is that controlled-circulation publications do not have the high expense of soliciting subscribers (nor do they give the Post Office the benefit of quite lucrative direct-mail solicitations at third-class rates). We do not suggest elimination of the disparity; we suggest merely that it is currently too great.

The present rate for publications with paying subscribers is five cents per pound; for controlled-circulation publications 31 cents per pound; and for association publications 47 cents per pound. As a basis for consideration, and subject to the technically detailed analysis which only the Post Office is equipped to give it, we propose tentatively the following framework:

For commercial publications with paid circulation .... 5c per pound.
For commercial publications with unpaid circulation .... 15c per pound.
For association publications with unpaid circulation .... 25c per pound.

We further suggest that these rates should apply only to publications which on an annual basis contain at least 50 per cent editorial material; to those published by a publishing company as currently defined by the Post Office; and that publications with partly paid and partly unpaid circulation should pay the rates applicable to each portion. This is an extension of the principle that operates now.

We repeat that we are not attempting to propose what the final rate structure should be in detail, but merely to put forward a frame of reference for working it out – no further increases, removal of the minimum charge, and a smoothing out of existing disparities.

The Committee heard a good deal from some periodical publishers on the subject of one claimed injustice in the rate structure. The complaint is that these publishers do much of the Post Office's work for it – pre-sorting magazines, bundling them in some cases into individual postal walks, delivering them aboard railway cars for shipment – and that the Post Office, by applying the full rate, is charging them for work which it does not perform.

We do not see how a rate formula could be structured to take these individual operations into account. The Post Office is running the equivalent of a street-car system, not a taxi service; it costs the same to ride for two blocks as for ten. The publishers are not compelled to undertake these sorting duties; they do it in their own interest, to ensure better service. We sympathise, but we are not inclined to recommend a change.

The above discussion does not refer to daily newspapers. In the main, they are not heavily dependent on the mails. We think the present charges are fair. The increase has worked a special hardship to readers in some individual cases, but we see no way to evolve a rate formula which can be tailored to meet the special situations of particular newspapers at a particular point in time.

What we do urge to assist these newspapers – and almost all weekly newspapers – is the earliest possible resumption of Saturday mail deliveries. The "lost weekend" has hit some newspapers almost as hard as the rate increases. The unhappy experience of *Le Devoir* is reported in the Hopkins, Hedlin study and we will not repeat it here. The St. John's *Telegram* Friday edition, circulated widely through Newfoundland, suffered severe losses. And this is not simply a question of financial hardship on publishers. Ottawa's *Le Droit* formerly had a wide readership among the French-speaking population of towns in northern Ontario; the combination of increased rates and Saturday non-delivery has deprived many of these readers of their French-language daily.

Elimination of Saturday urban deliveries in February, 1969 is estimated to save the Post Office $13,000,000 a year. We hope it can soon be restored – to the benefit not merely of publishers but of all who use the mails.

Finally, a note which is probably not even necessary. We hope that the Post Office will vigorously pursue the efficiency studies which it now has under way. Some publishers told us that regularity of service is as important as speed. The Post Office now has an experimental station in Winnipeg which is trying out improved methods of mechanical sorting, stamp cancellation, and weighing of mail. We hope that what is learned there will speedily be applied throughout the country, and that the unions involved will be co-operative in the introduction of new methods.

Mr. Kierans in his appearance before the Committee was typically frank about this problem, and he rightly put the responsibility where it belongs:

> This is the result of the way we, the people of Canada, have looked at Post Offices. You know, we never give them the capital equipment, the advanced mechanization to handle these tremendous problems, and we are at the stage where the provinces were fifteen or twenty years ago if they hadn't built the great autoroutes and the interchanges outside of Montreal and Toronto. Can you imagine the old Cote de Liesse Road trying to handle the traffic that goes over the Metropolitan? But we are still at the old Cote de Liesse state.

We hope to see the Post Office building its own Metropolitan Boulevard.

3. Advertising

This study was emphatically not an examination of Canada's billion-dollar-plus advertising industry; but studying the mass media without any reference to advertising would be like building a skyscraper without using structural steel.

Because value is received, it is unfair to describe advertising as a form of subsidy to the mass media. What is not only fair but vital to realize, however, is that advertising is the overwhelming, the first, the chief source of revenue for the media; our research indicates that 65 per cent of the gross income of all newspapers, and 93 per cent of the gross income of the private broadcasting industry comes from this source.

Table 21 is a breakdown of advertising revenue, structured to highlight the growth rate of advertising as well as comparative revenues of the various media.

About half of all the advertising in Canadian media is placed by national advertisers, usually through advertising agencies. And so it was that our Committee received briefs from the Association of Canadian Advertisers Inc., the Canadian Advertising Advisory Board, and the Institute of Canadian Advertising. Officers of the Institute of Canadian Advertising also appeared before the Committee.

Needless to say, the Committee in the first instance was concerned with the inevitable question: do advertisers control and manipulate the mass media?

It seems clear that they do not. We heard dark hints that abuses exist, but we were unable to find any cases, nor were any documented for us. It was suggested repeatedly that the tendency to yield to such pressures is especially great in the smaller media organizations; but the isolated examples we heard about tend in our opinion to confirm the rule that the Canadian media do not bend before advertisers.

Table 21. NET ADVERTISING REVENUES AND SHARES OF MARKET IN CANADIAN MEDIA

Year	Radio Dollars	Per Cent	Television Dollars	Per Cent	Dailies Dollars	Per Cent	Magazines Dollars	Per Cent	Business Press Dollars	Per Cent	Weekend Supplements Dollars	Per Cent
1954	31,711,000	9.4	8,596,000	2.5	116,113,000	34.3	14,280,000	4.2	15,238,000	4.5	11,566,000	3.4
56	38,820,000	9.0	27,063,000	6.3	142,409,000	32.9	17,940,000	4.1	20,642,000	4.8	14,701,000	3.4
58	43,553,000	9.0	37,752,000	7.8	152,536,000	31.4	17,798,000	3.7	23,383,000	4.8	15,457,000	3.2
60	50,354,000	9.2	49,963,000	9.1	169,928,000	30.9	21,033,000	3.8	25,760,000	4.7	17,089,000	3.1
62	53,756,000	9.0	61,718,000	10.3	184,054,000	30.8	17,875,000	3.0	25,547,000	4.1	17,018,000	2.8
64	65,121,000	9.7	80,662,000	12.0	195,894,000	29.3	17,818,000	2.7	26,400,000	3.9	17,935,000	2.7
66	80,048,000	10.0	100,392,000	12.6	234,915,000	29.4	21,872,000	2.7	29,183,000	3.6	17,391,000	2.2
68	92,000,000	10.1	118,000,000	12.9	274,200,000	30.0	22,000,000	2.4	29,500,000	3.2	16,000,000	1.8

The point, of course, is that they do not have to; because broadly speaking the advertisers, their agencies, and the media owners are all the same kind of people, doing the same kind of thing, within the same kind of private-enterprise rationale. There is nothing sinister about it, nothing conspiratorial. Advertiser pressure is not necessary because the influence is there anyway—subtly and by implication.

It is not for this report to analyse the ground rules which go right to the heart of the private-enterprise system. It will be enough for us to remind consumers of the mass media of these facts of life. The advertising industry reminds us over and over again that it "makes good things happen." Media owners accept this conclusion, but they don't often say so—at least in public.

The Committee heard a great deal, much of it critical, about how advertising meets its social responsibility. Surprisingly, one of the most articulate expressions of concern came from a Toronto advertising agency president; but Jerry Goodis has undoubtedly created something of a reputation as a conscience for his industry. He told the Committee:

> What are the results of the necessity to build an audience of affluent consumers to serve up to the advertiser a more affluent or more efficient audience than the next man? Editorial content inevitably comes to serve this end. The measure of editorial acceptability becomes how does it fit, or will it interest the affluent. As a consequence the mass media increasingly reflect the attitudes and deal with the concerns of the affluent. We don't have mass media, we have class media – media for the middle and upper classes.
>
> The poor, the old, the young, the Indian, the Eskimo, the blacks are virtually ignored. It is as if they didn't exist. More importantly, these minority groups are denied expression in the mass media because they cannot command attention as the affluent can.

Although Goodis's agency belongs to the Institute of Canadian Advertising, the I.C.A. representatives who appeared before our Committee were inclined to play down their social responsibility. Dennis Jotcham of Foster Advertising Limited clearly felt that advertising follows rather than leads public taste: "We try to go along with public taste, public demand, and fill consumer needs and they are there and they are in existence, but we follow trends rather than set them."

After agreeing with Mr. Jotcham, George Sinclair, the president of Canada's largest agency, MacLaren Advertising Company Limited, spoke about advertising's responsibility in connection with "poverty-stricken Canadians." He told the Committee: "He knows damn well that he is deprived and he doesn't need advertising to tell him so, and I think it is a sentimental point of view to put that argument forward."

But Canada's most successful private broadcasting station, CFRB, took a different approach. Several days before the I.C.A. appeared, the Toronto radio station told us:

> It is within the power of advertising agencies to exert a profound influence on the life style of the Canadian people. The advertising they create, to a considerable extent sets the standards of taste and the levels of consumer demand for a nation.

The CFRB brief went on to raise another pertinent concern about advertising:

> The degree to which our advertising industry borrows from foreign cultures and attempts to persuade listeners or viewers to alter attitudes and habits unique to Canada should be of concern in the preservation of our own way of life... To the greatest possible extent, such agencies should be controlled by citizens of this country. The decisions which will affect profoundly the buying habits of consumers and the marketing procedures of our industries should be taken by those who understand and wish to protect those attitudes which distinguish Canadians from other inhabitants of the North American continent.

The facts are alarmingly simple. Approximately one-quarter of I.C.A.'s member agencies are American-owned, and collectively these agencies bill an estimated 37 per cent of the industry's more than $460 million billing. The present rate of growth of such American agency billing is 1.1 per cent per year. In other words, in ten short years yet another Canadian industry – this time advertising – will be more than 50 per cent in the hands of American interests. There is no apparent reason for thinking that this trend will not continue; in fact it is likely to accelerate because the Canadian agencies most likely to be taken over by American companies are those with the largest billings. There are at least two enormous continentalist pressures in the advertising industry. Regrettably, many small Canadian agencies look to American mergers for their economic salvation; but that is only part of the story. All too frequently, especially following takeovers, American owners instruct Canadian subsidiaries to advertise through the Canadian branch of the same agency which the parent company uses in the United States.

At the 1970 I.C.A. convention Andrew Kershaw, the Canadian president of the New York-based Ogilvy & Mather Inc., told delegates that "the trend to internationalization" (i.e. Americanization) "of advertising agencies is not a plot to take over the world." He is probably correct. Anyway, we will leave his reassurance and indeed the entire debate about economic sovereignty to other times and places.

Perhaps we are too concerned about advertising's potentially lost Canadian virtue. Virtue once surrendered can hardly be abandoned a second time; and a fairly effective case can be made that Canadian advertising agencies, through constant imitation, are now capable of turning out a sales pitch as bad as the best from Madison Avenue.

But we are being unfair and just a trifle coy. The Canadian advertising industry is certainly worth saving; but it will serve us best if it is Canadian owned and operated.

Meanwhile, we wonder about the adequacy of laws compelling Canadian ownership of the mass media if the mass media's single greatest source of revenue is controlled from a foreign country, even if that country is the United States – or maybe, in the case of advertising, especially if it is the United States.

One of the controversial practices discussed before the Committee was the manner in which the media have traditionally franchised advertising agencies – a throwback to the days when an advertising agent functioned as a sales agent for a publisher. The Association of Canadian Advertisers, among others, opposes the media franchise system because the modern agency works not for the publisher or broadcaster but for the advertiser. Yet the media impose stringent restrictions which can work a special hardship on smaller agencies. The Canadian Daily Newspaper Publishers Association's franchise, for example, formerly required that an agency seeking national recognition have $50,000 working capital; that it agree to a C.D.N.P.A. probe of its financial statement; that it have at least three accounts, bill at least $150,000 a year, and agree to spend at least $20,000 of this in newspapers.

We were happy to note that the C.D.N.P.A. in April, 1970 abandoned the old practice and replaced it with a simplified, and more lenient, credit rating system. We hope other media organizations will quickly follow this lead.

As a Committee we have been impressed by the activity of the Canadian Advertising Advisory Board, both in formulating a code of standards and in informing the public of the code's provisions. The Canadian Advertising Advisory Board is composed of the various media associations and the Institute of Canadian Advertising. We applaud its initiative, and caution it against reading too much into the relative lack of public response.

Most media organizations have their own house rules. We were especially taken by the Toronto *Star*'s handbook, *Advertising Acceptability Standards*. We quote from its introduction, which really says it all:

> When the public places confidence in a certain medium, this confidence embraces the advertising in it . . . .
>
> Good advertising tells the truth, avoiding misstatement of facts as well as possible deception through implication or omission. It makes no claims which cannot be met in full and without further qualification.
>
> Advertisements must be considered in their entirety and as they would be read in good faith by those to whom they appeal.
>
> Advertisements as a whole may be completely misleading although every sentence separately considered is literally true. This may be because advertisements are composed in such a way as to mislead.
>
> Advertisements are not intended to be carefully dissected with a dictionary at hand, but rather to produce an impression upon prospective purchasers . . . .

We endorse the application of such standards. At the same time, we are concerned about the question of how far the media can go in rejecting ads. It would appear that at the present time a newspaper can turn down advertising for whatever reason it may choose; and it may do so under no obligation to offer explanations. Surely it is about time this unsatisfactory state of affairs was studied, perhaps under the restrictive trade practices provisions of the Combines Investigation Act.

Perhaps we should refer to the decision taken earlier this year by the I.C.A.'s American counterpart to allow American advertising agencies actually to purchase, own, and operate specific media organizations. We cannot believe that this practice is in the interest of the public. We hope it will not be repeated in Canada, and we would urge the I.C.A. to act against any member who sought to buy into the media.

These reflections on the state of the advertising industry, admittedly random and incomplete, lead us to one specific recommendation. Of necessity, our study could touch only the fringes of this vitally important industry. We think a thorough examination is called for, and we propose that it be made.

Our opinion was confirmed by the provocative speech made by Ron Basford, Minister of Consumer and Corporate Affairs, to the American Marketing Association in Boston in September, 1970; and by the singularly up-tight reaction of the Canadian advertising industry to the ministerial needle. (At least, we hope it was only a needle.) We think that a Parliamentary committee—perhaps a Senate committee—could usefully put our advertising industry under the microscope. Everyone would benefit: the industry, the media, and most especially the people of Canada.

We see such a study as encompassing everything from the "tyranny of ratings" to what Mr. Basford called "advertising over-kill." But the main line of inquiry would be the one which Peter Doyle of the London Graduate School of Business put neatly into perspective in the *Economic Journal*:

> The main arguments that advertising has reduced economic welfare can be grouped into three. These are: that the bulk of advertising is uninformative and misleading; that it produces monopolistic restrictions on the free play of market forces; and thirdly, that high promotional spending has raised prices and costs unnecessarily.
>
> The main lines of defence are that advertising permits economies of scale in production and distribution; that it permits cheaper newspaper and television services; and that it stimulates competition in technical progress and higher-quality goods.

In a nutshell, then, we would like to know if advertising really does "make good things happen."

4. Public Relations

The public relations business has an image problem. And that's a rather remarkable state of affairs for an industry whose self-proclaimed function is to earn public acceptance for others. One generally accepted definition of public relations is the one the Committee received in a brief from the Canadian Public Relations Society:

> Public relations is the management function which evaluates public attitudes, identifies the policies and procedures of an individual or organization with the public interest, and executes a program of action to earn public understanding and acceptance.

Clearly, media relations will be an integral part of any public relations program. However, it is a commonly held misconception that media relations is all that P.R. is about. Regrettably, our Committee's interest in and concern about public relations as it relates to the media might possibly add to this misunderstanding.

In fact many public relations practitioners do little, if any, news relations work. They are more frequently involved in such diverse activities as community relations, corporate advertising, product advertising, membership recruitment, government relations, house organs, employee communications, fund raising, financial public relations, public relations counselling, and sales promotion.

But most people, if acquainted with public relations at all, tend to relate it almost entirely to its inter-activity with the mass media. The fact that to this date at least, an overwhelming majority of Canadian public relations people have a working press background, understandably contributes to this impression. But unhappily and unfairly, the image of the cigar-smoking backroom wheeler-dealer flak persists; and the industry so concerned about everyone else's public relations has not taken enough time to improve its own.

On July 7, 1969, the *Globe and Mail* editorially suggested that the Senate Committee on Mass Media would do well to "contemplate the men between the news-makers and the news." The same editorial suggested that "their opportunity to influence what the public reads, hears and sees is as great as it is subtle."

We wanted to find out if other newspapers shared the *Globe and Mail*'s concern. Apparently a great many do:

> A few public relations officers are useful; most are not. (Windsor *Star*)
>
> All material produced by public relations people (who sometimes try to disguise themselves as information officers) is suspect and only publications who care little for integrity and responsibility use it. (Ottawa *Citizen*)
>
> Perhaps nobody is as acutely aware of how much useless material is turned out by countless PR men as is a newspaper. The material arrives in floods daily and practically all of it winds up in the wastebasket. (Calgary *Herald*)
>
> There is a danger that public relations organizations become a barrier between the press and the sources of news. (Fredericton *Gleaner*)

The Montreal *Star* was somewhat more generous and perhaps more typical of the kind of response we received:

> Where public relations means easier access to reputable sources of information, then we find it useful, but much of what we receive does not meet this test.

If our Committee had to draw a conclusion based on what the newspapers told us, it would be that there is too much quantity and not enough quality received from public relations people.

As well as receiving the Canadian Public Relations Society brief, the Committee sought and received a number of briefs from leading public relations counsels from across Canada. In an introductory statement to its presentation, David Wood, President of the Canadian Public Relations Society, said: "All of our societies recognize the impact of media in influencing the public, and are therefore vitally interested in the quality and attitude of Canadian media."

The briefs we received privately were similarly indicative of solid insight into how the press functions. For example, this from the P.R. director of a large Canadian corporation:

> One hears of people saying that they have been misquoted by the news media, but the incidence of this, in the writer's experience, is minimal. Where a person is deliberately misquoted by the news media must be a matter of concern to the particular paper, magazine or whatever vehicle is involved, because it simply results in the client being more cautious in future. Generally, the media tell the story as they receive it.

And this from a P.R. man on the west coast:

> Few newspapermen may be aware of it, but an important part of a public relations man's practice of public relations is inside his organization, rather than outside. Explaining and even defending the news media's position or interest in the organization to its top executives often

occupies as much as 50 per cent of a public relations man's time. The knee-jerk reaction of the majority of businessmen when queried by the press for a statement or an interview is still "No comment." It is impossible to say how many businessmen's statements would never have been released if it were not for the advocacy of the public relations man, but the percentage must be extremely high. The quality and frankness of such statements may leave much room for improvement, since businessmen have a well-founded fear of blunt, unequivocal statements being distorted or blown up out of context by the news media. Moreover, few business matters can be reduced to simple black and white statements, a fact newsmen often find hard to accept.

It is estimated that there are about 1,350 Canadians engaged full-time in the practice of public relations. All but 400 belong to the Canadian Public Relations Society, an organization whose five stated objects add up to the pursuit of professionalism. The society is understandably proud of its recently established accreditation program. To quote their brief:

> To be accredited, an applicant must undertake special studies and pass written and oral examinations. The candidate also must meet high standards of experience, character and professional reputation in the field of public relations.
>
> The accreditation program is supervised by a three-man team of professional educators. Dr. Roby Kidd of the Ontario Institute for Studies in Education serves as chief examiner. Successful candidates are eligible to use the designation "CPRS Acc." following their names.

We hope this pursuit of excellence will one day stiffen the backbone of the Society. Certainly, it was clear from our hearings that for all kinds of seemingly practical reasons the organization has no effective way of disciplining wayward members.

The Canadian Public Relations Society has a code of ethics in which Rule 2H reads as follows: "A member shall not engage in any practice which has the purpose of corrupting the integrity of channels of public communication." What, then, of the willingness of too many newspapers to allow advertising which appears as conventional editorial material but is not identified as advertising? Agreed, this is a newspaper matter; but when a Toronto-based public relations firm produces a series of feature pages in the Toronto *Telegram* and Montreal's *Le Devoir,* identified as advertising matter by an easily overlooked small disclaimer, it should also be a matter of concern to the public relations industry.

And was the industry upset? You bet it was. The then president of the Toronto branch of the Canadian Public Relations Society said at the time – and quite accurately – that "readers would tend to lose faith in the accuracy and objectivity of newspapers and reporters if the reader cannot tell what is advertising and what is important reporting"; and there was much similar hand-wringing before our Committee. But was anything done by the Society to the offending company – Public Relations Services Limited? Nothing. Absolutely nothing.

Meanwhile the Society's quest for professionalism goes on. We applaud the initiative but can only wish that some day it will be back-stopped by a code of ethics with teeth.

Perhaps one or two footnotes in conclusion. First, the public relations industry in Canada is still lamentably weak when it comes to involvement with the new electronic media.

Second, there are times when Ottawa seems to be alive with P.R. people performing useful functions albeit with something less than spectacular impact on major decisions. We agree with the Calgary public relations consultant who suggested: "The registration of P.R. people would add a little respectability to their work, and assist the legislator in his evaluation of the people making a presentation."

Third (and this may have less to say about public relations than about the general orientation of the press), Jack Williams, director of public relations for the Canadian Labour Congress, wrote as follows in the May, 1970 issue of *Canadian Labour*: "The major weakness of our movement now is a failure to communicate effectively with both the membership and the public at large." Soon after, the Chamber of Commerce Journal observed: "Evidence of the Association's co-operation with representatives of the nation's news media in presenting industry's thinking and reporting its contributions to the Canadian economy is the excellent share of publicity achieved during the year."

Public relations people, at least those who appeared before our Committee, take exception to the word "image" – preferring "reputation." But "reputation" or "image," we agree with the Toronto P.R. man who put the public relations business – and particularly its relationship with the news media – into this perspective:

> This strange relationship is perhaps a question of defining various shades of seduction. The PR man uses his skills with the news media on a very personal basis to get his story across to or alleviate criticism. The newsmen try to use this personal relationship to dig out the stories they really want from the PR man and his masters. If the PR man falls for this and gives out the "inside" story he will probably lose his job or his client. And if the reporter is too uncritical about the material he accepts from the PR men he becomes suspect within his own management. Both parties are therefore somewhat circumspect in their relationships, circling each other warily.

And what about the public? A recent issue of the Christian Science Monitor, after suggesting that public relations is an art which is becoming more efficient and important, concluded: "Public relations is practical politics – no more manipulative of public opinion than the citizens' credulity lets it be."

VI

EPILOGUE

1. And finally...

This has been a report to the Canadian people on the condition of the Canadian mass media, as seen by a Parliamentary committee after a year of study which we can honestly claim to have been conscientious. The Committee believes that there are a number of aspects of the media's structure and performance which are capable of improvement. We also believe that there is very little that governments can do – or even should do – to bring those improvements about. As more than one witness reminded the Committee, only the owners of the media, and the people professionally engaged in the media, can do that job; it is not a role for governments.

The report does contain some proposals for legislative and administrative action. But it contains many more recommendations (perhaps better described as exhortations, wistful wishes, and expressions of earnest hopes) for everyone else concerned: the owners of the media, their employees, their supporting services, and their audience. We thought it appropriate to end this report by briefly reviewing some of these suggestions and, to some extent, sloganizing them. The list below is *not* complete. It contains some ideas which are not spelled out explicitly in the report, and omits others which cannot be adequately summarized without distorting by over-simplification. It is a sampler rather than a summary, and we emphasize the importance of reading the report as a whole. But we believe this brief compilation fairly encapsulates the kind of thinking that has gone into the report, and consistently represents its tenor. For those who start reading at the back of any book, it is a tip-off to what may be found in the body of the report. Good hunting.

To the Government of Canada:
Set up a Press Ownership Review Board to represent the public interest in future mergers or takeovers of publications. Object: to ensure that the news business continues to be everybody's business.

Set up a Publications Development Loan Fund, so that the loudest voice in town won't inevitably become the only voice in town.

Remove the present exemptions from Section 12 A of the Income Tax Act. Somehow or other, we've arrived in the peculiarly Canadian position where our most successful magazines are American magazines, and we're moving inexorably toward the day when they'll be the *only* magazines we have. This may make sense in terms of economics; on every other basis it's intolerable.

Extend the provisions of Section 12 A to cover the placement of advertising on American-owned broadcasting stations. This will curb the pirating of commercial dollars by stations just across the border which accept Canadian money but don't play by Canadian rules.

Initiate a study of advertising in the media, to find out whether it's really true that Advertising Makes Good Things Happen.

Provide some postgraduate scholarships for journalistic specialists, so that the people who tell us what our world is like will be the best-informed people around.

Give some modest financial aid to *Canadian Scene,* which tells the Canadian story to new Canadians in fourteen languages, by way of the ethnic press. Twenty-five thousand dollars would probably fill the bill – and that's .833 cents for each person who gets the message.

Take a good look at the system of financing the Canadian Broadcasting Corporation. In particular, consider whether it wouldn't make sense to give the CBC five-year grants so that it can plan for the day after tomorrow, and remove the strait-jacket of the annual dole.

Give the Canadian Radio-Television Commission some more precise guidelines to follow on how much concentration of media ownership is tolerable. One overriding guideline: the public interest.

Give the C.R.T.C. jurisdiction over programming on closed-circuit television systems – the only form of "broadcasting" that is now under no jurisdiction at all.

Clear up the overlapping of authority between the Department of Communications and the C.R.T.C. where the interests of CATV operators run counter to the interests of common carriers. This is one of the areas where developments in technology have outrun social planning.

No more increases in second-class mail rates, on the principle that the free flow of information is vital to our national existence, and that postal-rate assistance is a subsidy to the reader, not the publisher. As soon as possible, restore Saturday deliveries.

To owners and operators of the media:

Here we indulge in some wishing.

We wish media owners, as an industry, would think again about the policy of maximizing profits by skimping on the quality of the product. The maximizing is their business. The skimping is everybody's business.

We wish the Canadian Daily Newspaper Publishers Association would put editorial quality on the Association's agenda, along with advertising sales. If ethical and professional standards aren't the business of publishers, whose business are they? Two ways to get going: support the formation of a national Press Council, and finance the establishment of some university scholarships for bright journalists.

We wish the Canadian Association of Broadcasters would re-read the Broadcasting Act of 1968, especially the part about the national broadcasting system and the place of the private broadcasters in it. Then we wish they'd get off the defensive; develop a positive policy of research and information; and keep on lobbying for what they believe in.

We wish the C.D.N.P.A. and the C.A.B. would get together with the Institute of Canadian Advertising and the Association of Canadian Advertisers on a serious study of the social consequences of advertising. Are our ills really cured by consuming?

We wish English-language broadcasters would ask French-language broadcasters why it is that the top four TV shows in French Canada are made in French Canada. Maybe they have more going for them than just the language barrier.

We wish French-language newspaper publishers would send a few staff reporters into English Canada. It's an interesting country too.

We wish all newspaper proprietors would put their names at the top of the editorial page – not just the name of the company, but who really owns the paper? The people have an interest in knowing who it is that's talking to them.

We wish broadcasting bosses, public and private, wouldn't wait to be pushed by the C.R.T.C. We wish they'd provide fuller opportunities for Canadian talent to develop in Canada – by more regional programming on the networks, by more low-budget programming everywhere. Their employees have plenty of ideas, not just for new programmes but for new *kinds* of programmes. Are the bosses listening?

To absolutely everybody in the media:

Get together and set up a Press Council; you do have something besides profits to protect.

We wish working journalists would remember that if they don't demand better newspapers and better broadcasting, no one else will. So stop griping; start organizing. This goes for editors too.

The press is an institution. Institutions resist change. But change is the constant of our time. We hope media practitioners will agree with us that their prime job is to prepare the people for the shock of change.

We hope the media will not be reluctant to embarrass the powerful. If the press is not a thorn in the side of the Establishment, it's a wart on the body politic. Try thinking of the press as the loyal opposition, or a countervailing force.

Never, *never,* NEVER print a press release intact.

To sundry friends, supporters, and sparring partners of the media:

The Canadian Press: Think some more about the advantages of direct Canadian reporting from the world's news centres, so that the news we get from abroad is told by observers who speak our language. We've calculated the costs; it is impossible to compute the benefits.

The public relations fraternity: Not surprisingly, you are held in most esteem where your real function is best understood. What's chiefly needed is a little work on your own image, which is a trifle fuzzy around the edges.

Local police forces: Reporters aren't policemen, and policemen aren't reporters; please try to keep that distinction clear.

Magistrates and public prosecutors, especially in cities with underground newspapers: Your job is to enforce the laws impartially, not to use local by-laws to muzzle newspaper editors who happen to have long hair.

The universities (at least four of them, regionally distributed): Set up full-scale faculties of journalism and television arts, and raid the upper echelons of the media for top-flight communicator-teachers. In the next few years there will be at least a thousand jobs a year in journalism and broadcasting. If those who fill them are to be professionals, they'll need professional training.

To the Canadian Broadcasting Corporation:

(Why single out the CBC? Doesn't everybody?)

Please do more to give us a genuine choice of programmes when we switch TV channels. If CTV comes up with *The Nurses,* must you respond with *The Interns*?

You *are* giving us a genuine choice on network radio; don't let anyone change that. But you might do more (on television, for example) to let the people know how good a service CBC radio is.

It now costs one dollar to give us fifty-four cents' worth of television programming. Can you thin out the overhead to provide more programme per dollar?

If you're staying in the commercial business (as we think you should) review the effectiveness of the commercial sales department and its commercial acceptance policies.

To the Canadian Radio-Television Commission:

Try every means to involve the people in policy-making. For starters, make your public hearings more hospitable to the public.

Get moving on a public-relations programme to explain what you're doing, to both the broadcasters and the people.

Match your technical research with depth research into the social implications of broadcast programming. Is there a working model of community cable-casting that can be professionally assessed? Does anyone really know whether TV violence is socially damaging? What are the kids learning from the tube, anyway?

Please re-think the cable blackout proposal.

On Canadian content, full steam ahead.

To the public:

Don't shoot the messenger – he didn't make the bad news, he just delivered it. The media really do reflect the society around them.

Tell your local newspaper publisher you'd like him to organize a Community Press Council. He might get a better idea of what his community expects from the paper – and you might find out that it's doing a better job than you think.

Tired of the same old programmes on the tube? There's a channel on your cable system that's reserved for community programming. That means you. So rally your bird-watchers' group, approach the cable owner, and go into show business. Communicate!

Remember that freedom of the press is basic to all our freedoms, and that the greatest danger to press freedom is public apathy. So if the media bore you or bother you, don't just sit there. React. How? Not just by doing what four out of ten Canadians do now, which is to talk out loud to the television set. It can't hear you. Telephone the owner. Write to the editor. Call in on the hot line. Speak to the advertiser. Praise the performer. Some newspapers and magazines are beginning to open their pages to the people. They call it "participatory journalism." So participate.

This Committee is concerned about the lengthening odds on our cultural survival. If you think this country has an identity worth preserving, you can help to shorten the odds. Again, how? By letting the owners, the artists, the writers, the producers, the editors know that you care.

Above all, maintain a healthy skepticism vis-à-vis the media. We don't mean cynicism. The media are human institutions, humanly fallible. But in our observation they're in the hands of people pretty generally devoted to doing an honest job of information. Don't expect the moon from them, but don't settle for moonshine either.